To Sam and Yvie

Sam, I started writing this just a day or so after you were born, and after I had held you for the very first time in my arms. I had always said, albeit with a laugh, that I didn't want to be a grandfather until I was sixty, but there I was at fifty-eight as happy as I could possibly be.

In every life there are moments you remember and treasure as long as you live, and for me your birth was one of the greatest. And I knew then that I had to do what I wished my grandparents had done for me: to record for you my life just so that you would have some idea of where your grandfather came from, what made him like he is.

And then, to cap it all, Yvie, you arrived and lit up my life yet further, doubling my pleasure at being a grandfather.

That life of mine has not been grand or famous; in many respects it has been quite ordinary. But it's me. Hopefully, God willing, we will have many years in which we will be able to play and to talk, to go places and do things together, and in which I can watch the two of you grow and hopefully help you whenever and however I can. But just in case things don't work out and I can't quite get round to things, here is me.

Foreword

As I write, I am 73, retired, married with two children and two step-children, two grandchildren and two step-grandchildren. I was a teacher for twenty-one years in state comprehensive schools, and then retrained in my mid forties as an actor, but continued to tutor privately.

This is a memoir of my younger years up to the point I started teaching. Hopefully, even if my story is very much for my family and friends, it is also for Dunstable. It is not an exhaustive social history of my times and you may be surprised to find certain things not mentioned. That is either because I did not experience them, have forgotten them or did not consider them essential to my story. There may also be things which you consider inaccurate. That is maybe down to my memory or to my limited experiences. Apologies. There again, it means I may have stirred a few memories within you which, hopefully, can't be a bad thing!

Note: Throughout the text where I have given modern equivalents of monetary values, it is been thanks to *https://www.measuringworth.com/calculators/ukcompare/*

Contents

Me, November 1949

BORN...

... Free

I was 'born free'. That is nothing to do with the film[1], it's just that had I been born ten months previously, it would have cost my father a pretty penny in terms of hospital fees. Mum and Dad – Mavis and Haydn Parrott – had married on 29th April 1944 and had a year together, given Dad's RAF duty shifts, before he was posted to India just as the war in Europe was coming to an end. He came back a year later in April 1946 with the new Labour government under Clement Attlee in power promising, among other things, to bring in a National Health Service (NHS) making all medical treatment, whether through a GP or a hospital, dentist or optician, free at the point of delivery, *from the cradle to the grave*. Before that, the cost of treatment meant that everyone except the wealthiest avoided seeking medical help if at all possible. Many working class men belonged to a state insurance scheme which entitled them to the services of a GP, but this did not cover dentists and opticians, nor did it cover their wives and children. Hospital births, which were recommended in 70% of all cases, cost 5 guineas (five pounds five shillings[2]) or five times what Mavis was earning per week at the council offices. The NHS was

---

1   *The story of Elsa the lioness and the Adamsons who reared her was made into the film "Born Free".*
2   *The equivalent now to earnings of over £600.*

finally implemented on 5th July 1948 which, you may calculate, was just one month before I was conceived. Perhaps the coming of the NHS is what spurred Haydn and Mavis to try for me. Whatever the case may have been, I can say that thanks to the NHS, just ten months later I was born 'free' on 3rd May 1949 on a Tuesday at 2:15pm, weighing in at 8lb 13oz (4kg), in what is now the Luton and Dunstable Hospital.

Tuesday's child, according to the old rhyme is *full of grace*[1]. In my case that certainly didn't mean that I would be elegant or able to dance! Hopefully, though, I may have some of the alternative meanings of kindness and goodwill. In Houghton Regis Parish Church on June 26th I was christened Roger Vernon – a middle name I have never much liked – Parrott: not the greatest of surnames, being open to name-calling and general teasing along with imitation squawking. I quickly learned – and especially on becoming a teacher – that if I made fun of my own name at the first possible instance, that took the wind out of the sails of those I had to teach and keep in good order: "Where do parrots go for an education? To a polytechnic!" Or "Why do parrots always do well? Because they succeed!"[2] In fact, the name is unlikely to come from the bird but rather – and appropriately, given my future aptitudes – from the French name for Peter: *Pierre* and its subsequent variations of *Pierrot, Perrotet, Perrot, Parot* etc, and was first noted in William le *Perot* in 1277. Some of my family in Dunstable liked to tease my parents that they had, in fact, named me after a second-hand and house-clearance merchant in Albion Street called Vernon Rogers! When I was later to turn to acting, I asked the

---

1   *Monday's child is fair of face, Tuesday's child is full of grace, Wednesday's child is full of woe, Thursday's child has far to go, Friday's child is loving and giving, Saturday's child works hard for a living, But the child who is born on the Sabbath day Is bonnie and blithe and good and gay.*

2   *"Polly – technic"; and "suck-seed", for those not on the same wave-length!*

principal of the Webber-Douglas Academy, Ralph Jago, if it wouldn't be better to change my name – I had it in mind to go on stage as 'Roger Vernon'. But no, he thought Parrott had the advantage of being "memorable" and so it stayed.

Mum went into the Luton and Dunstable Hospital on Monday 2nd May. She had already given up her job at the Council Offices since maternity leave did not exist then: mothers were expected to be at home with their children. And Dad? In those days there was certainly no paternity leave and Dads were not allowed anywhere near the birth, it being thought inappropriate for a male and non-clinical professional to be present at such an intimate and, it must be said, more risky time than nowadays. Dad spent the next morning at work and, finding that Mum's labour was progressing, was given leave to have the afternoon off. So there I was, bloodied and swaddled, and probably, as Shakespeare would have it, *mewling and puking* after a feed, cradled in my mother's arms and ready to meet a relieved and joyful father. Back at home, my mother was to be visited regularly by a health visitor or district nurse. I would also be taken in my brand new Silver Cross pram to be tended at a local clinic where I was weighed and my general health checked. And that pram was the first sign that my parents would always buy quality when and if they could afford it. Mum would even leave it with me inside on the pavement while shopping, something people would just not do now for fear of theft or abduction. Or being reported to Social Services.

And that's my version of events.

But are childhood memories real and as and when they happened? Or are they memories of incidents recounted in later years by a parent or a.n.other? Ultimately, I don't think it matters and, wherever they come from, they still remain an important part of my consciousness. In these baby and toddler years I was, naturally, totally oblivious of the wider world and certainly not aware that, in the United Kingdom, I was born into the last years of that radical, post-war Labour government who were to lose the 1951 general election, giving way to Winston Churchill (again) and the Conservatives. In the year of my birth, Enid Blyton published her first *Noddy* book and her first *Secret Seven* novel; Graham Greene's *The Third Man* appeared, as did George Orwell's *Nineteen Eighty-four*; and the Ealing film industry issued *Passport to Pimlico* and *Whiskey Galore*. *Twelfth Street Rag* by Pee Wee Hunt and his Orchestra would be the most popular record for seven weeks since 7th April; Rodgers and Hammerstein's *South Pacific* along with Arthur Miller's new play *Death of a Salesman* were on London's West End stages, while Laurence Olivier's film of *Hamlet* won the Oscar for Best Film.

It is difficult in a piece like this to encompass all the differences that existed in the year that I was born compared to nowadays. The following is by no means exhaustive, but something of a guide as to just how things have changed...

In 1949, television was in its infancy and, if you were lucky enough (we weren't) to own a set, there was only the BBC with one hour in the afternoon[1] and one and a half hours of programming in the evening[2]. When programmes were increased in the coming years, there was still no television between the hours of 6pm and 7pm, an hour known as the 'Toddlers' Truce'. This was thought to be a useful timing whereby parents could put children to bed without the distraction of television either to

---

[1]   3rd May 1949: 15:00: *"Your Wardrobe"* – *presenting fashion ideas to women; and at 15:30 "Children Learning By Experience".*

[2]   3rd May 1949: at 20:30 *"Inventors' Club"* – *the best inventions of the month, followed by a film "The Beloved Vagabond" with Maurice Chevalier and Margaret Lockwood at 21:00. The News was as 22:00 but in sound only for fear an real person might not give a totally impartial view of the news!*

the children or to the parents themselves! It was to be abolished in 1957. A wireless (aka radio) took time to warm up as, like television, its main workings were based on several very fragile valves which powered up slowly. We had never heard of FM, of stereo and certainly not of digital radio, and cameras still had rolls of light-sensitive paper film; similarly, there were no tape decks, CDs, computers, word processors and *rock music* was more probably a lullaby sung to a baby in a cradle.

Such language differences abound between then and now: then a *chip* was a small fragment of wood or stone, or a fried stick of potato, *hardware* meant screws and nails, and *software* didn't exist. There were no laser beams, no photocopiers, dishwashers or tumble driers, electric blankets or air conditioners. Tea came in loose leaves, not bags, and, like packets of cigarettes, contained series of small picture cards to collect; no-one spoke of cholesterol, organics, microwaves and takeaways. Cigarette smoking was fashionable, but other, less legal habits were relatively unknown: *grass* was what was mown on a Sunday, *coke* was either drunk or used to heat the house, and a *joint* was the piece of meat you ate on Sundays or a body hinge such as the knee. In relationships, people married first and then lived together; there was no contraceptive pill, no *house husbands*, no young men wearing ear-rings except perhaps for those we called 'gypsies'[1], and someone who was *gay* was the life and soul of the party.

I shall speak later about the house into which I was born, but look further afield and you would have seen lots of small shops (with personal service by counter staff) and no supermarkets; there was little pre-packaging and most things were sold loose and taken away in brown paper bags; meat was cut in front of you and then wrapped in greaseproof paper. Shops were not open on Sundays and there was also a half-

---

1   *'Romanies' or 'travellers'*

day closing every week: in Dunstable it was Thursday, while Luton was Wednesday. There were lots of pubs with very limited opening hours and no Wetherspoons; there were red telephone boxes but no mobile phones; Lyons Corner Houses and other individual cafés and teashops served refreshments – Starbucks and other high street chains had not even been thought of. Individual car ownership was rare compared to nowadays and we travelled on buses, trams and trolley buses, and steam trains which had separate, individual compartments for eight people. Coal was the principal fuel for these trains, for heating in the home, for generating electricity and for powering factories, giving us at the same time smoke and *smog*, a thick, dirty, noxious mixture of smoke and fog.

There was respect for authority, and deference to rank, age and seniority. Policemen were on the beat, abortion and male homosexuality were both illegal and there was capital punishment – execution by hanging – for murder. Families would always eat together, and would later listen to the Light Programme, the Third Programme, or the Home Service[1] on the wireless for which a licence was needed[2]. Women for the most part did not work except in the home and, unlike nowadays, very few wore trousers. There were no package holidays – most were spent at the seaside of the likes of Blackpool, Scarborough, Torquay, Southend and Bournemouth. Britain then had a population of 36 million as opposed to some 67 million as I write. In society at large, and particularly with the influx of men and women from the Caribbean to boost the labour force, there were the beginnings of racial tension. We had a King (George VI, father of Queen II and grandfather of our present King Charles III) and as I've already said, under the NHS, everything for our health was

---

1   *Later to become BBC Radio 2, Radio 3 and Radio 4.*
2   *This was later to switch to become a television licence.*

completely free. But I cannot begin to look at the vast field of medical science except to suggest that almost none of the procedures we today take for granted – *in vitro* fertilisation, gene therapy, joint replacements, and transplant surgery for but a few examples – existed then; and most cancers were a death sentence. I would say that the major advances in the last seventy years have, for ordinary people, been those in medicine and technology. Medicines, including vaccinations, have multiplied exponentially; preventative care – from nutrition to toothpastes and from vitamins to statins – has soared. Average life expectancy for men has risen from just over 65 in 1949 to just over 79 in 2015, and for women it has risen from over 70 to nearly 83 in the same period. Likewise, infant mortality has improved greatly: 30 deaths per thousand have decreased to 6, whilst post-neonatal mortality is down from nearly 9 deaths per thousand to 2[1].

And now, a simple exercise for you: look around your home. Remove all the electrical gadgets, save for the radio and lighting (accepting that light bulbs have changed to more energy-saving ones); throw out your mobiles in favour of one sturdy, black bakelite landline; swap your electrical cooker for a gas oven and hob; get rid of all the plastics, substituting mainly wood with some metal and possibly some bakelite; remove the fitted carpets, replacing them with a single rug on the bare floorboards in each room; reinstall a fireplace with chimney in each room and pull out all the central heating radiators, piping and boiler, not forgetting the bath itself, and make sure the tin bath is still hanging on the hook outside the back door – oh, and there are, of course, no showers. Throw out any clothing, including footwear, not made of cotton, leather, wool or silk i.e. natural materials (no synthetics), along with any disposable

---

1   *Office for National Statistics.*

nappies and pre-packaged food stuffs. Bin all biros and felt-tips in favour of fountain pens, bottles of ink and pencils, and attempt to find a typewriter complete with ribbons, carbon paper and flimsy for copies.

Welcome to my 1949!

... *into a World*

I think it safe to say that 1949 saw a world of great uncertainty and no little danger.

Four years before I was born, the Second World War in Europe had come to an end, soon followed by the war in the Far East. You might have thought, mightn't you, that everyone would have been thoroughly sick to the back teeth of fighting? With over 60 million people dead? Not a bit of it. In the month surrounding my birth, Chinese communist forces under Mao Tse Dong were fighting to establish a people's republic in China; in Vietnam a civil war existed between the communist Viet Minh supported by China and the Vietnamese National Army supported by France; whilst in Malaysia, a communist insurgency caused a state of emergency to exist. In India, independence from Britain, granted in 1947, had given way to vicious inter-communal violence mainly between Hindus and Muslims, and the assassination of Mahatma Gandhi, as the country partitioned into India and Pakistan. In the Middle East, the newly-founded state of Israel was fighting on three fronts (Lebanon, Egypt and Syria) to secure its existence, whilst in South Africa we saw the dawn of the era of apartheid in which the majority native black and coloured peoples would be cruelly discriminated against by the minority white Afrikaaners for the next 40-odd years.

This was four years after the USA had brought the war in Japan to an end by detonating nuclear bombs over Hiroshima and Nagasaki and, in the race for armed dominance, relations between the United States and the Soviet Union[1] had begun to deteriorate rapidly. There were heated disagreements over the postwar status of Germany, with the Americans as the richest and most powerful of the western allies insisting on German recovery and eventual rearmament, and with the Soviets steadfastly opposing such actions. In June 1948, the Soviets blocked all ground travel to the Allied Occupation Zone of West Berlin[2], and only a massive airlift, conducted mainly by the USA, Britain and France, of food, fuel and other necessities, sustained the population of the zone until the Soviets relented and lifted the blockade – within 9 days of my birth, not that I was in any way aware of it all – on 12th May 1949.

One of the consequences of this increase in tension between the Soviet Union and its 'Empire' of Eastern European states was the formation in April 1949 of the North Atlantic Treaty Organisation (NATO) by representatives from the major western states[3]. The main part of their agreement was *an armed attack against one or more of them... shall be considered an attack against them all.* On the opposite side of what had become known as the 'Iron Curtain', the Soviet defence alliance, the Warsaw Pact, was formed and another war began: the Cold War, full of threats and ultimatums, spying and negotiating, words and nuclear weapons. This was to dominate international relations and Britain's defence budget and strategic diplomacy for the first forty years at least of my life.

What a wonderful world!

---

1   *Russia, plus the satellite countries it had largely occupied after the war: Poland, East Germany, Hungary, Czechoslovakia, Romania and Bulgaria.*

2   *Berlin was in the Soviet Zone, or East Germany, and was itself, like the whole of Germany, divided into four occupied zones.*

3   *Belgium, Canada, Denmark, France, Iceland, Italy, Luxembourg, the Netherlands, Norway, Portugal, the United Kingdom, and the USA.*

... *into a Country*

In the Britain of 1949, the country was in the fourth year of the uniquely radical Labour government of Clement Attlee. And broke. Rationing[1] – which had been introduced during the war – was still in force for things such as petrol, clothing, meat and sugar. A quarter of British homes had no electricity and many no telephone or indoor toilet. Most families listened to the wireless for their entertainment, as hardly any homes had a television[2]. Cooking was done from scratch – there were no prepared meals – and Mum could only buy fresh items that were in season and most of what she bought was largely made or grown in the UK. Living in Dunstable also meant that I was within the three counties of Beds., Bucks. and Herts.: all more agricultural than industrial.

There were only just over a million cars on Britain's roads – compared to over 33 million[3] as I write – no motorways, and petrol rationing remained until 1954. This made the car an unaffordable luxury and most people used public transport to get around, just as Dad bussed to and from Luton every day of his working week: neither he nor Mum ever learned to drive. Nonetheless, zebra crossings were introduced in Britain a month before I was born. Air travel was mainly for the rich and there were no package holidays or mass travel. If you had to go abroad, usually for reasons of work or extended travel

---

1   *A system introduced during the war whereby, in order to buy most rationed items, each person had to register at chosen shops and was provided with a ration book containing coupons; and the shopkeeper was provided with enough food for registered customers. Purchasers had to take ration books with them when shopping, so the relevant coupon or coupons could be cancelled.*

2   *There were only 14,500 TV sets in the whole country and only one channel: BBC.*

3   *Department for Transport, March 2021.*

such as emigration, journeys which we now can do in a matter of hours took days and weeks as most people traveled by ship. The amount of money you could take out of the country was strictly limited to £25.00[1] per person. In today's terms, this may seem a large amount but these were the days before package holidays and credit cards: everything – hotel, restaurants etc – had to be paid for on the spot in cash. And if you did travel, suitcases were for carrying, not for wheeling. The best ones were made of leather and they weighed a ton even before you put anything in them! There again, only wealthy people could afford to buy them, and they could also afford to hire porters to carry them!

Although much changed after the war, there remained great camaraderie and pride in one's country. You knew your neighbours well and had a sense of belonging, of community. People were trusting: doors were left unlocked, if not open, and belongings were modest, largely from a wartime 'make do and mend' philosophy. Perhaps because there were far fewer goods around to steal or vandalise, there was less opportunity for crime? After the war, reconstruction, rationing and the general shortage of materials meant that there was little left for non-essential items such as furniture, and 'utility' cupboards, tables and chairs were made as economically as possible.

Britain was still predominantly a 'white' country whose men wore suits and hats; ladies wore dresses, gloves and hats, and workers wore cloth caps. Men's hats would be raised or touched to greet ladies, and seats on buses or trains immediately given up if a lady found herself standing. There was little 'leisure wear' and the term 'teenagers' had not been invented. Much of daily life was thick and heavy: our coins, our shoes and coats, our suitcases and our leather footballs (particularly when wet!). Swearing in front of ladies or children was not

---

1   *Approximately the equivalent of £2,500 in today's wages.*

acceptable and our books, plays and films were all heavily censored for language or acts deemed unsuitable or indecent – and nowhere more so than on the BBC (there was no ITV then). Anything that might be even slightly suggestive was vetoed: George Formby singing about what he did *With My Little Stick of Blackpool Rock* being but one example. Anything that could possibly be construed as mocking religion was also banned.

Domestic life was, on the whole, very 'proper'. Divorce was rare and unthinkably shameful for most folk. The 1945 film *Brief Encounter* encapsulated the domesticity and restraint expected of, and so often found in, middle-class couples: when a chance meeting between a woman married to a dull husband and a charming doctor leads to romance, it does not result in an affair and, in the end, she returns, correctly, to the dull husband. Pay was mostly weekly and in cash. Husbands often kept how much they earned to themselves, handing their wives some weekly money for 'housekeeping'. A few, on the other hand – and mainly working class too – would hand over their pay packets to their wives who would take charge of the rent and all other household expenses and give the husband his pocket or 'beer' money. But it has been noted by Andrew Marr in his *A History of Modern Britain* that despite the country being *awash with cheap handguns, struggling with profound resentments about shortages and with a thriving black market,* serious crime statistics actually fell in the late 40s and early 50s. Some might also put it down to the introduction of National Service – compulsory military serve for young men introduced properly in 1949 and which lasted until the beginning of the 60s

Authority in general was largely respected and for the most part accepted, whether it be from a police officer, a park-keeper, a school teacher or, indeed, anyone in a position senior to one's own. A policeman might clip a youngster's ear if he

found him scrumping[1] and corporal punishment from a slap at home to the cane in schools were all commonly accepted – and expected. We spent pounds, shillings and pence[2], measured in yards, feet and inches[3], and weighed in pounds and ounces – though coal came in hundredweights[4]. There were no politics on the BBC and live election meetings would be attended by hundreds if not thousands of people depending on the size of the local hall or theatre.

But – and perhaps thanks to the American money of the Marshall Plan pumped into Britain and other European countries to help them rebuild – in 1948 London still staged the first Olympic Games after the war, the railways were nationalised, and the ship *MV Empire Windrush* brought a large group of Afro-Caribbean immigrants to Tilbury near London with the intention of a much needed enlargement of our post-war workforce. It also marked the start of a large wave of immigration into Britain. In June 1949 and just over a month after my birth, a novel was published which has, perhaps, even greater resonance today than it did in the age of the threat from the Soviet Union: George Orwell's *1984*. Does a dystopian, authoritarian society in which a ruling elite controls the media, the broadcast news and all personal information ring any bells? Worth a read. At Cambridge University, the first stored-programme computer, EDSAC, ran its first programme; Legal Aid[5] – now greatly reduced – was introduced; and, given

1 *Scrumping was the stealing of apples from a tree in someone's garden or orchard.*

2 *There were twelve pennies to a shilling and twenty shillings to a pound.*

3 *1 yard = 0.91m. There were 3 feet to a yard and 12 inches to a foot. These would be divided into eights and sixteenths for very small lengths.*

4 *1 pound = 454g. There were 16 ounces to a pound; 14 pounds to a stone; and 112 pounds to a hundredweight.*

5 *Financial help to some who could not otherwise afford to bring cases to court.*

that we, as I write, have just left the European Union after nearly fifty years of membership, Winston Churchill had only recently made a speech at the University of Zurich in 1946 in which he said:

There is a remedy which... would in a few years make all Europe... free and... happy. It is to re-create the European family, or as much of it as we can, and to provide it with a structure under which it can dwell in peace, in safety and in freedom. We must build a kind of United States of Europe.

... into a Town

I was born into a town with a tremendous depth of history, an area in which settlements had existed since prehistoric times as evidenced by the remains of an Iron Age hill fort, and Bronze Age remnants of an older fort at Maiden Bower between Dunstable, Totternhoe and Houghton Regis. Dunstable is a town which is nearly 2000 years old and is first recorded as the Roman town of *Durocobrivis* or 'hill market'. Its history is, of course, still there, though subsequent years and especially the second part of the 20th century have not all been kind to Dunstable. No longer a borough with all the rights and responsibilities that involves, its council is thereby much reduced in status and its shopping seemingly a mass of closures and charity shops. For me, it has lost much of its character and, while various social and cultural organisations do their best to give Dunstable a life, its lack of funding and past amorphous, sometimes destructive growth amply reflects the age in which we live.

Founded on the Watling Street known commonly as the A5 from London to Holyhead (though bypasses etc. have changed this) at a point where it crossed the Icknield Way, this crossroads was the foundation of all that Dunstable was, being the main route out of London to the Midlands, the North, Scotland and North Wales. In my boyhood, I walked and cycled many miles on these two roads and through surrounding villages such as Totternhoe, Eaton Bray and Edlesborough. *Durocrobrivis* itself survived until the middle of the Dark Ages when it was successively raided first by Saxons and then by the Danes and is not mentioned in William I's Domesday Book as it was then still a mass of burnt ruins. By 1109 it was a crossroads town again, this time established by Henry I who granted its first charter in 1131. This status led to the borough incorporated by royal charter in 1864 that I knew, particularly through the work of my father and grandfather on the Borough Council.

But why is it called Dunstable? The popular theory is that it refers to a robber or highwayman called Dun who used to staple (i.e. tie to a ring attached to a stake in the ground) his horse there. Another variation is that the lawlessness of the time (the later Dark Ages?) was personified in a thief called Dun. Wishing to capture Dun, the King – unknown, but probably of Mercia – stapled his ring to a post daring the robber to steal it. He did, and the ring was subsequently traced to the house of the widow Dun. Her son, the robber, was taken and hanged to the final satisfaction of the new community which bore his name.

The first recorded name of the settlement on these crossroads is the Roman *Durocobrivis*: a fort made of planks or, some say – and I think this a more likely origin of the name – a market by a Dun or hill fort (The Chiltern Hills or Dunstable Downs). This had changed to the Anglo-Saxon Dunastopol (the boundary post of Duna) in the 9th century and hence the beginnings of the modern name of the town. It could also well be that 'staple' comes from the French *étape* or stopping place – and a crossroads is frequently that, as well as a trading point: a 'staple' diet was originally the principal commodity of the local food market. There again, what may appear to be a stake with a tying ring, or 'staple', on the town's coat of arms is likely – according to some though personally I have my doubts – to be an ale-warmer, attesting to the town's status as a place on the A5 for travellers to stay. In less ancient times, the town was still known as *Dunstaple* well into the 19th century.

In 1132, work started on the Augustinian Priory which was finally consecrated in 1213. The town's importance grew under Henry III when he granted permission for a tournament site to be established in Dunstable, one of only around nine licensed sites in England. Tournaments in this period were mock battles between rival armies held over a large area of land. Scholars estimate that the local site was along the foot of Blow's Downs. Dunstable was also the site of one of the Eleanor Crosses erected in memory of Edward I's wife in each place her funeral procession stayed overnight on its way in 1290 from Lincoln to Westminster Abbey in London. In mediæval times, the church survived two major fires and throughout its history – thanks largely to its position between the Watling Street and the Icknield Way – has welcomed several monarchs including Edward III, Henry VI, Henry VIII, Elizabeth I, Charles I and Victoria.

Much of my boyhood was spent connected in some way to the Priory Church: through the Ashton Voluntary Primary School and my favourite teacher, Mrs. Pratt; through the 3rd St.Peter's Cub Pack and Scout Troop, through confirmation into the Church of England at the age of 12 and by taking part in Easter Monday 'pilgrimages' to St.Albans, walking the thirteen miles between the Priory Church and the diocese's Cathedral.

The Priory Church has been at the centre of much of Dunstable's history. During the Tudor age, in 1533, it was at Dunstable Priory that a court annulled the marriage between

Henry VIII and Catherine of Aragon, the first of his six wives. The Queen refused to appear and the court's decision was announced in her absence in the Lady Chapel of the Priory. This historic act failed, however, to save it from dissolution by Henry six years later. Much was destroyed, leaving mostly only the church you can see today. In the middle part of the 17th century, the church suffered from both sides in the Civil War (1642-51). In 1643, it endured action by Parliamentary forces who also destroyed the Eleanor Cross. In 1644 there were *great outrages... during divine service* when Royalist soldiers plundered the town and, opening fire in the church, shot at the minister and wounded several of the congregation. This century also saw the town struck twice by the plague, by accusations of witchcraft, and also by the actions of highwaymen, holding up the relatively new stagecoach service which was making good use of the Watling Street going from London to Birmingham and Litchfield. The burgeoning stagecoach services also gave rise to three well-known buildings on the Watling Street in which you can still see the arched entrance to a back courtyard for the coaches to enter: The Duke of Bedford's Arms (later to be Grove House, the 'Council Offices'), The Saracens Head in High Street South (where I would celebrate my 21st birthday) and The Old Sugar Loaf in High Street North (where I was to try my hand at hotel work in the kitchen during the summer holiday of 1963 when I was 14).

The early 18th century saw the death of Frances Ashton who, along with Jane Cart, were two great benefactresses of the town. It was thanks to Frances Ashton's legacy that both my primary school and secondary school came into being. In the 18th century, lace-making was the prevalent cottage industry but by the first quarter of the 19th century, it was replaced by straw plaiting, serving the growing hat manufacturing businesses of which there were nine by 1823. The coming of the London to Birmingham railway in

1838 was the death-knell of the regular stagecoach service. Dunstable North station was opened at the top end of High Street North in 1848 for services between Dunstable and Leighton Buzzard, while ten years later another station in Church Street, Dunstable Town, opened for trains running from Dunstable to Luton. By these branch lines, Dunstable was then connected to towns on the two main routes from London northwards. I would use the Leighton Buzzard link to go fishing in the Grand Union Canal, and the Luton link for an afternoon in Wardown Park. In 1871, the Borough Council began a tradition which has lasted ever since and which was an annual feature of my days in the town: the 'Statty' fair, so called because it was inaugurated by statute to be held on the fourth Monday of every September. My two schools opened during this latter half of the 19th century. In 1864, the Ashton Elementary Schools, later to become the Ashton Voluntary (Aided) Primary School by the time I joined in 1955, came into being in Church Street, followed in 1888 by the Ashton School – eventually 'Dunstable Grammar School'. A favourite childhood haunt of mine, the town library, in my days run by the lovely and caring Miss Eileen Payne, opened in 1928 and it is during these post-First World War years that several shops I remember oh so well first came into being: Tilley the butcher, Stevens the ironmonger, Herington the chemist, Stott's the furniture shop, Charlie Cole for cycles and toys, Robinson for hardware, Buckle's for gentlemen's outfitting and Moore's for ladies' clothing.

With the advent of the Second World War, the Meteorological Office moved to Dunstable from Kingsway, central London, in 1940, thereby providing war service (secretarial) for my mother whose parents had refused to allow her to 'join up'; and for Dorothy Sprittles, who was later to be married to my father's brother, Keith, and hence to become one of my Aunties. Dunstable was spared bombing attacks during the war, save for its high street being once strafed by a German fighter in 1940 and for a stray bomb landing on Northfields School's playing fields.

By 1949, the town into which I would be born was doing its best to cope with the after-effects, both social and economic, of the war which had finally come to an end in 1945. Not being born in time, I missed out on the victory celebrations towards the costs of which the County Council had been kind enough to award local councils two shillings per child.

At this time, the Borough Council's thinking was focussed almost uniquely on the building of houses not because of local bombing raids, but due to bombed-out overspill from Luton and areas of London. A quick response to the loss of homes, the first 'prefabs' arrived in the town in May 1945. These were single-storey houses which had been made in sections in converted aircraft factories and only needed assembling on-site on previously installed foundations, and often by German and Italian prisoners of war. Weatherproof, warm, and well-lit with cooker, sink, fridge, bath, boiler and fitted cupboards, they were usually ready for living in within a couple of days. I remember in particular playing in the ruins of some disused prefabs which had been built opposite 'The Jungle', an area of bushes and undergrowth where Michael Harwood and I would play some ten years later.

A quarter of a million pounds[1] had been set aside for the construction of post-war housing schemes and the Beecroft Estate in the north-west of the town got off the ground, with more pre-fabs being erected on the Downside Estate land to the south. More pressure was placed on the council's planning by the fact that the Old Brewery in High Street North had been

---

1   *Now about £25 million in today's wages.*

occupied by squatters. These squatters had earlier, in 1946, been *forestalled*, according to the *Gazette,* when over 1,500 Polish troops moved into what the squatters had their eyes on: the then vacant army huts in First Avenue. By the end of 1947, however, the Council was facing what my grandfather termed the *penalty of progress*[1] when, thanks to the national quota system and rapid progress on Beecroft, the Council was prevented from negotiating the further contracts needed to build more homes.

The Council's desire to build more homes was stifled, however, by questions over the boundaries of the borough. It had been confirmed in May 1947 that Dunstable should remain separate from Luton which was later to be given County Borough status. That the Council had been successful in maintaining Dunstable's distance from its larger neighbour Luton was the Post Office granting Dunstable its own postmark. To the west, Totternhoe and Eaton Bray were anxious not to be swallowed up in a Dunstable expansion and a government minister had vetoed in their favour, leaving the Council confirmed to what my grandfather called *a sprawl along the Watling Street*[2] – the Beecroft estate to the north-west and Downside to the south-east.

This situation had eased by the April of 1948, when permission for building 50 more homes was granted by the government, provided that as many as possible were let to agricultural workers. And this at a time when there were well over 600 families on the waiting list. These people had to amass points for such things as the number of children, the condition and size of their present dwelling etc. That doubts were raised over Council members' integrity when considering housing allocation points was not surprising and much fuss was made in June 1948 of the refusal by the then Chairman of

---

1   *Dunstable Gazette: 28/11/47.*
2   *Dunstable Gazette: 28/01/49.*

the Housing Committee to make public the points accrued by those who had been given council houses.

Meanwhile, various environmental groups[1] – yes, even in 1949 – successfully contested in the High Court the proposed redevelopment of the Green Lanes area by the Rugby Portland Cement Company who wanted to excavate the chalk deposits. Neither did the company's idea for an atomic shelter some 150 feet under the Downs (presumably so they could benefit from the mining) come to fruition.

One building project which steadfastly refused to make progress, however, was that of a War Memorial. That Dunstable had lost people fighting in the war was indisputable, but the economic situation of the immediate post-war period meant that the cost of living was high, people were not well off and, if anything, life was harder after the war than during it – certainly the rationing situation worsened dramatically. By the beginning of 1947, public donations were limited to a single contribution from the Dunstable Repertory Company thanks to a performance in the Town Hall, and the project was viewed with considerable indifference. Equally reluctant to cover the costs, though keen to see the town have a memorial, was the Council which had just added to the steadily increasing cost of living by putting the rates[2] up 8%. It eventually came into being in Priory Gardens and was opened in 1952. Elsewhere, there were thoughts of closing the weekly cattle market which took place on The Square – though that would eventually happen in my sixth year, 1955.

The town was nothing but democratic though, with a public meeting in June 1947 deciding in favour of a local poll or referendum on whether the Union Cinema should be allowed

---

1   *The South Beds Preservation Society, The Council for the Preservation of Rural England, the Commons and Footpaths Preservation Society and Totternhoe Parish Council.*

2   *Modern Council tax*

to open on Sundays. The answer was a firm *Yes* though my grandfather also felt that the choice of film might be tempered in view of it being shown on the Sabbath!

For the week in which I was born, the Dunstable Borough Gazette of Friday 6th May 1949, recorded that this was a town whose population had risen to 17,547 and where 1,835 bottles of orange juice and 643 of cod liver oil had been issued to babies and young children. The orange was for the provision of Vitamin C, but also contained vast amounts of sugar which helped to rot our teeth as soon as they arrived, whilst cod liver oil provided vitamins A and D but also, it was said, served the all-pervading principle that regular bowels were the key to well-being. Arthur Chattell (*Cycles and Wireless*) advertised a Murphy television 'receiver' for £70.12.2 with a smaller screen (10 inches) for £46.8.0, whereas a good radio in a mahogany cabinet would have set you back £26.7.8[1]. though you could have spread the cost by paying £6.10.0 deposit followed by 9/6 weekly[2]. Watching a play by the Dunstable Repertory Company in the Town Hall would have cost between 5/- and 2/6[3]. There was also a new invention at the time – a *biro*. Nowadays they are comparatively cheap to buy, but John Simpson in his *Days from a Different World* quotes his uncle showing him this latest piece of technology and informing the young Simpson that it cost £1.14.10[4].

The Saturday previous, the A5 running through Dunstable (no M1 yet!) had been packed with coaches from Wolverhampton and Leicester heading to Wembley for the FA

---

1   *About £6,600, £4,400 and £3,000 in todays wages respectively. Given that Mum had been paid about £60 a year for secretarial work at the Council offices, it is clear just how expensive these were!*

2   *About £600 and £45.00 respectively.*

3   *About £23.00 – £12.00.*

4   *About £165.00 in today's wages.*

Cup Final which Wolves won 3-1. Inside the Gazette for the week there was also an encouragement to *Vote for PARROTT* on May 12th. This was not for the new-born me, but for my grandfather, Harold William, who was *The People's candidate who offers Service [and] Experience...* and who would put *Dunstable before Party* as he was standing again after already 24 years' service as an independent councillor for the municipal elections in the Icknield Ward, including three years as Mayor from 1943 to 1946.

... into a Family

I had the immense good fortune of being born into a loving and caring extended family which, although very close, was in no way on top of each other. My mother would see her sister, Eve, regularly, but it's fair to say that my father saw his three brothers but rarely, despite the fact that they all lived, for the most part of their lives, in the same town, Dunstable. Each knew the others were there and could always be called on in need. Apart from the families of the spouses (those who had married into the Estwicks and the Parrotts), I knew one great-grandmother, four grandparents, one great-great-aunt, four great-aunts and three great-uncles, four aunts and uncles, seven cousins, and four second cousins, but no brothers or sisters. They say you don't miss what you never had. When, however, later in life there were problems between my parents and my first wife and me, partly due to me being the sole focus of their attention, I asked them why they had not had any more children and thereby lightened what I perceived to be my sole load. Their answer was vague – talking of personal issues was not what they did – but Dad did hint that Mum had had a few problems having me and *didn't want to go through all that again.*

Thomas Collins Child, Ellen Alice Leslie, Doris, Evelyn. c1895

Leonard joins up
11th August 1915

33215 Private
Estwick 1915

Leonard and Evelyn,
married in 1921

Leonard's service record in France
from 17th October 1915

It is sadly traditional that many families only manage to get together for what is called 'Hatch, Match and Despatch'. Unfortunately, christenings are all too rare these days, and marriages are also much fewer than in my youth. But whenever the family can get itself together, even for a funeral, that gathering always gives me a great sense of pleasure, of togetherness, and of optimism for the future.

... into the Childs and the Estwicks

On my mother's side of the family, her mother, Evelyn Alice Child, – my Nana – was born in 1894 in Aldenham, Hertfordshire, where her father, Thomas Collins Child, was a tailor of the old school who would sit cross-legged on a bench to sew. And in these days long before the birth of the NHS, that was also a transferable skill for, if Evelyn or Alice cut her finger badly in the kitchen, her father would sew it himself rather than spend money on a doctor! Her mother, my great-grandmother and the one I called 'Mummisgranny' was Ellen Alice Child, née Wright. She was born in 1862 and lived to be 93 – an exceptional age in 1955. I remember going to her small terraced house in Aldenham when I was about four years old and asking what the little silver trails were that criss-crossed the tiles on her kitchen floor. Mum quickly shushed me: I learned later that they were traces of slugs. I still have her recipe book, written in her own hand and in that of her daughter, my Nana, as well as with contributions from my mother.

From the age of 14, Evelyn went into 'service' in the vicarage of St.Mary and All Saints in Potter's Bar. The Reverend Jacob Forrester had moved there with his wife, Theresa, in 1900 and Evelyn joined them eight years later, working as a domestic maid, helping with their three young children and as an assistant in the schoolroom – until she met and married Leonard Estwick.

According to Mum, Nana would have given me the chimney off the roof if I had asked for it! She was gentleness and kindness itself, but I knew that for only the first eight years of my life. I remember Mum coming home and saying how upset she had been to see her mother gasping for breath inside an oxygen tent in hospital, where the cancer finally killed her. But she had a sparkling sense of humour, telling me one day, when I was only about five and she was preparing a goose for cooking, to go and tell Granfy that she was *stuffing its arse*. He was tickled pink! Sometimes she took me to services at the Priory Church. On one occasion I needed her comfort more than ever when, at the age of about seven, having sliced my finger with my father's wood-chopping axe (I was trying to be 'helpful'), Dad had bussed me to the Luton and Dunstable Hospital where it was patched up with several stitches. As we sat down in Church for the evening service, I put my hand on the back of the seat in front of me just as a rather large lady in a big hat sat down, squashing my newly stitched and bandaged finger as she did so. Having had good behaviour, especially in church, drummed into me from birth, I managed to stifle the squeal of pain. That memory is also tinged by the fact that it was one of the last times I was with Nana. Soon after, she was admitted to hospital and died just before her 63rd birthday. I do, however, remember Mum coming to me quite tearfully saying how I wouldn't be seeing Nana any more. Somehow I understood or just accepted – I don't know how – cried a little in tandem with her, and then carried on.

Nana had a sister, Doris Elizabeth Child, who also went into 'service' but who never married. Whether she had had boyfriends or not, I don't know: no-one ever mentioned it. Occasionally later on in life, when talking about another single woman, she'd come out with *She died without ever having known the pleasure*. Whether she said that in all innocence, or perhaps because she had been in a relationship and "known the pleasure", I do not know. In the years up to the Second World War, it was not uncommon for well-to-do families to employ live-in staff, and the higher up the social scale you were, the more staff you had. Doris had entered service like her sister when she was fourteen, working as a maid in a large house and rising to become a house-keeper and then to a 'lady's companion': someone who acts almost as a paid friend but who is there to attend to whatever the lady needs or wants. Her lady happened to be rich (of course) and a great lover of opera. Consequently, Doris had seen more operas than most people get to see, but had always dreamt of going to La Scala, Milan.

When Nana died[1], Doris moved to Dunstable from Watford to have the upstairs of no. 128 Luton Road to herself and to cook and clean for Granfy, her brother-in-law. As a way of saying thank you to her, Granfy took her to Italy, and to the place of her dreams, La Scala, Milan. Before that, though, when the Second World War came, Doris and her lady parted company – I know not why but think it was due to her lady moving abroad, possibly to the USA and Doris not wanting to break her links with her sister Evelyn. She took on a regular job in charge of the newspaper and sweet kiosk on Watford Station. As such, I was told, she was well able during the war to bring to Dunstable a goodly supply of cigarettes – *Du Maurier*, mainly. I remember visiting her at the station kiosk when I was about seven and walking away with an armful of American comics one of her newspaper suppliers had given me – much to Mum's disapproval as I was never normally allowed comics such as the *Dandy*, *Beano*, *Lion* or *Eagle*. I had to read *books*! I have to say, though, I found little pleasure in the comics. My

---

1   *12th October 1957.*

sense of humour has always been verbal rather than physical and I've never been a fan of science-fiction

When I was young, I couldn't say 'Aunty Doris': it came out as 'Aunty Dor' instead. And so she remained – though by her later years that had been shortened to just plain 'Aunty' and she was known as that even to people beyond her family. Doris, like her sister Evelyn, was sweetness and light. Nothing was ever too much trouble for her and she was effectively another Nana, particularly after Evelyn, her sister, died. She was also the victim of one of those awkward questions children ask quite innocently but which can be quite embarrassing: in my case it was "Aunty, why have you got such fat legs?" Aunty just smiled, not knowing what to say, while Mum went bright red, tut-tutted and, gritting her teeth, snapped "You don't say things like that!" and packed me off to bed. After Granfy died, and with his second wife, Irene, living at 128, Doris, who had always enjoyed as much company as she could get, took on a new lease of life and moved to spend her final years in the companionable life of a Dunstable care home, The Chilterns.

The village of Walkern in Hertfordshire was no agricultural idyll, a report having been given to the Hertfordshire Sanitary Authority in 1875 which was highly critical of the living conditions and of the incidence of several cases of typhoid fever directly attributable to the deplorable situation. The main cause was overcrowding due to the greed of landowners who would not build more cottages and therefore accommodation being far short of demand. And it was here, twenty years later in 1895 that Leonard Wright Estwick, my Granfy, was born, the second son of Isaac and Edith. Issac, in turn, was the third of ten children born to Thomas, a brick maker, and Priscilla. Leonard was born into a family of agricultural workers and retained a love of the open air whilst training and working in a growth industry: mains electricity supply, eventually becoming a foreman for power cable works. But before that at the age of 20 and on 11th August 1915 – before conscription came in in January 1916 – Leonard volunteered and signed on the dotted line for the King's shilling. After basic training, he went to war in France on 17th October, firstly with the 6th Lancer regiment. I remember the spurs he'd kept adorning the mantlepiece at 128 Luton Road, the ones he gave me and which, to my great regret, I went and lost. Leonard then became part of the Royal Warwickshire Regiment 15th (Service) Battalion (2nd Birmingham). A Service Battalion is one that provides combat service support to a brigade group and its elements, and is able to fight in a defensive role as well as provide the logistical support vital to sustaining the operations of the other units within the brigade group. The mud and trenches of northern-eastern France had swiftly proved the end of cavalry charges and horses had become beasts of burden, supplying shells, food, ammunition and other necessities to the front lines.

As 33215 Private Estwick he was stationed first at Ailly le Haut Clocher in November 1915, moved to Longueval in the Somme and thence to Vimy Ridge, near Arras, in April 1917. Two years of supplying his fellow troops had one good effect: it kept Leonard away from front line fighting. But that was not to last. After the battles of 'Wipers' – the anglicised slang pronunciation of Ypres – in October 1917, he fought in the second battle of Passchendaele. The 15th Royal Warwickshire Regiment in the centre had had considerable success in clearing Polderhoek Park and capturing Polderhoek Château. However Leonard's battalion was so far in advance of those on either side, the Company Commander holding the Château feared they may be cut off in the event of a German counter-attack and decided to withdraw from it into the grounds. The Germans quickly reoccupied the Château, swept the ground with machine-gun fire and then counter-attacked to such an effect that the battalion was pushed back to its original start line. And

33215 Private Estwick was wounded. His name appears on the Nominal Roll of Walking Wounded from noon on the 26th October 1917 to noon on the 27th, though whether he had been shot according to the Roll or, as Granfy always maintained, hit by shrapnel from a shell is not clear: he once told me he still had a fragment in his left shoulder. After recuperation, Leonard re-joined his unit in time for the defence of Nieppe Forest near Merville in the April of 1918, fought in the battle of Albert during the second battles of the Somme, saw action which overran the Hindenburg Line and then took part in the final advance through Picardy at the beginning of November 1918.

Leonard, in common with the majority of those who had fought, never spoke of his experiences in the war, save for the mention of his shrapnel. And I, being young and naive, to my regret never asked him.

With the war over and after a short engagement, Leonard married Evelyn Child on 24th December 1921 at Aldenham Church and began their married life in Watford. Their first child, my mother Mavis, followed nine months later on 27th September 1922, and her sister Evelyn Edith on 26th April 1925. The family moved to Dunstable and to number 128 in the Luton Road in 1933. The house always seemed to me to have a good-sized garden, though later, as an adult, I peeked over the fence when the place was up for sale and it seemed then very modest! Nevertheless, Leonard was a keen gardener and provided a steady crop of vegetables for the family, especially during the 1939-45 war. He also grew tobacco. His shed reeked of the sharp acridity of creosote and the cloying headiness of tobacco hanging to mature and mellow from the roof or squashed in a press before being sliced and eventually shredded for cigarettes. Leonard seemed to survive happily on it although my father, in one comment made in all innocence, declared it to be the *roughest shag* he'd ever had.

Life was not always easy for Evelyn, Mavis and Eve, especially when Leonard's work with the Bedfordshire, Cambridgeshire and Huntingdonshire electricity company, later to be known as the Eastern Electricity Board, took him out of the country and into Egypt where he was part of a team installing power cables. There was the occasional moment which helped to lighten their lives, though, such as when a distant and deceased Uncle Albert had been cremated in Watford but had previously insisted that his ashes be scattered in the grounds of Dunstable Priory Church which he had known as a child. Nowadays, funeral directors would see that as no problem and make the appropriate arrangements, but this was 1935 and it had been left to his nearest and dearest to arrange that his ashes be posted to 128 Luton Road. 12-year old Mavis was in her room when she heard an anguished cry from the hall and rushed down the stairs to find her mother half way between tears of sadness and tears of laughter amidst a pile of dust.

"Uncle Bertie's all over the hall" she wailed.

The postman had forced the brown-paper package through their letterbox and it had split, showering his ashes all over the floor.

When the Second World War arrived, Leonard combined his garden and his mains cable installation skills – not to mention working outside in all weathers – in one good project: an air-raid shelter or, as Granfy preferred to call it, his dugout. Although I remember fondly clambering down its ten brick steps and entering the dank coolness of its room in the post-war fifties when it served as a store for his eating- and cooking-apples, its original purpose was clear. After the steps and beyond the wooden door was a space about 6ft long by 6ft wide by 5ft deep – it must have taken hours and hours to dig! The walls were bricked and a concrete slab some 6 inches thick formed the roof. On either side were mounted two wooden racks which could each have held a person and their bedding and it was reckoned he, Evelyn, Mavis and Eve would have survived just about anything other than a very close or direct hit. He had to have it approved by the Air-Raid Precautions wardens and entered on their list of private shelters, though its use must have been mercifully minimal as Dunstable was spared any bombing raids, unlike Luton 5 miles to the east with its factories, such as Vauxhall Cars, which had converted to manufacturing tanks.

Harold William Parrott
c.1910, aged 17

*Sarah and Harold in 1925
with Haydn (nearly 3) and
Keith (c.7 months)*

*Sarah and Keith (3rd, 4th from left), Harold (back, with glasses) and
Haydn (front right) in 1930 on Worthing beach.*

Keith and Haydn at Bexhill 1934

... into the Beartons and the Parrotts

On the other side of the family, Granny, Sarah Bearton, was born in Northall, Buckinghamshire, to Charles William Bearton, a dairyman, and Anne, *née* Smith. I should really have said Sarah *Smith* as she was the first of five children and, to her dying day, carried the shame – to her – of being born 'the wrong side of the blanket', i.e. before her parents married. In those days, if parents were not married, the child took the name of its mother, regardless of whether they married subsequently. This maternal name was entered on the child's birth certificate, marking him or her out formally as illegitimate, and was used for all practical purposes such as schooling until, for Sarah, such time as she married. It was only at that point that she was allowed to change her surname and then to that of her husband. The Bearton's had four other children: Annie and Frances ('Annie and Fannie') who were never to marry, Ronald, and finally Stanley, who followed his father into 'milk' and, from a roundsman, rose eventually to become Managing Director of Lea Valley Dairies – and my godfather to whom I was to look up tremendously. When Charles and Anne and the four younger children moved from Northall into Cheval Place, Knightsbridge in 1899, Sarah stayed in Northall with Anne's sister, Ruth (born in 1877) who, probably to Sarah's public advantage, was to remain a Smith to the end as she never married. Ruth and Sarah later moved to 123 West Street, Dunstable, and Sarah worked as a laundry assistant in the White Heather Laundry.

I would later know Aunt Ruth as my great-great-aunt and always looked forward to visiting her and to going back in time, it seemed. 123 West Street was a tiny terraced house which still retained, though out of use, the gas-light mantle in the centre of the living room ceiling and its two chains for regulating the supply of gas. The front room containing the stereotypical aspidistra was, as was common in those days, never used except for entertaining formal visitors such as the local vicar. Equally, you never used the front door (opening into the front lounge) but always approached Aunt Ruth's up the passage between 123 and 125. This led through and round to her back door, the back garden with a little pond in it and the outside privy or lavatory. The upstairs – though I never went up there – was accessed through a door in the wall of the living room next to a set of drawers, set in the wall and under the stairs, in which, it was said, Ruth kept her own laying-out clothes. In those days before the rise of the modern funeral director, people often made their own arrangements – as was the case with Uncle Bertie's ashes. Ruth was a 'layer-outer'. If someone died, it would, be 'send for Ruth' and Aunt Ruth, Granny's aunty, would do all that was necessary to present the deceased in as neat, as pleasant and as appropriate a way as possible before the undertaker arrived with a coffin. Ruth and Sarah were to remain very close all their lives, with Ruth being as much of a mum as an aunt.

Jennifer, Stanley Bearton's daughter, Granny's niece and my father's cousin, remembers how, when they were bombed out in London during the war and her father stayed behind to manage the dairy, she and Dorothy, her mother, came to live with Sarah and Harold Parrott at 103 Luton Road. Ruth would always come down on a Monday to help Sarah with the laundry: firing up the bricked-in copper in the kitchen and stirring the washing with a big paddle. In the final rinse, Ruth would stir around a little blue bag. Its ingredients were synthetic ultramarine and baking soda, and the original squares weighed an ounce and cost 1 penny. Made by Reckitt's, who had been in the blue and starch business in Hull, even before they started importing French ultramarine in the 1850s to make the new blue rinse additive at their English factory, it disguised any hint of yellowness and helped the household linen look whiter than white. The Little Blue Bag also formed part of Granny's first-aid cupboard in that, being alkaline, it was used to ease the pain of wasp stings and insect bites.

Granny would ring out the washing by hand and then Ruth would wind the large wheel which turned the heavy wooden rollers of the iron-framed mangle in the conservatory, to squeeze the remaining water out of the washing before hanging it on the washing line. And, of course, they didn't forget to steam a good suet pudding in the copper while it was hot.

Sarah – along with husband Harold – was a constant and devout Christian and would provide her own accompaniment to the day's household chores, humming the *Old 100th* or singing *Tell Me The Old, Old Story*, or *Jesus Wants Me For a Sunbeam* as she went round the house; her favourite hymn, though, was *The Day Thou Gavest, Lord, Is Ended*. She loved being in her garden, tending her flowers and, in her later years, being with her grandchildren. She was also a founder member of the Inner Wheel Club of Dunstable: the charity-minded club for the wives of Rotarians such as my grandfather.

As with my maternal grandfather's family, so with the paternal or Parrott side: my great-great-grandfather, James, was, at least by the 1851 census, an agricultural labourer in Chalton, Bedfordshire, although the 1841 census had given his profession as a Police Constable. James went on to have eight children with Mary who, typically for the area, was a straw-plaiter, her plaits going on into Dunstable and Luton for the straw hat industry for which her grandson, my grandfather, was later to make cardboard boxes. Here, though, I am concerned with only two of them: Kate Gurney and William Parrott. William, their seventh child, would become a printer in East Molesey, Surrey, and marry Miriam Chandler who would give birth to my grandfather, Harold William on 27th May 1893, but sadly die of complications ten days later. Incapable of both working and caring for a new-born baby, William placed him in the care of Kate, James' child no.4 who had married George Gurney, an electrician. They lived at 34 Victoria Street, Dunstable and, in time, adopted Harold as their own. William later remarried one Harriet and lived at Teddington, Middlesex. Thus my father and his brothers had three Grans: Gran-in-London (Anne Bearton, Sarah's mother), and two on their father's side: 'Gran-in-Victoria-Street' and 'Gran-in-Teddington'.

By the age of 15½, and after an education in the local Wesleyan day school and in Luton, Harold, known popularly as 'Rall', went to work in the warehouse of a local hat factory. With the outbreak of the First World War, he was sent to Commer Cars where he worked in the stores as a warehouseman. His eyesight had been poor from childhood and it was this that was to keep him out of uniform – and safe – throughout the 1914-18 war. But with his father, William, dying shortly before the end of the War, Harold inherited £400[1] which, along with his close friend Arthur Jackson, he invested in a cardboard-box

---

1   *About £130,000 nowadays when compared to wages.*

manufacturing business in a former bus depot in the Luton Road, Dunstable: *Parrott & Jackson*. One of the main industries in Luton and Dunstable from the earliest days of the eighteenth century had been the manufacture of straw hats. For these were required yards and yards of 7-strand, plaited straw which, as with Mary, James' wife and from my mother's remembered poem (see in the Appendix), was the principal home industry for many women and children. The hat industry needed boxes and, while Parrott & Jackson were never big enough to cope with the largest of manufacturers or to compete with larger box concerns, the business survived and expanded into what had been William's trade, printing. From what Keith, Harold's second son and future partner, said, Harold never did have that good a business or financial brain and the company was frequently in debt. Nevertheless, the aspiring young business man was clearly a good match for Sarah Smith / Bearton and they married on 19th April 1919. Haydn William (my father) arrived on 5th November 1921 and (Charles) Keith followed in 1925. Keith described Granny and Grandad to me as "the last of the Victorians". Sarah and Harold were indeed very strait-laced, very 'proper' , very strict on behaviour and politeness, and regular in church attendance at least once on Sundays: either the Methodist Church on The Square, or, earlier on, the Baptist Church in St.Mary's Gate. Babies and how they were made and arrived in the world were never talked about and so, when Keith was due, Haydn was packed off to Sarah's mother, Anne Bearton or 'Gran-in-London' in Ryecroft Street, Fulham, for a week or two. As children, both Keith and Haydn were smacked when naughty and once, when Keith was having a tantrum and kicked out repeatedly at his mother, Sarah kicked him back! On one occasion – and this during my lifetime – when their drains were blocked, the problem was found to be caused by condoms obviously from the young couple next door. Granny remarked to my mother:

"Dad and I never used such things. We used self-control!"

It was in 1925 that Harold, then 32, took a step which would colour the rest of his life. On the run-up to the municipal elections in November 1925, the following appeared in the *Dunstable Gazette*:

LADIES AND GENTLEMEN,

At the request of a large number of the Burgesses I gladly offer myself as a candidate at the forthcoming election. I am the nominee of no party or organisation and therefore claim to be purely independent, as may be seen from the ladies and gentlemen who have signed my nomination papers.

Being a life-long resident in the Town, and one who has always taken a keen interest in its affairs, I will, if elected, **work and vote** for the **further advancement and prosperity** of the **Town**.

It is usual at election times to make all sorts of promises, but I refrain, as one realises that they are much more easily made than fulfilled, but such schemes as the **Cottage Hospital, Housing**, the encouragement of **New Industries to the Town**, would receive my whole-hearted support.

On these grounds I respectfully solicit your vote and support on November 2nd. Remember, you can vote for **Two Candidates** and one of those votes will be much appreciated by

Yours faithfully,

Harold William Parrott

Three weeks later, the following appeared in the same newspaper:

TO THE ELECTORS OF THE CENTRAL WARD
LADIES AND GENTLEMEN

I now take the opportunity of thanking you for your kind support at the poll on Monday. I very much appreciate the confidence you have placed in me, and will make it my earnest endeavour to be worthy of it. Always at your service,

Yours faithfully,

Harold William Parrott

And so began a career on the Dunstable Borough Council which would last for nearly four decades. In his early years, he served on committees which do not ordinarily exist today such as the Fire Brigade Committee – at a time not far removed from the period when firemen had to catch the horses in the field before the engine could set out. He served on Allotments (before it became 'Parks'), Street Lighting (before they had electricity), Rating (before it was taken over by the Inland Revenue, now HMRC); Survey (now 'Planning'); and the Sanitary committee (now 'Public Health'). That he sat as a steadfast independent is evidenced, it is said, by the individual way in which he assessed the needs of the town. I could not begin to say how he voted in national elections before the war, nor how he voted in the all-important post-war election which saw Churchill toppled by Attlee and the Labour Party. Possibly rather paternal in the running of his own business, one of his strengths on the council was in bringing more industry to the town and its people. Yet he was also very aware of the effects the Great Depression was having on the working man. Fortunately for Dunstable, its industries were varied and the Depression had little effect on the town and its people. Nevertheless, he was instrumental in ensuring that the Hunger Marchers who passed through the town in 1932 received a good welcome and places to sleep for the night. That same year, after seven years as a councillor, he was elected an Alderman for a period of six years and two years later became the Chairman of the Finance Committee, the senior committee of the Council. It was also during his time on the 'Industrial and General Purposes' committee that he and the council succeeded in 1934 in attracting AC-Sphinx[1] to the town, something he described as a *"turning point"* in the town's industrial progress which had been static for a few years.

Harold would always put Council work before everything else. And it has to be noted that these were the days before day-time meetings, before councillors could claim allowances – often almost a salary – and committees and council were in the evening after a full day's work. Harold also kept business totally separate from his home life. He never talked of it with Sarah – in fact, he didn't even tell her when the business moved from the old former bus depot to the other side of the road! How much Sarah or Haydn or Keith would have seen of him, can only be imagined, but there must have been some spare time as Raymond and Alwyn arrived in 1930 and 1935 respectively.

Harold always also made room for an annual holiday. Until 16th March 1935 when a Mr. R.E.L.Beere of Kensington paid seven shillings and sixpence[2] to be the first man in the UK to take the test and pass – there had been no driving test, and Harold was happy to potter around in the family car, though not on long journeys. One of his employees, a lorry driver called George East, would always drive the family off on holiday to places like Southsea or Bexhill. Harold's poor eyesight, however, and his complete lack of interest meant that after 1935 he no longer drove, never took the test, but retained

---

1   *Later AC-Delco, a division of General Motors making sparking plugs.*

2   *7/6 = 38p but about £66 in today's wages.*

the car and the services of George East up to the 1939-45 war and the consequent tight restrictions on petrol rationing.

Sons no. 3 and 4, Ray & Alwyn, were brought up very differently from Haydn and Keith, partly because of the effect of the war and partly because Sarah clearly struggled, largely on her own with Harold out both at work and at Council meetings. Ray and Alwyn were always getting into trouble, either at home or with the neighbours. This behaviour was totally unlike the gang and drugs problems we read about so much today, or even of the 'juvenile delinquent' behaviour of the fifties and sixties. If anything, and according to Ray, it was probably no worse than in the *Just William* books: they were boisterous to extremes, disobedient and would have been considered, for the 1930s and forties, quite disrespectful in the way they spoke. Their activities and what they wanted to do would come before everything, and everyone around was expected to tolerate their disregard of others' sensitivities. Invariably this came about because of their love of sport, particularly football and cricket. Balls would fly everywhere regardless of flowers, green-houses or people, and he and Alwyn would be forever climbing over fences in search of said balls – their careless feet trampling tulips and crushing chrysanthemums – which, of course, only worsened the damage already caused by the balls. They were clearly more independently-minded than Haydn or Keith, and were awkward – *bolshy* according to Ray – over church attendance.

When the war came and evacuees arrived in Dunstable, the free time they had for their fun and games increased greatly as they could only attend school 50% of the week in order to allow time and space for the incomers. Yet Ray also remembered feeling very proud as he walked up Church Street on VE day in 1945, to hear his father's Mayoral victory speech echoing over the Town Hall tannoy – although in that same evening, he and Alwyn lit a bonfire on top of Blows Downs[1] and would celebrate the victory themselves by sending a flaming tyre rolling down the hill towards the houses below!

It could be said that Ray and Alwyn 'grew out' of such behaviour into responsible adulthood – or, that the pressure from their ultra-respectable, churchy, civic-minded middle-class 'Victorian' parents won the day. But that would not be until after Ray at 17 took it upon himself to book a Costin's coach for a Luton Town away football match at Blackpool, leaving his father possibly to pick up the bill if it all went wrong. Fortunately, he managed to sell all the seats. When I asked Ray some sixty-odd years later how much personal education he was ever given about life and the opposite sex from Sarah and Harold, he recalled only a proposed day out in Ashridge forest[2], along with a male friend and two girls. The sum total of advice from his mother was:

Councillor Harold W. Parrott, Mayor of Dunstable 1943 (courtesy Dunstable Gazette)

---

1   *Hills on the east (Luton) side of the town, now an SSSI managed by the Wildlife Trust for Bedfordshire, Cambridgeshire, & Northamptonshire.*

2   *In the Chiltern Hills on the Herts, Bucks and Beds Borders and now an AONB, run by the National Trust.*

In Grove House Gardens for recruitment drive c.1943   (courtesy Dunstable Gazette)

At the Town Hall for a military parade, c. 1944 (courtesy Dunstable Gazette)

Ray, Alwyn, Keith, Sarah, Haydn and Harold Parrott, 1945

"Keep yourself to yourself and remember it takes two to make a bargain."

In 1939 and with war looming, Harold was made Chairman of the Emergency Committee and responsible for planning the town's efforts to maintain accommodation, supplies, and support for the war effort, for mobilisation and for the families of those worst affected by its outcomes. With the advent of World War II, part of the Parrott and Jackson works was commandeered by the authorities for storing aircraft engine parts and so the printing part of the business was suspended. But it was after 18 years of service to the Borough Council and in 1943, a year of optimism that the war was going in favour of the allies and against Nazi Germany, that Harold was elected Mayor of Dunstable and was to serve for three years until 1946. Proposing speeches reiterated his gift for organisation and Harold in turn made it clear from the outset that he expected to organise the peace celebrations. Which he did. But before that, much of his time was spent in leading the town's fund-raising for the war effort, for the Red Cross and for the *Salute the Soldier* campaign, in leading and organising commemorations and thanksgivings, and in setting the example of growing as many vegetables as he could in his spare time! Frequently he exhibited at the local Garden Show held at Evelyn Road School by the Luton Road and District Ratepayers Association – indeed, the *Dunstable Gazette* of 8th September 1944 commended the Mayor for winning two cups for food growing: one for potatoes, the other for *general vegetables*. His leadership of the Borough Council was focused mainly on looking ahead and encouraging as wide a range of industry as possible to come to Dunstable, on the building of houses to accommodate the growth in population caused by some three or four thousand evacuees from London, and on the allocation of that housing between competing claims from families in need and ex-servicemen attempting to re-establish their and their families' lives in the post-war years.

Harold was later to describe his war years as Mayor as *grim* with a lot of *flag days and welfare work*. Two years later in 1948 he was made a Justice of the Peace, later to chair the Bench for several years. His sense of doing what was right also came to the fore in the council deliberations over the level of rates (now Council Tax) imposed by the council. Even though, thanks to an intervention by the Exchequer, the rate had come down by 3d in the £, a reduction of 1.25%, as Finance Committee chairman he warned against any complacency:

"I feel that a desperate situation, such as the country is in and the present time should be met by desperate measures in order to keep the council rate as low as possible, compatible with the efficient maintenance of local government."[1]

---

1   *Dunstable Gazette 27/03/1948.*

1948 was a particularly difficult year for the Council's housing policies. Over 600 people were on the waiting list and permission to build another 50 dwellings was conditional upon the council letting as many as possible to agricultural workers – a figure of 25 out of the 50 was mentioned. Harold voiced his concern with this restriction on the grounds that, despite the county being largely agricultural, the borough of Dunstable was mainly industrial. There is some evidence to suggest that the figure was reduced to twelve out of the original fifty[1]. Further pressure on the council came from the British Legion in support of ex-servicemen when they demanded *clarification* of the points system used to allocate council housing. Harold was firmly on the side of those demanding all available information claiming that would "clear away the many misrepresentations of facts which are spattered about the town". This, the then chairman of the Housing Committee, Councillor Hillman, steadfastly refused to give and threatened to resign if forced, only to be told by Harold that it would show *very bad taste... to threaten the council*. The system was not clarified on the grounds that it would divulge personal details about the applicants.

He was again elected Alderman in 1951 and chaired a succession of committees. It was during the fifties that the end of the Town Hall was decided in favour of a new Civic Centre (later the Queensway Hall) to be built on the Park Estate, the land which my friend Michael and I called 'the jungle' and which, along with the fields, disused prefabs and the old fire station lay between Kingscroft Avenue, Dorchester Close and the park, Grove House Gardens. Harold was reluctant to see the Town Hall go, was determined that it should be used as

---

1   *Dunstable Gazette 30/04/1948.*

long as possible[1] and no doubt pleased that it was used by BBC radio in 1959 to broadcast an episode of *Have A Go* with Wilfred Pickles. Harold was also delighted to accept the role of the new Hall's first Entertainments Officer – although his taste in entertainment were decidedly traditional and it would take the decision to appoint a professional manager before "entertainments" extended to the likes of reggae music and boxing contests! That said, it seemed that Harold was very much in favour of new growth in the town as he appears to have supported the widening of Church Street – despite the demolition of two historic coaching inns, the Red Lion and the White Hart – and the gutting of the central town on the eastern side of the A5 to make way for the Quadrant, a concrete and glass shopping centre to which I have referred elsewhere as, sadly, *a mere ghost of its planners' original but limited aspirations*. And this within a few years of the opening of the M1 motorway and the consequent halving of the traffic

Harold's Past Mayor's badge   Sarah's Past Mayoress' badge

1   *Dunstable Gazette 15/10/1957.*

*Harold's silver casket commemorating his appointment
as a Freeman of the Borough of Dunstable*

flowing through Dunstable. and the resulting effects on Dunstable's economy.

In 1959 and 'Father of the Council[1]' at the age of 66, the Dunstable Borough Council conferred upon him the highest honour a council could then award: the Freedom of the Borough which, according to the relevant Act of Parliament, was for *persons of distinction and any persons who have rendered eminent services to the borough*. It carried with it no privileges whatsoever – as Grandad pointed out "I still have to pay my rates[2] " – save for an engraved silver casket and an illuminated scroll, crafted by a master illuminator at Waterlow's[3] and which was an artistic masterpiece. Grandad left these to my father who, in turn, and to avoid having to insure them further,

---

1   *The longest continuously-serving member of the Council.*
2   *Local taxes, now called Council Tax.*
3   *Local printing works.*

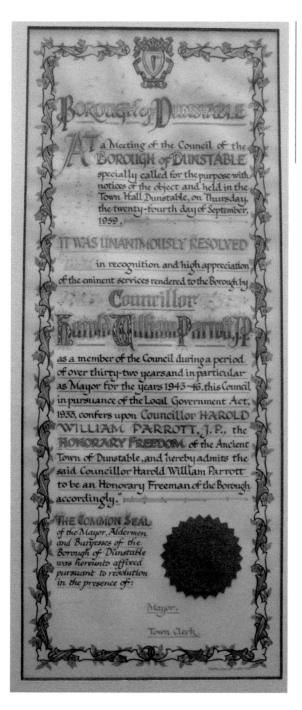

Harold's illuminated scroll upon his appointment as a Freeman of the Borough of Dunstable

placed them on loan to the Town Council. I have now gifted them both to the Council and they are now on display in Grove House, along with the Past Mayor's and Past Mayoress' medallions. The ceremony was conducted in the old Town Hall which would in itself have pleased my grandfather and I watched avidly as several councillors rose to support Grandad and praise his character and his work. His own reaction was only to be expected by those who new him well:

"I love my town as I love my country, and whatever I have done has been a pleasure for me to do."

I was only slightly peeved when, afterwards at the reception, Granny queried whether I should be there at all given that alcohol was available!

When he retired from the council in 1966 after some 40 years' service, the Borough Council then further conferred upon him the title of Alderman Emeritus, effectively making him a member of the council for life.

That I looked up to him is beyond question. I never experienced the closeness I felt with Leonard Estwick, my Granfy, but was immensely proud of being a member of the Parrott family with this man, my Grandad, as its head. I never experienced personally his work on the Council, on the Bench as a Magistrate, as a Rotarian or, indeed, as the founder chairman of the Dunstable Girls' Choir, but I envied and warmed to the speeches made in his honour when he was made a Freeman of the Borough of Dunstable. In the heightened formal language called for by the times and the occasion, it was said that he was a *"force to be reckoned with in debate"*; that he always showed respect to others and was *gracious in defeat*; that he was able to *criticise and accept criticism on differences without rancour*; and that he worked with *sincerity and impartiality*[1].

---

1   *Dunstable Gazette.*

"Whatever inroads into his home life and leisure his public work may have occasioned over the years, he had made those sacrifices as he considered them the duty of a British citizen, who had the heritage of this great democratic country at heart – always anxious to preserve its freedom, justice, self-government and free speech... How fitting that Councillor Parrott was a member of the Dunstable Rotary Club whose motto 'Service Before Self' was the very essence of his dynamic personality."[1]

... *to Mavis*

Mavis, my mother, was born on 27th September 1922 the first of two girls to Leonard and Evelyn Estwick. She was later to wonder why she only had been given the one Christian name when her father was Leonard Wright, her mother was Evelyn Alice and, to make the contrast greater, her sister was Evelyn Enid.

At primary school from 1927 to 1933, the poverty suffered by some families was evident to Mavis in that she could remember children who had to share the same pair of shoes – meaning that only one could come to school on any one day, especially when the weather was bad. Standards of hygiene and cleanliness were, in some families, quite low and hair nits could be a problem. Many's the time she remembered having her and Eve's hair washed in vinegar and then combed through with as fine a comb as possible in order to remove the eggs – these were days long before the chemical solutions obtainable nowadays off the shelves in *Boots*. Mavis was intelligent, read and understood well, coped easily with arithmetic and

---

1   *Councillor W.T.Lack, also a former Mayor – and Deputy Head of the Grammar School.*

possessed a logical, organised way of thinking and of explaining those thoughts. Consequently, she had come to the conclusion that the one thing she wanted to do above anything else was to teach and for that she would need, in 1937 at the age of fifteen, to sit the entrance examination for Luton Girls' High School. This was not to be and Mum often talked to me about the following conversation she remembered almost verbatim:

"Mother and I have been talking," began her father. He looked flustered and had difficulty looking at Mavis in the eye. "She says you're thinking of becoming a teacher. What on earth…?"

"Go easy, Len," said her mother, but that only made Leonard more ill at ease.

"Can you tell me" he tried his best to sound neutral, reasonable, "why you think that's the right way forward for you?"

"They do say that I'm good enough in my English, in my Mathematics and in all my other subjects, especially History and Geography. And when I had a talk with them, they thought I would get into the High School quite easily. It's only a bus journey away and I'd be able to do my English and History and maybe Geography as well and they would be enough to get me into teacher training college. I might even come back to Evelyn Road[1] as a teacher – just think of that! Wouldn't that be good? Wouldn't you be proud of me? I mean, I…"

"Wait." Leonard sat down heavily in his armchair by the fire. "What about your sister? What about Eve?"

"Shall I get her down?"

"No, Mavis. This is between ourselves."

"You must realise, don't you, Mavis," her mother interrupted, "that Eve doesn't have the same ability as you. You know that.

---

1   *Primary School in Dunstable.*

You're constantly helping her with her arithmetic and when you offered to correct all her spelling mistakes, well, she just burst into tears. I don't think she'd get in, herself."

"Evelyn, you know that's not really the point." Leonard was feeling very uncomfortable.

"Isn't it?" Evelyn didn't understand.

"I don't know," said Mavis, beginning to have doubts, "I've tried to help her as much as I can. Surely she could sit the exam, too."

"Yes, she could, but I don't think she'd ever pass it." Len was still skirting round the main issue.

"But you said to Mum that that wasn't the point."

"Look, the point is – and we can'tspend all evening on this – I've always tried my best, so has Mum, to treat both of you equally..."

"We do love you both the same." Evelyn offered.

"Er... well, yes... of course we do. But the point is..." and Leonard tried to regain the unsentimental initiative, "I can't – I won't – send *you* to the High School and *not* your sister."

"Then I'll help her as much as I can," said Mavis, her eyes starting to water. "Mum, Dad – you know that this is what I've wanted to do for some time. Why, why are you against it?" Leonard looked away, his face colouring, his breath slightly snorting in frustration. Evelyn looked from one to the other:

"Oh, Len, you can't leave it like this..."

"Alright," said Leonard, getting to his feet and staring Mavis straight in the eyes. "You want an explanation? I'll give you one and then I'm going straight out down the Club. I'm sorry..." and he paused to gain breath and keep his embarrassment and anger in check. "I'm sorry, Mavis, but the High School costs, and if I pay for one I'll have to pay for the other and I just can't afford for the both of you to go. And so neither of you will."

And with that, he stalked into the hallway, grabbed his coat and hat, and slammed the front door behind him.

Missing out on the education her intelligence deserved, Mavis left school that same year and, in common with many other girls of that age and situation, followed the archetypal secretarial route of typewriting and shorthand. In these, she progressed quickly, gradually building up her accuracy and speed on the typewriter. She would have a small apron tied round her neck and to each end of the carriage, hiding the keys, so that she learned to touch-type: to be able to type accurately, looking at her notes and without having constantly to look at the keys in front of her. Her shorthand soon rose beyond the merely acceptable level of 40 words per minute and up to 60wpm. She still retained these skills into her later years – perhaps not with all the old speed and accuracy, but still sufficient to hold an office post in her late forties after not working for twenty years.

Before then, however, her skills were put to other uses during the war – but not until there had been another 'scene' at home. When the Second World War began on 3rd September 1939, Mavis was nearly 17 and had been working in the Council Offices as a junior shorthand-typist – which, as she once remarked, was perhaps more of the 'junior' and less of the 'shorthand typist'! Leonard had soon got over his embarrassment about the High School and was soon to be occupied digging his air-raid shelter. Eve was doing reasonably well at school, but nowhere near the standard needed for Luton High. Mavis, meanwhile, had noted the formation of the Auxiliary Territorial Service (ATS) which had its roots in the Women's Auxiliary Army Corps formed back in 1917, the year Leonard had been wounded on the Western Front. Sure that her father would be proud to see her in uniform as he himself had been – she announced, on her 18th birthday, her intention to join the ATS, units of which were to be attached to (male) units of the Territorial Army. Whilst they were not to be in the front line or, indeed, see any active service,

Leonard was torn between his pride and his wife, who *so cried and screamed and carried on*, according to Mavis' memory, at the thought of her daughter going off in uniform. Mavis could even quote the example of the future Queen, the Princess Elizabeth, in uniform, driving and maintaining lorries. But no, Leonard, siding with her distraught mother, refused point blank.

It is difficult to say what effect both this and her father's refusal to send her to Luton High School may have had. So many of us gain confidence from the skills we have and the use to which we put them: we identify ourselves in terms of what we do in life. That Mavis never had a career probably made her more anxious about the things that she did do, like her later work as secretary for the Dunstable Business and Professional Women's Club (they allowed a certain number of 'housewives' to join.) and managing the box office for the Operatic Society. These did come after she had, in 1962, been plunged into the local limelight as Mayoress, a greatly successful experience which, I am sure, did a great deal for her self-confidence.

So, after this latest set-back, what did Mavis do? Did she assert herself? Scream back? Walk out? Run away? Not a bit of it. That's not how things usually happened then, perhaps unlike today. No, she buried that dream in the back of her mind along with the teaching and did the next best thing. When it moved to Dunstable in 1940, she joined the meteorological service and wore the uniform of a part-time volunteer in the Civil Defence.

Later at Bracknell in Berkshire and now in Exeter, Devon, the meteorological service – the 'met' – was situated until 1960 at the Dunstable end of Green Lanes, next to where the Council would, after the war, build the Beecroft estate. The met provided a weather-forecasting service for the Army and the Air Force, while the Navy had their own set up. Mavis soon settled in and would spend her war years both typing and in front of a teleprinter – in all probability, handling weather forecasts for the Dambusters to D-day and Dresden – not that she would have known it at the time! There again, her mind may well have been elsewhere while she walked out with a certain Haydn William Parrott from just a hundred yards down on the opposite side of the Luton Road. They would have known each other from growing up in close proximity and, although they went to different schools, would have played in the same Luton Road 'rec'.

Haydn Parrott and Mavis Estwick, c.1941
Memento photographs for each other to carry with them when they were parted during the war.

The HOR radio-receiver Haydn would have used at Chicksands 'Y' station and the W/T Red Form with the letters he would have heard via Morse, written down in groups of 5

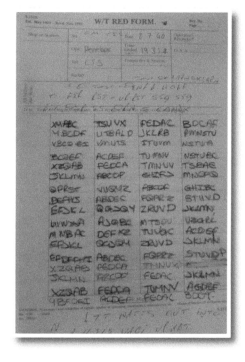

from L.toR.: Sarah & Harold Parrott, Peggy Estwick, Charlie Claridge, Anne Crawe, Haydn & Mavis, Eve Estwick, Jennifer Bearton, Leonard & Evelyn Estwick. Haydn & Mavis' Wedding, 29th April 1944.

Haydn, 2nd from right standing with the WEC RAF group , New Delhi, India 1945

Haydn's RAF Service and Release book, with comments from his Commanding Officer

... *to Haydn*

Haydn William, my father, was born on 5th November 1921, the first of four sons to Harold and Sarah Parrott. Although Haydn was the eldest, it would very often be Keith, brother no.2, whom Sarah would use as a yardstick. If a question arose as to someone's age or when a certain event took place, her calculations would inevitably begin with "Now, how old's our Keith?" Haydn attended the Ashton Elementary School and was clearly thought of as trustworthy and responsible, as his was the job, alone and at 11 years old, of taking the school's dinner money up Church Street and along High Street North to Grove House, the Council's headquarters, there to pay it in. No Health and Safety, or Risk Assessments, in those days! Perhaps less crime too?

At the age of 11, Haydn passed the entrance exam for the Grammar School but not sufficiently well enough to qualify for a scholarship and Harold couldn't afford the fees, and so he went to Britain Street Secondary. Later, Keith was to pass with a scholarship but, just as with Mavis, if one couldn't go, neither would. After school and leaving at 15, Haydn joined the engineering staff of Dunstable and Water Co., played cricket for the town and was an active member of the Wesley Guild of the Methodist Church. After war broke out and when he was old enough, Haydn joined the Royal Air Force Volunteer Reserve (RAFVR) and trained as a wireless operator. I have to say, from the outset, that he never flew and never even saw any fighting, let alone took any part in it.

In 1941, after learning all the dots and dashes – *dits* and *dahs*, he called them – up to a speed of some twenty to thirty words a minute at RAF Compton Bassett training camp, 1216268 Leading Aircraftman (LAC) Haydn Parrott was posted to Chicksands Priory in Bedfordshire. The Crown Commissioners had bought the Chicksands estate in 1936 and subsequently rented it out only for it to be requisitioned later by the Royal Navy. After nine months the RAF took over operations and established a signal intelligence (SIGINT) collection unit there, known as a Y Station or WOYG – War Office Y Group. Chicksands at its peak had 200 receivers in operation – amongst them Haydn's – and provided nearly the entire Air Ministry's supply of German Airforce strategic communications interception. While at Chicksands, he was billeted[1] at the home of a Mr. and Mrs. George Matthews in Clophill, a couple with whom he was to remain friendly for many years after the war.

Haydn would do his eight-hour shift, sitting in front of his radio set, an American HRO[2], valve-based, shortwave, general coverage, communications receiver, his headphones on, a pencil in his right hand, his left turning the large, bakelite, tuning knob seeking any German morse transmissions. In front of him would be a pad of thin, flimsy paper, printed in red and divided into a grid. Each box would hold five letters and he would tune his set until he came across a transmission. He would then, at extraordinary speed and unerring accuracy, note on the pad, in groups of five, the letters he heard being transmitted. When the message finished, he would tear off the grid he had been working on, put it in a wooden tray in front of him, and tap his pencil on the tray to alert the sergeant in charge. That paper would then be collected and, along with others, handed to a motorcycle courier who would then take them. Away. You didn't ask why; you didn't ask where. Haydn, in common with all the others, had signed the Official Secrets Act, the breaking of which in war-time could well mean the death penalty. In fact, this interception of German wireless

---

1   *Compulsorily lodged – if you had the room, you could not refuse to put up a serviceman if asked to.*

2   *Originally HOR and known as "Hell Of a Rush", but because of the pronunciation of 'HOR', it was changed to HRO: 'Helluva Rush Order'.*

traffic was passed immediately to the Government Code and Cypher School at Bletchley Park, which is where they broke the codes of the Enigma machine, later to prove instrumental in the defeat of Nazi Germany.

Haydn used to say that he could recognise what was known as a man's 'fist' – the way whoever was sending the message was tapping the *dits* and *dahs* of the Morse. He said it was like recognising someone's voice. This could be useful in terms of linking messages one to another and even in terms of geographical positioning. Dad later taught me, in addition to the international distress call sign SOS (… _ _ _…), how my name was spelt: dit-dah-dit [R], dah-dah-dah [O], dah-dah-dit [G], dit [E], dit-dah-dit [R] (. _ . _ _ _ _ _ . . . _ .).

He must, however, have found time to attend dances held in the Town Hall, or down at Totternhoe Memorial Hall on a Saturday evening and, for half-a-crown (2/6)[1] each, to court and eventually marry Mavis on 29th April 1944, The Dunstable Gazette's front page proclaimed *Mayor's Son Bridegroom* and *one of the biggest war-time wedding congregations Dunstable Priory Church has seen* under a photograph of the two sets of parents, Sarah and Harold, and Leonard and Evelyn (Leonard insisting on wearing what he thought to be 'proper': a winged collar with his tie), Peggy and Eve Estwick, Mavis' cousin and sister as Matrons of Honour, and their two bridesmaids, Anne Crawe and Jennifer Bearton[2]. The Best Man should have been Haydn's brother Keith, but he had just been posted to South Africa for flight training in bombers. Fortunately for him, the war was to come to an end before his training did! Consequently, one LAC Charlie Claridge filled the breach. According to the *Gazette*, my future mother *made a radiant picture in ivory figured satin with a long train… and a*

---

1   *Worth about £2.50 in today's money.*
2   *Daughter of Stanley, Sarah's brother, and Haydn's cousin.*

veil lent by a friend. Now, when I look at the picture of the four bridesmaids and Mavis in their dresses, I can only wonder how, in wartime and when so much was rationed, they managed to get the coupons to buy the dresses or the material to make them. Were they hand-me-downs or second-hand, perhaps? I remember Mum (Mavis) telling me once how she, her mother and her mother-in-law-to-be[1] saved food coupons in order to be able to make a small wedding cake for their reception tea in the Parish Hall near the church.

Their honeymoon was spent in Blackpool, a town, according to urban legend, that Hitler did not want bombed as he wished to have it for his personal playground after the planned German invasion of England. As the area was used for military training, some of the small hotels were paid to keep a certain number of rooms available at all times for the intake of military personnel, but many used to risk it and let the rooms. If, like Haydn, you had booked your accommodation you were all right. Blackpool, during the war, still had a lot going for it and Haydn and Mavis had the choice of dancing in the Tower Ballroom, or going to *On with the Show* on the North Pier with such stars as Jewel and Warris, and Tessie O'Shea, or perhaps to the Grand Theatre for a Noel Coward play. There were, of course, also the beaches which, unlike many which had been fortified against invasion, remained open, the pier, the promenade and bandstand. Whilst their room was comfortable enough, eating was less easy and gave good cause for amusement as none of the breakfast plates were flat on the table and, when you tried to cut your food or bread, moved around alarmingly. The landlady apologised, saying that it was the war and she could only get 'seconds' for crockery.

---

1   *Evelyn Estwick and Sarah Parrott.*

One of the many sad consequences of war is that it separates those who love each other. Haydn and Mavis had but a year in which he could spend as much time with her as his leave from Chicksands Priory allowed. Home was a bed-settee in the upstairs front room of 128 Luton Road. Living at home with her parents gave Mavis some company when Haydn was away and avoided the expense of finding a house. Togetherness such as it was, was not to last long, however, as in May 1945, just as the war in Europe was in its last days, Haydn, now 23 was posted out to New Delhi in India as a wireless operator with the South East Asian Airforce, leaving Mavis, now 22, to join in the VE Day celebrations without him. There in India's capital, he was part of the Wireless Experimental Centre (WEC). This was one of two overseas outposts of Station X, Bletchley Park, to which Haydn had already contributed from his Y Station at Chicksands Priory. Situated at Anand Parbat, then outside the capital, Delhi, the WEC was staffed by members of the Intelligence Corps, the British and Indian armies and the Royal Air Force, and was used partly as a wireless intercept station for Japanese coded transmissions. There were three outstations, and also about 88 listening wireless sets around India, and several mobile Y-stations.

It was in India that Haydn acquired the name of Bill. Apparently, none of his colleagues had ever come across 'Haydn' as a name before, thought it strange, asked for his middle name and shortened 'William' to 'Bill'. And so he became known. Whilst in New Delhi, 'Bill' Parrott played piano for Church Parade, kept goal for the RAF football team and was awarded his corporal's stripes. He also made what was to be a life-long friend in Jack Thornton. The two lost contact after demobilisation, but got back together again after Haydn was televised rolling – throwing, rather – oranges down Dunstable Downs on a Good Friday and Jack sent a letter to the Council Offices at Grove House addressed to Bill Parrott – it took them a little while to work out who Bill was.

When demobilised in April 1946, his commanding officer noted:

The above named airman has at all times shown himself to be a keen and conscientious worker. Of excellent character, he is intelligent and can be recommended to any future employer

Back in Dunstable, Haydn returned to employment with the Gas Company whilst at the same time following evening classes in accountancy which would eventually lead to his post as an export clerk at George Kent Ltd, an engineering firm in Luton.

... into a Home

Mum and Dad's – and my – first real abode was number 57 Waterlow Road in Dunstable. This was up a slope leading westwards off High Street North. Keith, Dorothy and Cheryl had a similar house near the bottom of the hill at number 16. A three bedroom terraced house with a front room, living room and kitchen, built in the last quarter of the 19th century, it had a tiny front space, a small back garden and a 'back passage' between us and Mrs. Megs Jasper at number 59. The passage (our houses were joined together above it) led to both our back doors and gardens.

On opening the front door, you immediately found yourself in the front room or lounge and standing not on carpet but on linoleum, or lino[1] for short: a cold, unwelcoming covering for bare floorboards in the days before floorboards were fashionable or the arrival of wall-to-wall fitted carpets. This room, in common with many front rooms of the time,

---

1   *Made from resin and oil with fillers and on a material base, it came in various colours and patterns, but was prone to cracking.*

was hardly ever used and was kept for special visitors and Sunday afternoons. The decoration was lightly flowered wallpaper which was not washable or even wipeable. It went up as far as the picture rail, from which no picture ever hung (Mum thought they gathered dust), and down to the wooden wainscoting. Dad had decorated the room himself – the first time he'd undertaken this sort of work – with tutorial help from Leonard, his father-in-law. Mum stood in the background, fearful less the distemper used for the ceiling should penetrate the old sheets Leonard had brought with him to cover the furniture which could not easily be moved out.

The focus of the room was the open fireplace, the murky black depths of which were shielded from view by a Mum-embroidered peacock-patterned fire screen. It also hid a small two-bar electric fire for use when the front room might only be used for an hour or two as there were no radiators, no central heating. A small set of fire tongs (poker, shovel and brush) dangled in a stand on the right behind the fender – a wooden barrier whose purpose was to stop loose coals from running beyond the hearth and on to the lino. But there was a rectangular rag-rug of many colours that Mum had made during the war and while Dad was away in India. Round and above the fire was a tiled fireplace and mantelpiece on which stood the only noise in a silent room: a ticking clock, wound with a large key, and situated between two brass candlesticks given as a wedding present.

In the alcove to the right of the fire stood a small rectangular table, with a drawer under (containing the telephone directory – a very thin affair in those days). On it stood a large, black, bakelite telephone on top of a crocheted doily. We were Dunstable 1056[1], the number a clear indication that the town,

---

1   *But you could not dial numbers; you had to speak to an Operator and ask her to connect you to another number. Long distance could take ages to connect; international had to be booked in advance. As Dunstable and technology grew, the number went to 61056 and then to 661056.*

with a population of 17,547 did not have that many private telephones: many people relied on the familiar red call box on the corner of the street. To own a telephone was considered quite a status symbol; there were no answerphones – and no mobile phones for another forty years at least! To the left was a small bookcase. Behind the table was a standard lamp with a tasselled shade, wired to a two-round-pin plug, red wire positive, black negative, and no earth.

The small table was second-hand, but Mum and Dad had saved hard and had managed to save both coupons and money to buy a small three-piece suite of which they were so proud it was hardly ever used, despite the antimacassars protecting the backs from the heads of men who used oil or *Brylcreem* in their hair. Computers did not exist and information had to be gathered through encyclopaedias – in our case, single volumes such as *Enquire Within*. Mum and Dad were later to discuss getting the *Encyclopaedia Britannica* in all its twenty-odd volumes, but decided against it because a) of its very high cost, and b) even with easy-pay plans, there was no way that they would have anything other than the debt of the mortgage.

Through a door, past the stairs going up to the right, and into the living or dining room with the kitchen beyond. A utility table and four chairs sat on the lino opposite another fireplace, this one actively burning coal and sending thick smoke up the chimney and occasionally out into the room. The coal was delivered by a coal merchant, complete with leather jerkin and cap for protection, who would heave the sacks of coal off the flat bed of his lorry and carry them on his back up the passage and round to the back where Dad had built a small coal store. He'd then hand Mum a slightly grimy bill and grin, the whites of his teeth and eyes contrasting with his coal-dusted face. In front of the fire and behind the fender, though, was a fire guard for when I was able to toddle about. To the left of the fireplace and on another second-hand table partially covered by another crocheted doily stood the wireless ready to bring Dad the daily news, sports reports and occasionally some music. Mum would occasionally have it on during the day but that wasn't her habit as in those days you sat and listened to a programme rather than have it on as background – and Mum would always be too busy doing something. There was no television – in fact, in 1949 there were barely 4 or 5 television sets in the whole of Dunstable! Neither did we have a gramophone/record player, not even for the 78's.[1]

Under this table, covered by a cloth both to keep it dust-free and to hide its relative 'unsightliness' was Mum's old, second-hand typewriter. Under the cover also lay a small stock of carbon paper and of flimsy[2], for copies. On the other side, in the corner, stood my pram for which I still possess the blanket with a large 'R' embroidered on to it. There was a window looking down a path past the kitchen and a tin bath hanging on the wall. When I was born, we did not have a proper bathroom, but Dad had plans to convert the smallest room above the passage when they had the money to do so, Clearly this took time as, to begin with, I had my evening wash in the tin bath on top of the rug mat in front of the fire with water Mum had heated in the kitchen.

It was clear when I was a toddler that Mum liked to be in control and to make sure she knew where I was and what I was doing. Routine was everything, whether it was my feeding, my

---

1   *Large discs made of shellac and played at 78 revolutions per minute (rpm) via a needle and a large bell-shaped horn or speaker. Vinyl records came mainly in two types, the 33rpm album and the 45rpm single (1 track per side) or EP (extended play) with 2 tracks per side. No CDs for another 40 years!*

2   *Very thin paper used with a carbon sheet to make an instant copy of what you're typing.*

toileting, my sleeping or the weekly round of visits. Hence, I spent a deal of time in my secondhand, wooden (no plastics or metal tubing) highchair, not only for meals but after, when I and the chair had been swabbed down and wiped clean, as a play contraption. The base was unhooked from the chair part and hinged round and forward to form a table on which I could play with paper and crayons, plasticine and toddler-style jigsaws. Another advantage was the hole in the seat under which a potty could be slotted and I could be toileted with minimal fuss and disruption of Mum's routine. As soon as I could eat properly, my high chair became redundant and I was moved to the dining table.

Against the wall on the side of the staircase was the utility[1] sideboard. The surface supported two earthenware biscuit barrels, white with a blue-and-yellow loop pattern and with wicker handles, a brass tray and an ash tray (both Mum and Dad smoked), all on the obligatory doilies. Inside its cupboards, neatly arranged over two shelves stood the (for 'best' only and consequently hardly ever used) six pale green dinner plates, side plates, bowls, cups and saucers, a milk jug and a sugar bowl all of which were Mum's status in the world when or if anyone called. Add to those various other bowls and jugs, four wooden 'utility' egg-cups which I still have, half-a-dozen sherry glasses along with a bottle of sherry already two years old, plus one set of yellow-frosted and gold-banded, glasses complete with their own similarly decorated jug. In the drawers above was the decent cutlery set, including fish knives and forks, along with carvers and serving spoons, a neat pile of cotton serviettes, three silver serviette rings (mine was all ready for me for when I was old enough), two white table-cloths (the one a present, the other colourfully hand-embroidered in

---

1 'Utility' goods – *mainly furniture and clothes – were cheaply made and mass-produced after the war.*

the corners by Mum, and a pile of small, crocheted doilies for standing things like the milk jug or pot of jam on the tablecloth or on a tray. Very little else was put in these cupboards and drawers: there was no cork screw (they never had wine), no sets of glasses for different drinks, no other bottles and no fruit bowls.

But: tucked away in the drawer to the left hand side were our ration books, a feature for the first five years of my life. For such things like sweets, sugar, meats, canned and dried fruit, chocolate biscuits, treacle and syrup, jellies, soap, tea, eggs, cheese, coal, rice, tinned tomatoes and peas, sausages, butter and margarine, you had had no choice but to register with a particular shop whose name was then stamped inside your ration book. So when I went shopping with Mum we would start walking up High Street North towards the centre, calling at G.A.Waller Ltd for bacon at no. 25, then move on to The World Stores at no.18 for any sugar, butter or cheese, and then up and over the cross roads and into High Street South to A.E.Fisher at no.32 for our meat. In the 1953-1954 Ministry of Food Ration Books which I still possess for the three of us, eggs were no longer rationed.

Everywhere were little shops, although Woolworth's always seemed big to me. There were no supermarkets at all in Dunstable until I was 22[1]! But shopping was not a straightforward experience. As well as paying the advertised price, Mum had to present the necessary coupon(s) and was not allowed to buy more than the coupon(s) for that week or month permitted as in this post-war period, everyone could buy only so much and rationing was a way of trying to ensure that everyone had their fair share. That there was also a black market in all manner of goods goes without saying. Then

---

1   *The first to open on 28th September 1971 in Dunstable was a small Tesco at 71-77 High Street North.*

there was often added frustration for Mum as for everyone else since having the coupons did not mean that the goods would be in the shops: there were frequent shortages and moreover the Government could also change the *amount* you could have for a coupon at any time. I have to say that, as a young child, I was totally unaware of any scarcity or deprivation. Mum must have struggled and queued to get the food she wanted, but I slept on and played on, oblivious to the difficulties she faced and about which she never, to my memory, complained.

Perhaps if we wander through the archway, down the steps and into the kitchen, since this is where the differences between 1949 and today will be most apparent. On the right was a door, bearing my mother's pinafore (not the coat/wrap-around variety as she thought this too 'common') leading on to the side path to the garden – and round to the 'back passage'. Next to this was the large stone sink with a wooden draining board. The sink had just one tap for cold water, plus a spout that led from a wall-mounted gas-fired water heater called the 'geyser' or the 'Ascot', smaller and less noisy than Granny's. Under the sink and behind a little curtain on a wire were hidden her cleaning materials, bucket and scrubbing brush. Cleanliness was next to Godliness – especially so far as your front door steps were concerned! In the corner was the copper, a large drum bricked in and with a waste pipe connected to the drain outside. This was where Mum would do her weekly wash – always on a Monday, though why that was, I think, owes more to tradition than to practical necessity. Since there was no such thing as a motor to help her, Mum had to move, turn, rub and generally clean the washing herself – probably with the aid of a large wooden 'paddle', the copper only serving as a container with a plug. Really dirty items – like my nappies – would be rubbed up and down a ribbed scrubbing- or wash-board[1] to torture the dirt out. She rinsed, again by hand, in the sink before putting all the sheets, clothes and anything else through the mangle which she had stationed outside the door on the side path. Without a spin-dryer, of course, everything had as much water as possible squeezed out of it between the wooden rollers of the mangle as she turned the handle on the large wheel at the side. Later, she would get a much lighter model with modern rubber rollers which were more easily adjustable. Had we lived near Queensway in West London, Mum could have tried the first launderette which opened on 10th May, ten days after my birth. When all that had been done, the washing would go out on the line which stretched the length of our back-garden and which was supported in the middle by a wooden clothes' prop. At times of bad weather or urgent need, she would drape the articles in question over a wooden 'clothes' horse' which was already old when she got it. Like two three-barred gates, it was 'hinged' with thick woven tape which enabled it to be closed completely or stood at about a 120° angle in front of the fire in the dining room.

Against the far wall stood a gas cooker: a mottled grey-enamelled iron frame with white panels in the door and at the sides, a rack on high over the hob for drying or warming plates, and a grill between the oven and the hob, the whole supported by four almost elegantly curved, little legs. Next stood a cupboard for tinned goods with an enamel surface – no laminates, granite or other fancy worktops then for food preparation – and on which rested the bread board: there was no sliced bread in 1949. Saucepans were stood on a shelf to the left of the cooker and above another small cupboard with a drawer and storage for plates, dishes, cups and saucers, and kitchen- and everyday-

---

1   *A board made up of rounded rungs against or on which the soapy washing would be rubbed vigorously.*

cutlery. There were no mugs and, as a toddler, I was taught to go straight from a feeder beaker to a cup and saucer. There was no dishwasher, no washing machine, no micro-wave (no ready-made meals either), no food mixers or blenders – no electrical gadgets of any kind, in fact. Neither was there any cling film; tin foil was around but Mum rarely used it. The kettle – not electric but heated on the gas – had a removable whistle on its spout; tea was loose leaves spooned into a warmed teapot, boiling water added and left to brew; coffee was a concentrated liquid and came out of a bottle marked *Camp*, redolent of Empire with the picture of a Scottish military officer being waited on by a turbaned Indian servant.

We didn't have a freezer (there was no frozen food) or even a refrigerator – we didn't get one of those until 1957 when I was 8 – but Mum did have a tiny cupboard with a metal gauze door called a meat safe, and a cold slab (a small piece of marble about the size of an A4 sheet of paper) for milk, butter and cheese to stand on: just like Granny and Nana had. Milk was delivered daily except for Sundays and was stored in a bucket of cold water, in the sink, or outside if the weather was cold. Mum and I shopped for food regularly, several times a week – most days, in fact (except Sundays of course when virtually nothing was open) and usually in small portions which would be eaten within a couple of days. She wouldn't tolerate left overs, saying

"It won't keep!" Consequently, she didn't have storage jars, or many dishes or basins for keeping food. But that was also perhaps her displaying the wartime mentality of never letting anything go to waste. The one exception was Sunday lunch as Monday was traditionally the day to eat the remains of the joint (when rationing permitted!) cold with maybe just the left-over vegetables heated up: a favourite of mine being 'bubble-and-squeak'[1].

---

1   *Vegetables (usually green) chopped up, mixed with mashed potatoes and fried.*

Her cupboards did contain things like cornflakes and porridge oats (there certainly was not the choice in breakfast cereals that exists today), jam, syrup, flour, sugar, a couple of tins of fruit, some sultanas and currants, loose tea leaves – there were no tea bags – a tin of powdered eggs left over from the war (and which she was to keep in her cupboard for many more years to come), salt, vinegar, tomato and brown sauces, custard powder, rice, semolina, and the bottled coffee. There was no pasta, and herbs were not common except mint and parsley. She kept no spices save perhaps a little cinnamon and nutmeg for cakes. I should add that we had no chocolate, burgers, fizzy drinks, or fast-food – McDonalds did not exist and it wasn't to be until the early 60's that Dunstable had a Wimpy bar. Moreover, there was not the great string of additives in food. These have been developed to preserve food longer and to enhance flavour and consistency. Tinned vegetables and fruit were common enough, but the vast majority of food Mum bought was fresh and, without refrigeration, had to be consumed within a short period of time. All in all, food – and our diet – was probably healthier despite rationing still being in place, and I for one was certainly not aware of any shortages. We certainly didn't go hungry nor do I remember ever feeling poorly fed. It cannot have been easy at times for Mum to cope, but cope she certainly did – and very well, too.

The back-door in the kitchen led to the side path with the tin bath on the wall and also the lavatory set into the end of the kitchen but entered from outside. Out in the garden, the tiny lawn was cut by Dad first with a hand-me-down pair of shears, and then later with a push-and-pull lawn mower. Other than that, his pride was always in the roses he managed to get. He never knew that much about them, just that they were his favourite, and he would dead-head them regularly and prune them diligently. With both his father, Harold, winning prizes for growing vegetables on his allotment near the factory during the war, and his father-in-law, Leonard, growing vegetables, fruit and tobacco in his garden, Dad was never short of advice – and second-hand garden tools. Though it has to be said that in those days, tools lasted a great deal longer and were replaced very sparingly.

But back inside and upstairs. 57 Waterlow Road had two bedrooms whose drawers and cupboards would invariably smell of mothballs and lavender, and a small third room which would become the bathroom. To begin with, my own room had a Victorian washstand complete with ornate jug and bowl resplendent on it. Lino was on the floor along with the ubiquitous rag rug, this one made by Aunty[1] during the war and given to Mum and Dad when I was born along with a woollen hat, booties and top she had made for me. Aunty was a great knitter of everything from the ordinary jumper to hats and socks via gloves and the dreaded woollen swimming trunks when I was older – the sort that, when you emerged from the water, would droop alarmingly, sagging somewhere between your knees! Of course, whilst socks may today be thrown away as soon as they develop any holes, mine were always mended in order to last as long as possible. Mum would 'darn' them, a process by which she used a proper darning wooden 'mushroom' inserted inside the sock and over which the offending hole was stretched, and sewing which was more like using the woollen thread (not the modern silk/cotton/polyester stuff) firstly to link two opposite sides, and then by weaving the thread over and under, to link the other two sides. The only other items of furniture were a nursing chair for Mum while she breast fed me, a small set of drawers for my clothes and a small cupboard for cot linen and for what toys I had. I say "what toys I had" not to complain about their fewness but to make the point

---

1   *Aunty Dor(is), Nana (Evelyn Estwick)'s sister.*

that there was nothing like the volume of toys by which many children are submerged nowadays. And plastic, so far as toys were concerned, did not exist. I possessed various rattles and assorted noisy things (not Mum's favourites!), teething rings, two rubber ducks for the bath (there was a third made out of a sort of rubber – it may have been sorbo because it had a strange smell and I refused to have anything to do with it), some small board books, bricks or wooden cubes with pictures on some sides, numbers or letters on the other, and Peter. Peter was a little stuffed dog, the size of (but not looking like) a Yorkshire terrier, that was given to me by Jennifer, Uncle Stan and Aunty Dorothy's daughter. The bricks later grew to encompass a few other shapes along with arches, encouraging more elaborate assembly – not that I remember being that interested. Later came a spinning top the handle of which I pumped up and down to wind it up and make it spin faster.

This was, of course, the era of traditional bedding: sheets, blankets and eiderdowns. Just as with my cot, so Mum and Dad would put a blanket on top of the mattress, a sheet (not 'fitted': those weren't until much later) to lay on, then a sheet over, one or two blankets according to the season, and an eiderdown which was a bit like the duvets of today but which sat on top of the bedding, rather than draped down snugly over you. Feathers filled the pillows: we did not have any of the synthetic fillers common nowadays. By the time I came to have a proper bed, it was then that I felt the cold of the lino on my feet first thing in the morning and why slippers were so necessary – and an annual Christmas present. Lack of central heating could also be seen by the frost on the *inside* of the windows during winter and the steamy breath in front of you when you woke up – and was why a good, warm dressing gown was equally necessary. One constant worry Mum and Dad had was, in cold weather, the possibility of the pipes freezing.

Lagging, if we had it, was only strips of brown sack-cloth, not the far more effective synthetic tubular foam coverings we get today. There was no central heating, of course, just the fire in the living room which would be allowed to go out at night – though Dad would often leave the trap door to the roof open to allow what heat was in the house to waft up into the roof and keep the tank and pipes from freezing.

I remember nothing of my toilet training, save for the white enamelled metal pot with a blue handle and edging, traditionally shaped like a 'gazunder'[1] and without any of the ergonomic plastic designs now common place for a toddler unsteady on both his feet and his bottom. Then there were the one or two lapses in my training that embarrassed Mum and offended the olfactory sense of others. It was by that time, too, that I got some pleasure out of being able to reach the wooden handle on the end of the chain that you pulled to flush the loo, the water rushing down from the cistern or tank perched as high as possible on the wall to give good pressure in the downward swirl of water into the pan – no low-level cisterns with suction process and save-water, small-flush option. Loo paper was more like thick tracing paper with *Izal* printed through it. It was rough – some might say harsh – and not terribly efficient, unlike today's soft, many-layered tissue. It also had a particular smell which to me is that of damp and draughty outside lavatories.

So far as washing was concerned, I don't think I, as a young boy, ever had more than one, maybe two, baths a week even when Mum and Dad had had the bathroom installed. And neither did Mum and Dad. A wash every morning, yes, though I was often told off for only having *a lick and a promise* as Mum called it, i.e. a very quick wipe over the face with the flannel – I was only too pleased to get out of the freezing-cold

---

1   *A slang term for "Goes Under" – i.e. kept under the bed.*

bathroom!. Yet we considered ourselves clean and well cared-for nonetheless: a very different regime from the now common daily shower. Toothpaste came in a red tin: *Gibbs*, it was. Inside the tin was a round, pink block, and having bought the tin, you could then buy refills. You used it by wetting your brush, scrubbing it over the strawberry-flavoured block and then doing the same on your teeth. I think we were well into the sixties before our toothpaste came in squeezable Colgate tubes.

By this stage in our family's life, Mum and Dad had achieved the basis and basics of what they wanted: a house, with its mortgage as their only debt, thanks to their prudent money-management and to Dunstable Borough Council of which Grandad was a member; and a steady job with some prospects and a pension at George Kent Ltd., Luton, for Dad. Yes, Mum would have liked a career of her own but accepted, at least at this point in their lives, that being a housewife and a mother and a daughter was, indeed, her role. Mum's life was me and Dad, her sister Eve, and her parents Leonard and Evelyn Estwick; Dad not only had Mum and me and his parents, Harold (also on the council) and Sarah Parrott, he was later also to have the Council and its committees and, to begin with (until Mum put her foot down), his refereeing of local league football. His three brothers were all local and remained close even if they didn'tsee each other that often.

Families, of course, come and go, but houses last a deal longer. 57 Waterlow Road is still in existence, though, according to the website *Zoopla*, its inside has changed considerably – as one would expect. The front room and dining room are now one, with an extended kitchen. Upstairs, what was the third bedroom which was converted into a bathroom has now been converted yet again into a very 'compact' bathroom and a bedroom big enough for a cot. My parents paid £1,200 for it in 1947 which would be worth £184,000 in today's wages. In 2018, it was sold for a quarter of a million pounds – but that's property inflation for you! Every time I go to Dunstable, I always make a point of driving down the road, stopping outside and just looking. Pictures on Zoopla are all well and good, but dare I call and ask if I could have a look around, just to get a feel of the place nearly seventy years later? One day, perhaps, I might…

Four generations in 1949:
Ellen Child (85, 'Mummisgranny') holding Roger,
Mavis Parrott (26, Mum), Evelyn Estwick (54, Nana)

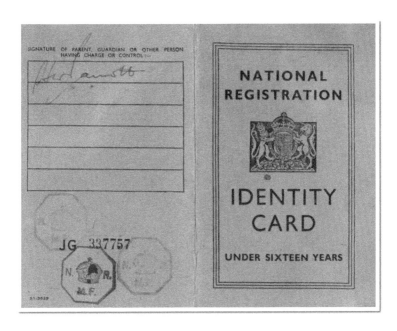

My ID card and number which became my first NHS number as well

My ration book 1953-4

*1951, Jaywick, with Nana and
Aunty Dor; and with Granfy*

1952 and Dad stands for election to Dunstable Borough Council

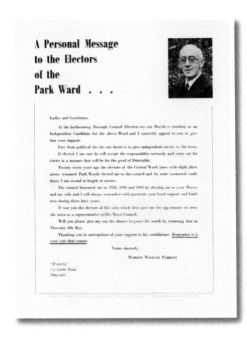

1952 and Dad stands for election to Dunstable Borough Council

1952
57 Waterlow
Road

1952
Christmas

1953 Broadstairs

1954 with Uncle Ray and Sooty

INFANT YEARS 1949-1954

Home and family

In Waterlow Road, life for me consisted of playing and shopping, both done daily. The only recollection I have of post-war austerity and rationing[1] was one day, at the age of about three out shopping with Mum.

"I want a bang of crisps!"

"You don't say 'I want'"

"*May I have* a bag of crisps?"

"What've you forgotten?"

"Please."

"No."

I knew better than to throw a tantrum, but all the same, I'd been through all the politeness hoops...

"Why?" And my lower lip trembled.

"Because I haven't got enough coupons, that's why." The rest of the journey home was quietly sullen. I may not have known exactly what 'coupons' were, but I did know that Mum's shopping was largely controlled by her giving shopkeepers a little book in which things were either crossed out or torn out. The crisps in question would have been Smith's, the ones with the little, blue, paper screw of salt inside, and the shop one I was

---

1   *Rationed: petrol, sweets, sugar, meats, canned and dried fruit, chocolate biscuits, treacle and syrup, jellies, soap, tea, eggs, cheese, coal, rice, tinned tomatoes and peas, sausages, butter, margarine. And the government could change the number of points or coupons needed for an amount of food.*

to know better in my later years as Mitchell's, a local newspaper and sweet shop in High Street North near the Grammar School. Everyone, including children, had, in addition to an ID card, a ration book with coupons worth so many points for the items covered. Clothes' rationing ended shortly before I was born and sweet rationing ended on 5th February 1953. I still have our three ration books left over after 4th July 1954 when all rationing finally came to an end and a full English breakfast would no longer be short of bacon – which, along with meat in general, was the last item to be rationed.

Before then, however, in May 1952, my father was to cement our links to the Borough of Dunstable by joining my grandfather on the Dunstable Borough Council. He stood for election, like his father, as a candidate independent of any political party – something that was then quite common in Dunstable. His election leaflet contained a recommendation to the Park Ward electorate from his father, hoping that they would support his son as they had done him. They did. Almost overwhelmingly. There had been an apology from the local Conservative organiser when the Young Conservatives defaced some of Dad's posters and stuck theirs over his. Today, it would be all over social media with threats of a court case. Dad was the sort simply to accept the apology and quietly carry on canvassing. And within a few years he was elected Alderman and was committee chairman of one of the council's most controversial areas: housing. He re-opened the waiting list and persuaded the council that it should, in part at least, subsidise the rents of the elderly from the central rates fund. And this against some very entrenched opposition from the Conservatives.

Days at home came and went with no upheavals or upsets beyond normal domestic life. Mum cooked, cleaned and cared; and Dad went off each morning soon after 7 to catch the bus to Luton and to George Kent Ltd. where, according to my birth certificate, he was then an 'export clerk'. His working day was from 8:30 to 5:00 and my time with him was very limited, especially given his council duties, except for weekends. He would then be off on Saturday afternoons, black shirt, shorts and socks in a bag with his boots, whistle, notepad and pencil, to referee local league football matches. Mum had added two bamboo sticks sporting yellow dusters as flags for his linesmen. My time with him was further limited by the strict routine Mum imposed on my early years so far as feeding and sleeping were concerned and she would follow diets, medication and toddler routines to the letter. Indeed, many years later and without this rigour applied to his diet in the days before Statins, my father might well have died years before he did, such was to be the level of his cholesterol.

Mum, however, was soon to put her foot down in another way: Council business could take two or three evenings a week – there were no paid day-time meetings in those days – and Dad had to choose between the Council and his refereeing. Which was no great decision, and his boots were hung up for good and Mum got her linesmen's flags back as dusters.

My infant years were, to my memory, blissfully happy with only a few events imprinting themselves on my consciousness. My earliest event on record is, according to my father's cousin, Jennifer[1], who, at the age of eleven, was at 57 Waterloo Road when Mum had just fed me and was changing my nappy[2]. As soon as she removed it, I apparently responded with a massive 'fountain'. Mum was terribly embarrassed and Jennifer was amazed as that was the first time, she tells me, that she had really understood that a boy was constructed differently from a girl.

1   Daughter of my Granny's (Sarah Parrott) brother, Stanley and Dorothy Bearton.

2   No disposable nappies in 1949: Mum had to wash all my messy, wet terry-towelling nappies by hand.

I wasn't aware until years later of the Festival of Britain which was to open on my second birthday. This, in 1951, was a major national and international event held on the south bank of the Thames in London and aimed at re-affirming Britain's place in the modern world after the destruction and hardships of the Second World War. Neither do I have any personal recollection of the Coronation of Queen Elizabeth II on 2nd June 1953 when I was four – except for watching it on Granfy[1]'s television – though apparently he did also pay for me to go to the children's tea-party in the Town Hall in celebration thereof.

One memory of that time, however, which is clear in my mind, is of Granfy buying his *Cossor* television, in order to be able to watch the televising of a coronation for the first time in history. This massive wooden box, taller than I stood at nearly four years old, had a screen about the size of a hard-backed novel and three bakelite knobs on the front for its volume, tuning and contrast. My recollection in particular is of the day when it was being delivered from an Austin van parked on the road outside. My eyes were looking past the blue budgie in its cage, through the net curtains, out of the window and onto the van in the Luton Road, anxious to see what a 'television' not only looked like but actually *did*; they were definitely not on where I was going. I tripped and fell, putting my hand into the fireplace It was very quick: perhaps my hand missed the fire itself, or it was very low, or someone grabbed hold of me just in time, or my hand wasn't in contact with the fire for above a second or two. Grandmothers always seem to be able to do or say the right thing at the right time and Nana[2] was no exception as, for some serendipitous reason, she happened to have a pot half-filled with cold tea on the table into which she immediately plunged my

---

1   *Leonard Estwick.*
2   *Evelyn Estwick.*

hand. I can bear witness to cold tea being a good antidote to burns as no scarring has ever existed. I also have some memory of the tiny, grainy, flickering, black-and-white images of the new Queen at whom we peered and marveled some months later, crammed together in front of this box, with Granfy occasionally and frustratingly getting in the way to tweak the knobs in a vain attempt to improve the picture.

One weekend activity to which I accompanied Dad was when he was duty organist for the Sunday evening services, in the local Methodist chapel at the bottom of Waterlow Road. Hidden by the red velvet curtain which shielded the organ from the rest of the congregation, I would perch on the bench behind him where he kept his music. There, I would become mesmerised watching his hands glide over the double manual surrounded by ivory-headed organ stops, with his feet heeling-and-toeing the pedals, and all the while a multitude of sounds wheezing dustily forth out of the pipes high above my head. Now, I think it a pity that it did not inspire me to learn the piano while we still had one at home.

Prior to that, on a Sunday afternoon, if we were going out for a walk which we usually did and I got wind of

"Where shall we go?", my toddler suggestion was always the same:

"The cemetery". Perhaps I liked the flowers; perhaps I liked the quiet; perhaps I liked the openness: I don't know. Did I have an infantile ghoulishness? I think not.

Nevertheless, toddlers have their ways and means and I formed my own little customs. When I was about 2 or 3, I acquired the habit of getting out of bed and coming downstairs when Dad was having his evening meal – we called it 'tea' then – with the words

"I tan smell sumsing tooking" and would only return happily to my bed if I were given a little piece of what he was eating.

That in itself is some evidence of how I learned at an early age not to ask outright for something unless I was prompted to do so: implying or suggesting seemed to work the trick. I should add here that I had trouble, to begin with, pronouncing my c's. In town I would want to go for a *tup of toffee and a take* and both Mum and I got terribly frustrated when, coming back from Nana and Granfy's on a bus near Dunstable Town station in the Luton Road, I proudly pointed out a *trane*.

"But there isn't one!" insisted Mum, gazing at the empty bridge and station.

"Yes there is! It's there!" I wailed. It took a little while for Mum to realise that I was talking about a crane, not a train.

These were the days when most families remained nuclear, many remaining in the same area, if not the same town, as their parents and grandparents – indeed, I would later be the first member of the extended Parrott and Estwick families to go to University and live away from home. Besides seeing both sets of their parents on a Saturday, Mum would also go down and visit her mother, my Nana, during the week except on Tuesdays. Then, she and I would catch the bus from near the centre of Dunstable ('The Square') and head the three miles south down the A5 for the road up to Kensworth. There, in a caravan in a field and with – to my infant disgust – a separate chemical toilet, lived her sister, my Aunty Eve[1] and Uncle Ray, her husband. I could not understand how poo and pee could be left sloshing around, mixed with a pungent chemical. Such was the post-war housing problem in Dunstable that this was their first home together since getting married just before I was born. Eve's first job had been as an office junior at Whipsnade Zoo. Set further along from Dunstable Downs on the Chiltern

---

1   *Evelyn Smith née Estwick, my mother's sister, married to (Stanley) Raymond Smith.*

Hills and signalling its existence from afar by the large white lion carved into the chalky soil of the hillsides, the zoo was the first of its kind to to allow animals large open spaces rather than box them in cages – a precursor to the safari parks of today. It was there that she met Ray Smith, though Granfy[1] was far from happy when, on one occasion, bad snow meant that there were no buses and the staff, Eve and Ray included, had to sleep overnight at the Zoo. It had probably all been quite innocent – indeed, the Zoo authorities would have ensured that it was in those days – but Granfy took a lot of persuading as parental attitudes were very different in the forties and fifties.

But Tuesdays were not only Aunty Eve, they were also motorised travelling which, even on a local bus for about twenty minutes, was an ordeal for me, leading to bouts of travel sickness. Mum soon learned to dread the comment, *Isn't it hot in here?* She and Dad never learned to drive, never owned a car – thereby perhaps never accustoming me to motorised travel – and this sickness would last for about the first twenty years of my life, and longer so far as flight was concerned. In the meantime, though, we frequently had to get off early for me to be sick. This aversion to motorised travel could also on one occasion have been linked to my hatred of Eve's chemical toilet in the shack outside her caravan. Mum just did not know where to look late one afternoon on the bus home from Eve's when those two factors probably led to my pooing my pants. Her embarrassment was immense as the smell slowly but surely filled the bus and she had to sit there. with me stinking, until we got home.

I have almost no memory whatsoever of birthday parties. In fact, apart from on one possible occasion, upon which, in

---

1   *Eve's and Mavis, my mother's, father, Leonard Estwick.*

addition to the traditional sandwiches, cake and jelly, Mum had splashed out on some of the tiny 'iced gem' biscuits I used to love, I don't think I ever had any parties. Neither do I remember ever being invited to somebody else's. What I think is more likely is that parties were kept within families, rather than the bigger and more expensive affairs so many parents have to organise nowadays, often inviting the whole school class! But Mum just did not like entertaining, be it their friends, my friends, or even our family. The success of her hospitality was, to her, not guaranteed and therefore stressful in the extreme. Furthermore, the organisation of that hospitality – and the aftermath 'mess' it would, in her opinion, leave – would create tremendous anxiety in her. Flexibility was not one of Mum's attributes. To incur her wrath, I only had to invite the friend I was playing with in the afternoon to tea that same day. Mum would hate this with a passion and I would get told off through gritted teeth and in a harsh whisper so that my friend wouldn't hear. In fact, she never said no, fearing that that would cast a terrible social blight on her nature, but always bewailed in private that there wouldn't be enough – a sign that she was always extra careful with her housekeeping, the money my father gave her. To make sure we were all catered for, she would, for instance, cut the ends off her and my sausages to make them go round three – her, my friend and me. Dad's meal was sacrosanct.

Joan Bakewell, in her reflections on her later years entitled *Stop the Clocks*, speaks of a mother's work in those days as *cleaning and washing, dusting and polishing, shopping and cooking, washing dishes and ironing clothes. Her aim is to have the perfect house and having a child around threatens that perfection.* She must have known my Mum!

I was wholly unaware that this was still a time of scarcity and was totally oblivious to the difficulties Mum must have faced.

Mum cooked well but simply – very English, in fact: meat and two veg., virtually no herbs or spices and minimal mixing of ingredients save for baking cakes or the occasional stew. Fresh food was always her priority when available and meat invariably was the central focus of each plate whether it be the Sunday roast or its remnants, sausages, a meat pie, ham, bacon or fish – which was then not the more expensive semi-luxury it can be today!. No doubt I would also have had some rabbit stew – later, one of her best dishes – had not the deadly myxomatosis outbreak of 1953 taken rabbit off menus for the next ten years or more. Eggs, porridge, toast and cornflakes were the main staples of breakfast, with lunch being whatever she wanted or needed to get rid of while it remained fresh – we did not have a fridge until I was about 8 years old. The one thing I always had was a good appetite – I ate everything I was given. Granny[1] used to say that I had 'hollow legs' to be able to cope with the amount I ate. Mum was more graphic in some ways, harking back to the war during which nothing was wasted and, if there were scraps for whatever reason (potato peelings and the like), they would be put out for the local pig-farmer to collect. Hence she would occasionally refer to me as 'pig-bin'. How sweet!

Holidays

The one thing which came round as regularly as Christmas and birthdays was the annual holiday at the seaside. These were family affairs in the sense that they were spent in the company of either the Parrotts (Granny, Grandad and possibly Ray and Alwyn[2]) or the Estwicks (Granfy, Nana and Aunty Dor[3]). A

---

1   *Sarah Parrott.*

2   *Sarah and Harold Parrott and no.s 3 and 4 sons, Raymond and Alwyn.*

3   *Evelyn Estwick, née Child; Doris Child.*

bungalow would be rented for two or three weeks, although Dad, who had just two weeks holiday in the summer, would normally only take one week, leaving himself the other week to catch up at home on domestic tasks such as decorating. The costs would thus be shared more widely and Mum would have others on hand to help her look after me. Allowing extra time for me to be ill, we would catch the bus to Luton, my ticket being peeled off a wooden board by the conductor and with a 'C' for child stamped on it and a hole would be punched through to show that it had been used. Later, mechanical machines would be introduced whereby the conductor would ring up the fare on little levers, then wind a handle and your ticket would emerge to be torn off and handed to you.

From Luton, we would then catch the steam train to London St Pancras – I was never travel-sick on a train – and then from another London station, take a train to our preferred resort such as Jaywick, near Clacton-on-Sea in Essex, Thorpe Bay near Southend, and Broadstairs on the Isle of Thanet in Kent. All places were chosen for their genteel peacefulness, I think, rather than for any degree of 'life' – which, I think, did not exist as a criterion in the early fifties – at least, not for Mum and Dad who would never, ever, have deigned to go to a *Butlins* or a *Pontins* holiday camp, such a thing being, in their view, far too working-class. I therefore had all the time and space to ride donkeys, travel around in large three-wheeler bikes or 'social cars' and build sandcastles. Then there were the awkwardly convoluted gymnastics of having to undress and change into my trunks with a large towel wrapped around me before spending the morning or afternoon blissfully playing with sand and water and occasionally eating a pear and having a donkey ride. The only thing I remember really hating was my mother's insistence on rubbing me clean and dry with a rough towel and with all the sand still on me. I could now – if in masochistic mode – recreate the misery by rubbing my legs with coarse-grade sand-paper.

These, of course, were not the days of massive suitcases packed with clothes for every eventuality: cases were not of the lightweight construction common nowadays and had to be carried, not wheeled. Nevertheless, I would have my entire summer wardrobe with me: one pair of good shoes, one pair of sandals (always 'sensible', always Clark's or Start-Rite); three pairs of short socks, two pairs of shorts – buttoning on to my shirt in the first years; four pairs of airtex pants, a smart shirt and tie – possibly a bow-tie at that; two short-sleeved shirts, a warm top of some description and my raincoat. Not forgetting, of course, a pair of Aunty's knitted, saggy-crotch swimming trunks. This was not a lot for a small boy coming out of potty-training and Mum was frequently frustrated by my occasional 'accidents'. I could, no doubt, have been equipped with more had Mum been willing to shop around for lower prices, but both she and Dad preferred quality to quantity, and all our wardrobes were consequently limited in size and scope. Mum would shop at *Fosters* in High Street North, Dunstable for me, whilst she herself would patronise (Fred) Moore's shop in High Street South. Dad invariably went to E.H.Buckle & Son in Middle Row and was still buying his clothes there – though from the son, Philip, – some twenty years later when he told me to get myself a made-to-measure suit for my wedding to Helen[1] and to *put it on [his] account*.

But back to our holidays in the early fifties. Dad always traveled in his "best" holiday outfit: his demob suit to begin with but later a blazer, shirt and tie and trousers, and would have two or three more shirts with him, another pair of trousers and a light pullover. Mum had no more than two dresses, a skirt with two or three tops a cardigan and a summer coat. Not an anorak in sight! Whatever clothing I had, however, I still managed with annual regularity to spoil the beginning of

---

1   *To Helen Sinnett, on 2nd June 1973 at Cockington, near Torquay, Devon.*

Mum's holiday by falling into the sea, fully-clothed, off one of the groynes or break-waters. The only other item of clothing I associate with holidays was a pack-a-mac or plastic mackintosh which could be folded up small and put easily in a bag or even a big pocket when out for the day. Grandad always carried one of these and we could always tell when he had had a decent holiday – at least weather-wise – when and if he said "… and I didn't have to take my pack-a-mac out once!"

Writing this originally by a swimming pool in France, I noticed a young mother and her baby in the water. The baby would have been under two months old and she was bouncing him up and down in the water, dunking him right under, playing with him and then hauling him back up again, the little one revelling in the water and both in being under it and then rising up through it. How I wish that baby had been me and that I had learned to swim from the beginning! Neither Mum nor Dad ever swam, ever *could* swim – a rolled-up-trouser-leg paddle was usually the limit for Dad. It was not until 2013 and I was 64 that I finally learned to swim.

Bully Cows and a Milk Cart on a Hill

Regardless of what was going on in the wider sphere, my world was my immediate family and the town in which I lived: Dunstable. As a toddler, one day would probably meld imperceptibly into another, but Wednesdays were always market day. This was the weekly livestock market which, in various guises, had been around ever since Dunstable, or its Roman origin, existed. It took place on The Square right outside the appropriately named Noah's Ark café which we would patronise for my 'tup of toffee and a take'. I delighted in going round looking at the 'bully cows', as I called them, watching them being loaded or unloaded, snorting up and down the wooden ramps in and out of the lorries. I always went armed with a little wooden cricket stump so I could poke them. One day, however, they got their own back when a cow stamped in a pool of slurry and covered me from head to toe in stinking, dark green liquid. I screamed, Mum was angry and it was the end of the cricket stump. The market was by then in decline, however, and would close for ever by the time I was six in 1955. I find it rather apposite to note that the Noah's Ark, no longer a café, is now, as I write, the home of a veterinary surgeon's practice.

Looking back, I do feel that one of the habits I have now of having tea or coffee and probably a cake whenever we go out, be it for shopping, for a walk in a park, or visiting a place of interest such as a National Trust property, is down to habits formed in childhood in the Noah's Ark, and later, on Saturdays, in the coffee-mornings at the Methodist Church, also on The Square.

But I would and could play happily both in the garden and in the street as there was rarely a single car in Waterlow Road. They just weren't the sort of houses for people who owned cars – which were very much a luxury item then. On one particular occasion, this was just as well. Our local milkman – milkwoman, rather – had an early battery-powered milk cart – not a sit-in-and-drive one, but one with a long handle to be led by the milkwoman. This cart was equipped with a handbrake which, being curious – or some would say downright stupid – I found could easily be let off. The cart started to roll slowly back down the slope that was Waterlow Road towards the busy – for those days – High Street North or A5. Fortunately, a passer-by with great presence of mind managed to stop the cart and its contents before disaster occurred. I have no recollection of the consequences of this for me but maybe one just blocks out the bad bits. In fact, I do have some memory of

Mum and Dad's reactions to this being concentrated in their apologies to the milkwoman and to her company.

Nowadays and with more traffic in the road, I am tempted to think that the cart would have at least badly damaged some parked cars and that, in the ensuing legal recriminations and Health & Safety considerations, the parents would have sued the milk company for not ensuring that their cart was little-boy-tamper-proof!

Playing, whether in our garden, in Grove House Gardens or in Waterlow Road, inevitably led to falls and grazed arms and knees. There must have been something about my knees, or about medicine and hygiene in those days, as my grazes always took forever and a day to heal. Perhaps, though, it was more due to my being an inveterate scab-picker! Many's the time Mum whisked me off to Dr Hugo Stevens when my knee turned septic. His surgery was part of his elegant, double-fronted house, now called 'The Friars' on the corner of Friars Walk and High Street South and opposite what was then the Police Station. Unlike nowadays and the ubiquitous 'group' practices, Dr Stevens was on his own: you always saw him, he knew you and, moreover, probably knew all your family, too – and had done for years! He was an exceedingly tall man with a large, dark moustache and thinning dark hair swept back. I would find him in his surgery, his three-piece tweed suit bent over the solid oak desk, puffing away at the pipe clenched between his teeth, the banker's desk lamp casting a soft glow over the green leather desk-top, a stack of prescription leaflets in a wooden rack next to a thermometer in an antiseptic holder, an ink-well and an upright, mercury-filled blood-pressure gauge in its wooden holder with brass fitments and squeezy, spherical rubber pump, his fountain pen going backwards and forwards and all the time, his black labrador panting quietly behind the high-back, quilted and buttoned, leather captain's chair in which he sat and swivelled.

Antiseptic mixed with pipe smoke and dog is not an aroma usually associated with good health. He was a man, however, in whom I had complete faith and trust as a curer of all ills and we would go from his surgery to Flemons and Marchant, the Chemists in High Street North, who would make up whatever he had prescribed. I gather, though, he could, at times be quite brutally straight-forward as when, soon after having me, i.e. 1949-1950, my mother went to see him about losing weight. His response was that

"No fat people ever came out of Belsen[1]".

School

So far I was the sort of child who spoke when he was spoken to, who spoke to adults properly and sensibly, and who was keen on reading: *Books and jigsaws, please* was my standard response when asked what I would like for my birthday or for Christmas. My Uncle Stan[2], though, always sent me a postal order, usually for ten shillings[3]. Presumably I also had some sense of responsibility at the age of 4 or 5 as I distinctly remember being given half-a-crown to cut through the passageway from Waterlow Road to Small's Timber Merchants in Clifton Road and to come back clutching a clothes-line prop: a 6-foot piece of 2" by 1"[4] with a V slot cut in the top.

But now School beckoned. I only had to walk five minutes

---

1   *A Second World War Nazi concentration and death camp which, when discovered and liberated by British troops, was found to contain starving prisoners who were little more than living skeletons, such was their level of starvation.*

2   *Stanley Bearton, Granny (Sarah Parrott)'s brother, my great-uncle and Godfather.*

3   *Ten shillings – 10/- in 1955 is worth about £30 in today's wages.*

4   *2 inches by 1 inch or 5cm by 2.5cm*

round the top of Waterlow Road, turn right and right again into Chiltern Road, and to the Chiltern Road Infants' School. In 1954 the pre-schools, or nursery schools as they were called, were few and far between and by no means within the financial range of ordinary folk, so for most children, this would be the first day they had been away from home and from their mothers. Mum came with me on that first day and I couldn't wait to get there! Thereafter I walked the five minutes by myself, often meeting up with others on the short way,. Later on, Mum did tell me later that for the first few days at least, she would follow me, keeping out of sight, just to check that I got there safely.

With the advantage of hindsight, I can now see that, whilst Mum and Dad were delighted when I learned to read and gave me every encouragement, they had been totally content to leave everything to the school. Thirty years later and I would not have dreamt of sending my two girls, Sarah and Heather, to school without them being able to count or to read a simple book.

My first memory of a teacher is of one Miss Spraggins, who taught me within the first few days to spell my name and I went home delighted to announce that I was *ruh-o-guh-air-ruh*. My second memory is that the toilets were outdoors and had doors with large gaps top and bottom. The whole business with toilets is a mysterious minefield for little 5-year old minds and I hated going there. I also remember asking Mum how many times I should wipe myself with the rough Izal paper if I did go to the loo at school, and was told that twice should be sufficient. It wasn't. In the classroom, in straight rows behind tiny tables and sat on rickety chairs with canvas seating and backs, I started writing using chalk on slate. One thing we did which would stand me in good stead for minor repairs in the future: I learned to sew – not plaits of straw[1] but cross-stitch,

---

1   *See the appendix for my mother's poem.*

running-stitch and blanket-stitch on squares of binca material – small woven squares with tiny holes in a square pattern to guide where you put the needle.

In my report from Chiltern Road Infants' School, dated 1st April 1955 and shortly before we moved house and I moved school, Mrs. Briggs, the Headmistress, was encouraging, saying she would be *"very sorry to lose"* me and describing me as *a very apt pupil* who *reads well*. She was sure I would *do very well* (at Ashton Voluntary Primary School) and would be *a credit to [Chiltern Road] school*. Miss Spraggins noted further on a separate sheet that I had progressed to *Janet and John book II* page 30, was practising using the *Beacon Reader Book Two*, and listed the simple addition and subtraction number work of which I was capable.

Children Road Infants School closed in 1974 to become a teachers' centre. By 1982 and with less government spending on education and an emphasis on private enterprise, the building was bought by the independent radio station, Radio Chiltern. That then became a victim of corporate buy-outs, and the building in which, I, ruh-o-guh-air-ruh, first learned the three R's: to read, 'rite and do 'rithmetic, is now flats.

O tempora, o mores![1]

---

1   *Oh the times, oh the customs! (Cicero)*

1956 with Elaine and Kevin

1956 Ashton School Nativity Play, as a Page, kneeling 2nd from left

1956, Nana (Evelyn Estwick)

1958, Granfy (Leonard Estwick)

1958, (Great) Aunty Dor (Doris Child)

1958, (Great, great) Aunt Ruth

1958, Mum & Dad at
Paignton

2012, Hope Pratt celebrates her
100th birthday.

1958 at Ashton School

1959 at Ashton School

PRIMARY YEARS 1955-1960

The second half of the fifties was to pass me by in equal measure to the first half. Leaving an infant school to join a five-to-eleven primary school, little of what the world had to offer beyond the confines of Dunstable ever reached my awareness.

The writer Alan Bennett was of the opinion in his boyhood that life was generally *something that happened elsewhere*.[1] So it was for me in Dunstable. No wonder when I was out in town with Mum and Dad that we went to places such as the Noah's Ark, or the coffee-morning in the Methodist Church: it probably served to reassure them that God was in His Heaven and that their rather comfortable world would not collapse in on them tomorrow, regardless of Eden's ignominious attempt to take back control of the Suez Canal[2] from Egypt in 1956, or of the Soviet Union's invasion of Hungary[3], or of competition between the USA and the Soviet Union heating up: the race into space and to the Moon and in nuclear weapon superiority. And even if I was not old enough to comment on the sickly

---

1   *Keeping On Keeping On. Alan Bennett. Faber & Faber 2016.*

2   *The Suez Canal was a link for between the south-eastern Mediterranean Sea and thence in to the Red Sea and Indian Ocean and was a vital shipping lane for exports to and imports from the Indian sub-continent and the whole of the far-east.*

3   *In 1956, there was a popular uprising by Hungarians against their domination by the Soviet Union, which then invaded the country in order to 'restore order'.*

and ageing Winston Churchill giving way to Anthony Eden in 1955, or on some prominent names at the height of the British establishment found to be spying for the Soviet Union, I was still expected to speak when spoken to, to speak up, and to talk sensibly with people far older than myself and in many cases much older than my parents.

Things started in the fifties which were to mean a great deal to me in later life: Premium Bonds[1] were issued for the first time in 1957 and the first winners selected by ERNIE[2]. 1958 for me is the year when I – along with a lot of other youngsters, – started supporting 'ManU'. Half of the "Busby Babes", the youthful and brilliant Manchester United team, were killed in a plane crash in Munich on their way back from playing in the European Cup in Belgrade. Matt Busby, the Manager, survived – just – as did the legendary Bobby Charlton, and together they led Manchester United to be the first English side to win the trophy, ten years later at Wembley. And I was there! I think supporting Man U was initially the romance of the greatest club in the world, a great tragedy, and the desire to be a part of something, to identify with something big and important. Now, of course, that need to identify with, to be a part of something has diminished, but, despite their fluctuating fortunes, I still cannot shake off the need to follow them.

My interest in and love of the cinema began later but was centred on the great British films released in the fifties such as *The Dam Busters*, *The Bridge on the River Kwai*, *My Fair Lady*,

---

1   *A forerunner of a national lottery. You bought a bond (for£1) and waited for your number to be called for monthly cash prizes. Your bond is valid forever and can win multiple times!*

2   *Electronic Random Number Indicator Equipment. The original computer was the size of a van and generated 2000 numbers an hour, compared to the latest ERNIE which is the size of a personal computer and is 500 times faster, generating a million numbers per hour.*

the beginnings of the *Carry On* series and *Saturday Night and Sunday Morning*. In the USA, *Ben Hur* and *Around the World in 80 Days* won Best Picture Oscars, while back in the UK, Agatha Christie continued to write her detective books, CS Lewis his *Narnia* stories – I was to read them again forty years later prior to playing Lewis in *Shadowlands* at the Lyric Theatre in Belfast – and Ian Fleming continued to produce his *James Bond* novels, although I wasn't allowed to read them for another eight years! That I have always been something of a news addict was inculcated in me by my parents' insistence on watching it on television – when we acquired one. In September 1955, BBC television brought faces[1] to its news reading. Prior to this, there had been a feeling that visible news readers might have a personal effect on the way the news was presented, running the risk of bias. For an example of what this can mean, – you have only to watch Fox news in the USA or, for a more extreme version, the state-controlled television news service in North Korea – amazing performances!

The BBC also lost its monopoly of the airwaves when the new Independent Television Authority (ITA) began broadcasting, funded by advertising – the first ad. being for *Gibbs'* toothpaste. Our first telly arrived three years later in 1958, much to my relief as I remember feeling rather "out of it" compared to friends and family members. After all, the only telly I got to watch was when I went down to Nana and Granfy's on a Saturday. Three years down the road in 1960, Granada TV, part of the ITA, aired the first-ever episode of a television soap opera which is still running today: *Coronation Street*, though I have to admit to never following any of the available 'soaps'.

These were also the years in which I began to understand and to handle money – the rather obscure (at least to those from

---

1   *Richard Baker and Kenneth Kendall.*

other countries!) system of pounds, shillings and pence. 1956 was the last year the humble little farthing, a quarter of a penny or ¼d[1], was minted, eventually to be withdrawn from use. I now collect them, along with all pre-decimal coinage of the UK.

Other aspects of traditional life were also rapidly disappearing, such as telephone operators and their *Putting you through now* as STD – which then stood for Subscriber Trunk Dialling rather than a sexually transmitted disease – meant we could all just stick a finger in the appropriate holes, whirr the dial round and release it, and speak to Aunty Clara in Aston Clinton or Ellis Plumbers in Ellesmere Port without having to go through the Exchange. Policemen on the beat were fewer, as was their tendency to give an errant child a good clip round the ear. Not owning a car, we did not notice that drivers no longer received salutes from the breakdown motorcyclists of the AA or RAC. We still had a regular daily delivery of newspapers – early morning deliveries being a useful source of income for many teenagers – and also of milk (save for Sunday). And there were two deliveries of post – early morning and lunchtime/beginning of the afternoon – on weekdays with one on Saturday and with a standard letter or postcard in 1957 costing 2½d[2]. The weeks just before Christmas also provided ample opportunity for students home from University to earn money assisting with the increased delivery loads.

A New Home

In April 1955 and just before my sixth birthday, we moved from 57 Waterlow Road to 28 Kingscroft Avenue, Dunstable.

---

1   *In 1971, a modern penny (1p) replaced nearly 2½ old pennies or nearly 10 farthings, with 100p making £1.*

2   *"Tuppence ha'penny". In today's wages, 54p (Now in 2022 a first class stamp costs 95p and a second class 68p).*

This was to be the house in which I was to live so long as I called Dunstable my home and the second and last home of my parents.

Our new home was a three-bed semi with big, bay windows to the front, built in 1932 in a pleasant residential close near to the centre of the town and terminating in an unkempt wilderness of open fields leading northwards to Grove House Park and eastwards towards Vauxhall Motors. My main interest became a stretch of rough scrubland with bushes we nicknamed 'The Jungle' leading up past some dilapidated prefabs[1] to the fire station on the left and thence to High Street North, emerging more or less where Queensway does today. Dad had paid £2,500 for the house, having sold 57 Waterlow Road and taken out another mortgage through the Borough Council, of which he was a member. The monthly mortgage repayment cost him just over one week's wages – about £9.00[2] – at a time when he was paid £450[3] a year as an export clerk. Granfy[4], when he heard of the cost, told Mum that the mortgage would be like *a millstone round your necks for the rest of your life*. But his financial forecasting was no better than his football pools calculations. In any case, Dunstable was then reckoned to be quite an expensive area for housing, being just north of places such as Harpenden which was in the northern edge of the so-called 'stockbroker belt' of high-priced, luxury housing extending from the north of London, and round to the counties of Middlesex, Surrey and Kent.

---

1 *Short for 'Prefabricated' and applied to emergency post-war housing which consisted of factory-made and assembled walls, floors, ceiling and roofs which were subsequently erected and bolted together on site, on foundations which had been laid down by builders.*

2 *This is approximately £600.00 in today's wages.*

3 *This salary would now be approximately £30,000 per year.*

4 *Leonard Estwick, my mother's father.*

At this time, many workers like Dad were undergoing a change in the way they were paid and it happened about a year before we moved. George Kent Ltd, the engineering firm in Luton for whom Dad worked, decided to switch all its white- and blue-collar workers to a monthly pay cheque, rather than weekly cash in little brown envelopes. For Mum and Dad, even given the several months' notice they had had, this was considerably stressful as, refusing to have any debt apart from the mortgage, they had had to boost their meagre savings to be ready to cover a whole month's pay in advance of the changeover. I will say now that, throughout their lives, they were, unlike me in my working life, financially ultra-prudent. Neither did they ever discuss money in front of me or, indeed, anyone. There were times I thought them rather less than generous, others when they were only too keen to help out. And there were times such as when Mum had lent me the money to buy a new car (I'd crashed mine with them in it in France, shortly before I decided to give up teaching!) and then, when I announced I was leaving teaching to go to Drama School, she suddenly – and I am still grateful to her to this day – cancelled the debt.

Inside number 28, the water for washing was heated by a coke boiler in the kitchen but each room had its own electric radiant bar heater. The boiler was also the source of another instance of my giving a "helping hand" when, thinking that it looked a bit dead, I went and got a jam-jar of the paraffin that Dad kept in his shed. I opened the lid of the boiler and poured it in, jumping back promptly as the flames whooshed upwards and out, burning to cinders a tea-towel and a pair of Mum's stockings drying on the rack above. I was so shocked at what I'd done that tears of regret took a while to arrive but probably saved me from much punishment. Mum and Dad also seemed more than relieved that the outcome hadn't been much worse.

My bedroom was a great change from Waterlow Road in that it was quite large and actually carpeted – so no more cold lino under my bare feet! Dad was to build me a wardrobe[1] in the alcove to the left of the chimney breast – which was itself bricked in and tiled, with an electric fire mounted at just the right height for me to sit on the bed and feel the warm glow of the radiant bars – one brass switch for each of the two sections: put both on and you were cooking! But I wasn't allowed to. The amount of electricity it used made it an expensive luxury. I think they must have invested in a new bed for themselves because, before too long, I found myself wallowing in the expanse of a double bed all to myself. Bed-clothes were very different then. My sheets – and my memory is of synthetic or at least poly-cotton ones, rather than pure cotton, to save Mum ironing time – top and bottom were tightly tucked in with old-fashioned 'hospital' corners. I had two blankets, satin-edged or at the very least with big hems held by what were called 'blanket' – obviously – stitches. On top of those, there would be a floral-patterned, quilted eiderdown – a smaller version of today's duvet, only laying on the top surface of the bed and perhaps as much for decoration as for warmth. Finally there would be a bedspread designed to cover the whole bed, the most popular sort, at least later on, being the candlewick type. Next to my bed was a pale blue bakelite radio that Granny[2] had given me

Being forbidden to use the electric wall fire in my bedroom, I was delighted when, by about the early sixties, Mum and Dad had saved enough money to invest in an early form of electric central heating: night storage heaters. In these, special bricks were heated by lower-rate (*Economy 7*) electricity overnight,

1   *This was made on a 2x1 timber frame in the alcove to the left of the chimney breast, and covered in hardboard – not the strongest wardrobe I ever had!*

2   *Sarah Parrott, wife of Harold W.*

were hot in the mornings and gave off their heat steadily during the day. This frequently meant that, by the evenings however, the rooms needed some additional heating. Much later on they were to have gas central heating installed and Dad was to spend part of his retirement lump sum on double-glazing.

However, one improvement soon installed after we moved in was our first refrigerator. This was a gas-fired fridge, something which is not common these days. Once when I'd been naughty and Mum had said

"Just you wait 'til your father gets home!", I touched the cover of the gas pilot light and burnt my fingers. Mum took that as punishment for my naughtiness and I no longer had to wait for Dad to get in – though I remember such threats more as a form of words rather than as the portent of dire retribution!

Mum remained throughout her life very house-proud, the house sporting nary a speck of dust and the hoover requiring new drive belts on a regular basis. I've commented before on Mum's reluctance to entertain family, friends, or other children and to this reluctance I would add the fact that I was never allowed a pet. I used to love Pip, the Yorkshire Terrier Granfy acquired after Nana died – I don't think she had cared much for dogs either, as they always had had only a budgerigar. However, both Mum and Dad were, much later on in my life (1980's), only too glad to look after my Border Collie, Laika, when we went on holiday. Once, while a student, I was stupid enough actually to buy a parrot in a cage. He was an African Grey whom I called 'Percy'. On one occasion when we'd taken him to Mum and Dad's to be looked after when we (Helen, my first wife, and I) were going away – this was in the mid-seventies – Dad had his finger bitten by the bird and went to the Luton and Dunstable hospital for a tetanus injection. While there, he heard staff tittering that there was *a bloke out there called Parrott who's been bitten by a parrot.*

Eating and drinking

Mum would shop almost daily until the arrival of a fridge in 1957. Staple foods bought were bread – always white – meat, eggs, potatoes, carrots, greens, milk, tea, and syrupy welfare orange from the clinic in Kingsway (later the site of the 3rd St Peter's Scout Hut, later just houses). There was always, but always, enough to eat: I was never, ever left hungry and had certainly remained blissfully unaware of any of the privations of rationing in the first three or four years of my life. Mum, however, was careful to the point of being regimented in her housekeeping. If she had bought six eggs it was because she had already planned exactly how those eggs would be used: perhaps 2 for a cake and another three for tea for the three of us during the week, usually with some bacon and perhaps a sausage if the butcher had any – and she had the coupons. The sixth egg would be added to next week's supply so that, in addition to a sponge cake, a fruit cake could be made. It goes without saying that it was inured in me that everything I was served was 'good for me'. In later years, Mum's quasi-obsession with eggs and their quantity extended to rationing slices of sponge cakes when Dad was found to have high cholesterol.

My breakfast would usually have been cereal with milk and sugar. There was little choice: corn flakes (later Rice Krispies) or porridge – and that tended to be only in the winter. Occasionally I might have a boiled egg with buttered 'soldiers' (the use of margarine was regarded as being very 'beneath' us, despite what the adverts on TV said about not being able to tell the difference between a certain margarine and butter[1]) for dipping, but that was on Sunday mornings only and thanks to Granny.

1   *In the TV advert, many people supposedly could not tell the difference between the taste of Stork margarine and butter.*

Without doubt, the meal of the week, for which Mum pulled out all the stops, was always Sunday dinner – and we still had *breakfast, dinner* and *tea* then, it didn't change to breakfast, lunch and dinner for some years! Sunday dinner was always a roast: beef, pork or lamb; never chicken as it was too expensive in those days and would only be used at Christmas as a cheaper alternative to turkey. Small, individual Yorkshire puddings and plenty of gravy (made from the meat juices and the inevitable Oxo cube) accompanied the joint. This was always 'well-done' as there was never any pink meat or 'rareness' in Mum's cooking, and sat alongside roast potatoes and a couple of vegetables from: greens (*that'll make you grow!*), carrots, swede, cauliflower, broad beans, peas and parsnips. Marrow, braised celery and leeks were less common, as were onions – except in stews, or only very occasionally cooked whole for Dad who loved them. Turnips were never served as Mum thought them only good for pigs – a sentiment due partly to sheer snobbery and partly left over from the war, I believe.

We never had starters even for celebration or festive meals. Mum, for some obscure reason, was never one for soups and resisted any suggestion that that would be a good use for left-over vegetables. Her only purpose for those was that they should be eaten and finished off, there and then. But there was always a dessert which, on Sundays, was always pie or crumble and custard. The fruit was either apples, or gooseberries, with the occasional addition of blackberries or black currants. The other regular fruit was plums for which I had to count my plum stones using the rhyme:

Tinker, tailor, soldier, sailor, rich man, poor man, beggar man, thief, doctor lawyer, indian chief – supposedly to forecast your future position in life!

Desserts were also an integral part of every main meal and would vary from steamed puddings with a sauce or jam, semolina (with jam), tinned fruit, baked apples, rice pudding, rhubarb jelly, jam tarts, and then the much heavier, suet-based jam roly-poly, dog-in-a-blanket and the much-joked-about (not with Mum!) spotted dick[1] – all with custard.

Monday tea would be thinly sliced, left-over roast with perhaps bubble-and-squeak[2] or, in the summer, a salad of Cos or Webb's lettuce (there was no Rocket, Chinese leaf, or Iceberg) with tomato, cucumber and maybe some beetroot or spring onion, along with a generous covering of salad cream – mayonnaise and vinaigrette were unheard of. Tuesday's might be a 'sliced dinner' with the remains of the roast cut up and put in a casserole with potatoes, tomatoes and carrots. Or minced up and mixed with vegetables in a shepherd's (lamb) or cottage (beef) pie.

On other days of the week there might be faggots, peas and potatoes, sausage and mash, liver and bacon casserole, stuffed hearts, toad-in-the-hole, egg and chips (never often enough for me!), cod with peas and potatoes, kedgeree – most of my memories are from the post-rationing era of the late fifties and sixties when rationing was a thing of the past. Saturday dinner (lunch!) was invariably a bought meat pie, mashed potatoes and peas or baked beans.

Then there was always Spam! A type of pressed meat made mainly from pork, but one was never totally sure. Spam could be cooked – we even had spam fritters at the Grammar school: deep-fried, battered slices of spam which, by the time we came to eat it, had turned soft and positively dripped fat. Or it was eaten cold with vegetables, salad or in sandwiches. If Mum ever gave me sandwiches – perhaps on the very rare occasion I went fishing or out with the scouts for the day – they would

---

1 *These three would be made with suet pastry and required rolling in a cloth, tied and cooked in simmering water for a good two hours or more. The first was filled with jam, the second (dog-in-a-blanket) with mincemeat, the third with currants, raisins and sultanas.*

2 *Mashed potatoes mixed with left-over vegetables and fried in a pan.*

be cheese and tomato or cheese with a leaf or two of lettuce. And salad cream.

Sunday tea-time was always very traditional. Even though we would have it in the lounge in front of the television – BBC's Sunday serial and *Songs of Praise*[1] – there would always be a milk jug with a gauze cover weighted down by small beads – never a bottle (which would have been the height of common vulgarity for Mum) – sugar bowl, teapot and cosy, cups and saucers of the best china Mum had, along with matching plates bearing scones with butter and jam or sandwiches with a thin filling of *Shippam's Potted Meat* (or *Crab*) *Paste* (my personal favourite was Heinz's *Sandwich Spread*, a salad cream-based spread with tiny pieces of what I think were perhaps finely minced salad ingredients). There would also be a cake-stand with shortbread, sponge or fruit cake – whatever Mum had made fresh that day. All this would be finally crowned by the one thing I detested more than any: evaporated milk poured over tinned fruit!

As I write, I can honestly say, much to everyone's relief, that I eat everything. I never ate mushrooms as a child and still prefer to avoid them if possible. But I eat them if they are given me and, by the same token, hate waste in any degree.

Milk was one element of our diet which was not at all a favourite with me throughout the years I lived at home and I did not like cream. Mum had her milk delivered regularly as clockwork every morning. It came in foil-capped bottles and would be left next to the back-door step (tradesmen again!) before any of us had woken. She would leave out a couple of old tins or small containers which the milkman would place over the tops of the bottles to prevent birds from pecking their way through the foil cap and into the milk. The quantity

---

1   *A televised dramatisation of a classic of English literature; a programme of hymns from a church somewhere in the UK.*

varied between one and two pints, but it was always two pints on Saturday as there was no delivery on Sunday. Empties – and Mum would always wash the bottles thoroughly first – would be put out at the end of the day ready for the milkman and his early morning delivery – which was always in time for an early breakfast. If you were awake, you might hear the sound of the bottles clinking in their metal carriers and the unmistakeable sound of empty bottles being picked up and replaced by full ones. Then there was the colour-coding of the foil caps: gold for the full cream, Jersey milk, and silver for full fat which later turned to blue, along with green for semi-skimmed and red for skimmed: the colours we see today, though the gold has largely disappeared. One thing I couldn't stand was getting the thick, gooey gloop of pale yellow cream on my cornflakes, so I would always turn a new bottle upside down to dissipate the cream.

It has to be said that the proliferation of refrigerators which allow milk to be kept longer along with the rise of the supermarket, probably led inexorably to the decline in daily milk deliveries and by the 1990s, doorstep milk deliveries were doomed to be a thing of the past as most people bought their pints of milk in plastic litres. Certainly by the time I had effectively left Dunstable in the early seventies, 94% of people still received their milk by direct delivery. Now, it is less than 4% – though a recent news report at the time of writing did say that in a few areas, the glass milk bottle delivered to your door was making a comeback. One thing I never did was to obey the advert, seen on large hoardings about the town, which exhorted us to 'Drinka Pinta Milka Day'. I always knew, however, that milk originally came from a cow. I wonder how many children nowadays would swear that it is manufactured by and comes from Tesco and not cows and farms?

These were still, though, the days before calories and cholesterol, organics and obesity had entered our daily vocabulary. Microwave ovens were still to be invented and takeaway meals a thing of the future.

Diseases and Dentists

One of the biggest differences between now, well into the 21st century, and then in the 1950s is in health care. Practice may have changed nowadays but in the 1950s, a couple of bouts of tonsillitis and you would be sent by your GP (in my case, the much looked-up to, literally and figuratively, Doctor Hugo Stevens, he of the pipe and the labrador) to have your tonsils surgically removed. Thus occurred, at the age of seven, my first entry to the Luton and Dunstable Hospital since I exited after my birth in 1949. The event itself proved nothing to bother about, save for the wonderfully soothing effects of the copious amounts of ice-cream I was allowed to eat afterwards "to sooth the stitches", so to speak. Other than that, I did not prove a particularly good patient.

"I don't want the sides of my bed up!"

"Well you must."

"Why? I don't have them at home. I'm in a big bed now."

"In you go."

"But – " And I am unceremoniously pushed by the nurse on to the bed

"We don't want you falling out now, do we?" And with a couple of clunking clicks, I am imprisoned behind the railings. Then, when I was told to go for a wee, I went to the lavatory, saw the pot balanced on a wooden plank across the the loo, removed both and did it in the pan as was my wont at home. Wrong. They wanted it in the pot for sampling. Nurse was not amused. Again.

My next visit was for having sliced my finger with an axe (as I mention later in…*Grandparents and Other Relations*); the third, at the age of nine was to a Mr. Plewes, an orthopaedic consultant, because Mum was worried that I was walking pin-toed. His remedy was that I would grow out of it playing football. I did grow out of it, but not through playing football as I was useless. Other than that, Mum did her damnedest to get me every childhood disease that was going around. Chicken pox? Here's Roger to play with you. Mumps? Give me the address. Measles I caught at school in the normal course of events, and my abiding memory is fear of going blind – or so I was told – and being shut in a darkened room for a week with only Mum or Aunty[1] to read to me. No books, no jigsaws. Oh, the complete and utter boredom! I did, on the other hand, have copious amounts of *Lucozade* to drink as well as my favourite comfort food: poached egg on mashed potato.

In the early 1950s, Polio had been the great dread. It crippled thousands of children, and killed many. It wasn't unusual to see children with crutches or leg callipers, or even to hear of some who had been in an iron lung – a machine which helped you breathe when your normal muscles had failed. But in 1955 a programme of immunisation started which has totally eradicated the disease in the UK and throughout Europe[2]. I was spared polio, and also the threat of Diphtheria by the vaccinations and was also given the BCG jab against Tuberculosis, an unpleasant experience which left a circular scar of multiple needle holes on your arm. Of course, these were also times in which there was no transplant surgery and for many serious diseases, it was not a question of *if* it would prove fatal, but rather *when*. Penicillin, originally discovered by Alexander Fleming in 1928, was not used on a large scale until further development by the Americans during the War, and it became a vital factor in the improvement of health in the post-

---

1   *Aunty Dor(is) (Child)*.
2   *http://vk.ovg.ox.ac.uk/polio*.

war world. A positive aspect of the development of nuclear technology during the war had led to radiation therapy being used against cancer. The 1960s then brought hip replacement surgery – from which I was to benefit some fifty years later – and mass availability of the contraceptive pill. My mother was then a volunteer worker at the local family planning clinic round the corner in Kingsway. Whilst I once heard my father muttering something to her about bringing home some free samples (of condoms) and Mum shushing him knowing I was within hearing distance. Her rather strict moral code led, however, to her resigning in the early 1960s in protest at unmarried women being prescribed the Pill.

I have to work hard to achieve some memories, but a sensory one immediately comes to my nostrils even though I haven't smelt it for decades: the dentist's 'sleeping gas'[1]. All the time I had total faith in our GP, the imperious Dr. Stevens, I had nothing but fear and loathing for the dentist's work. I was registered at Lyle and Glenn's in High Street North and in particular with Mr. Glenn. Their receptionist, Rene – I think she was Mr. Glenn's wife – was the nicest person imaginable and Mr. Glenn himself did his absolute best to be sympathetic, but I would refuse to turn up, manufacturing the slightest excuse for not going. There was the ghastly brace that was placed between your teeth and ratcheted wide to keep your mouth open, plus that awful, black, rubber face-mask that was held over your nose to administer the anaesthetic gas –

"It's just like Journey Into Space" Mr. Glenn would say soothingly, quoting the popular radio programme, as his hand slowly but surely clamped the mask on my nose, its cavernous metallic smell sending me down a never-ending tunnel with dizzying speed and remaining in my sensory memory sixty years on. As I became older, fillings followed more fillings as

---

1   *Nitrous oxide* N_2O.

night follows day, with Mr. Glenn, in those extremely low-tech days, pumping his foot up and down on the treadle so that the dreaded drill would whirr and whine ever more shrilly through a maze of pulleys, grinding a hole in the offending tooth.

Grandparents and Other Relations

I grew up with a good sense of family. Some can be torn apart by deep-seated resentments or events or they can live so closely that they come to depend on the family as their social unit and there then arises an expectation on everyone always to be there, always to take part in whatever. My own family was always very positive but never claustrophobic in any way. They lived geographically close, in and around Dunstable and were always there, even if we didn't see them for months at a time. Nevertheless, the big occasions, 'hatch, match & despatch[1]', saw them out in force, of course. There were two occasions, however, when I was considered too young to join in – both funerals. The first was of 'Mummisgranny' at the age of 92[2], when I was 4. The second was that of her daughter, my Nana,[3] who had died on 12th October 1957 when I was 8. I cannot remember what I understood about death though I recall an older boy at school showing me his pen-knife in Kingsway on our way home and telling me how he used it to cut up dead bodies. Naive little me believed him – at least sufficiently to be bothered, even upset, for a while – but it was soon consigned to the back of my mind.

I always looked forward to Saturdays as family days. They invariably followed the same familiar pattern and one I grew to

---

1   *Births (Christenings), weddings and funerals.*
2   *Ellen Alice Child, my great-grandmother.*
3   *Evelyn Alice Estwick, née Child.*

love and in which I felt very much an integral part of both the Estwick and the Parrott families. The mornings were shopping and for my parents to socialise with local friends over coffee and a sausage roll. Lunch at home was invariably accompanied by the BBC Light programme's *Sports Parade* to allow Dad to relish what he might be able to follow later on in the afternoon when commentary on the second half of a league football match would be broadcast on the wireless, along with any other major event such as the Grand National or international athletics. Saturday afternoons usually meant Mum putting her feet up while Dad did some domestic chores: gardening, or perhaps a bit of DIY – less easy in those days when he didn't have a drill or a sander, and there were no plas-plugs[1] or superglue and the only jigsaw was the type that I did on the dining table.

Both before and after Nana died and on my own at the age of seven or eight, I would catch the Luton bus just outside the Alms Houses in Church Street, pay the tuppence[2] bus fare and get off at the Luton Road Post Office a mile away and walk the few yards to 'Maleesh', no.128 where she and Granfy[3] lived. They inhabited mainly the ground floor of the house, save for the upstairs bathroom. Their garden seemed very big to me when I was young. In addition to the tobacco I've mentioned before, Granfy continued to grow fruit and vegetables there. One year, he cut my name, along with that of my cousins, Kevin and Elaine[4] , into three young marrows and eventually we were each presented with this massive vegetable, mine with 'ROGER' scarred into the side. On one occasion I helped him 'muck-spread', throwing forkfuls of horse manure over freshly turned soil. On another, when Granfy was gardening and I was

---

1 *Holes in walls were made by hammering a Rawlplug bit and repeatedly twisting it to form a hole, then inserting a fibrous Rawlplug.*

2 *2d or about 40p in today's wages.*

3 *Evelyn and Leonard Estwick.*

4 *Mum's sister Eve's children.*

'helping', I turned the garden hose on him. I thought it a great laugh and he, lovely, tolerant man that he was, just stood there and laughed, got drenched and then went in and changed.

But back to my Saturday afternoons. Having arrived in the afternoon at number 128, Granfy always gave me a shilling – probably worth about two pounds in today's wages – to buy some sweets at the Post Office where I could choose perhaps a packet of *Spangles* or a sherbet dip, some flying saucers or a banana split, and maybe even 4 ounces (120g) of pineapple chunks, licorice comfits or rhubarb-and-custard flavoured sweets. Any odd copper left might just get me a gob-stopper as well! All loose in paper bags.

The living room was not big but seemed magically to contain the television to the left of the fireplace, two massive old leather armchairs, a table with four dining chairs, a sideboard, a budgie in a cage in front of the window and a large, round, brass tray Granfy had brought back from Egypt complete with a folding leg stand, all of which were dusted by a *Nenette* soft brush kept in a yellow tin container. There was also a concertina kept in the depths of the shelves by his armchair from which he would occasionally squeeze out the hymn tune *Rock of Ages*, despite one of the buttons being faulty. In the hearth would be a container of spills – thin strips of wood for lighting cigarettes and a pair of bellows for blowing air into the fire. In his later years, when his chest was getting bad – I think he eventually died of lung cancer probably caused by his home-grown tobacco – he also kept a screw-top jam-jar as a recipient when he coughed, gurgled and spat.

For tea, Nana always bought four jam doughnuts although there was only three of us. When we had had one each, she always urged me to have the last one. It had been made clear to me however that the polite thing for me to do was to offer it, first, to Granfy. He would then refuse and tell me to have it, and I would. If, on the odd occasion I did not offer it to him first, Granfy would take it from my plate and eat it himself. I soon learned. When I was older, I would have my tea sitting in one of the two big leather armchairs, my toast (which I had done in front of the fire with a twisted-wire toasting fork) and Marmite, and maybe a little celery or watercress, and tea balanced on a plastic tray, held on the broad arm of the chair by spring clips. It was from that position that I used to watch the old cowboy programmes on television: *The Lone Ranger, The Cisco Kid, Wells Fargo, The Range Rider*. Granfy always bragged that he knew how and why *The Lone Ranger* became the 'masked crusader" he was, but frustrated me by refusing to say. Later, it was usually the police series *Dixon of Dock Green*, probably the most unrealistic picture of police work there has ever been, but in those post war years when authority was losing its respect, it comforted those who still believed in it.

The one thing neither Nana nor I could do was to speak during the football results. Granfy did the Pools[1] and kept a large hardback, foolscap notebook in which he religiously copied down all the results, and woe betide us if we interrupted him! Yes, it was a form of gambling just as the National Lottery is today, but Alan Johnson, the former Labour MP, in his *This Boy* makes the point that for a host of people, it was Hope – the hope of winning hundreds if not thousands of pounds[2], a fortune in those days of post-war austerity.

After tea, Granfy would get ready to go out for his usual Saturday evening session of bridge at the Liberal Club in the middle of Dunstable. He always voted Labour, but the Club had good Bridge players and so that was where he went. There

---

1 A form of betting, forecasting the results of Saturday afternoon football matches.

2 £100 was the approximate equivalent in wages to £5,500 today. One of the largest wins in those days was £152,300.18.8 in 1961 and worth over £7,500,000 today.

was at least one time that he had stayed on drinking after the then legal drinking hours, The club had had a 'lock-in', arguing that it was therefore no longer subject to licensing laws, but Granfy and others were prosecuted and Mum's dad found himself up in court before Dad's dad and other Dunstable magistrates for out-of-hours drinking. I think I remember Mum saying he was fined £2.00.[1]

After tea, Granfy would sit ensconced in the big armchair in his dark, striped, three-piece suit, watch and fob chain in the waistcoat, with a clean white shirt and detachable collar held in place by a stud at the back and one in front, his bow tie hanging loose and allowed me to shave him. He possessed something that was still quite rare in those days – the late fifties – an electric shaver, a Ronson it was, and I would spend ages running it over his face, then stroking his face with my fingers to make sure all was smooth. I would then apply the Brylcreem to his grey hair and comb it into place for him. When I think about it now, it seems a strange thing to have done, but I thought nothing of it then – indeed I used to look forward to doing it. Maybe it was all akin to the 'grooming' you see chimpanzees doing to each other: I always felt we were very close. It was during one of these occasions that he mentioned the piece of shrapnel in his shoulder left over from the First World War[2]. Now I wish that I had asked him about his experiences and written about them, but I doubt if he would have talked that much as those who had been in the trenches of the Western Front rarely did.

Early on in the evening, Mum and Dad would have arrived for about an hour. I would sit in my armchair, the crumbs of my tea on the spring-clipped plastic tray on the arm of the chair, Granfy opposite neatly groomed for his evening at the club, Nana still at the table and Mum and Dad also perched on the

1   *About £100 in today's wages.*
2   *See the earlier piece about Leonard's First World War experiences.*

dining chairs. I paid little attention to what was being said as television was still a great novelty: we didn't have one at home until 1958 when Dad, as was often the case in this early days of television, rented one from Radio Rentals. Anyway, soon after Jack Warner as PC George Dixon bade *Good night all* from Dock Green, we would bid our own farewells and good nights, leave number 128, 'Maleesh', and walk the hundred yards or so down the Luton Road, crossing over to 'Waverley', number 103, and Granny and Grandad's.

Arriving at 103, Granny, in several layers of clothing, her thin grey hair plaited, coiled and pinned over her ears, and gazing through small, thick spectacles, would let us in, hugging me warmly, her whiskery face tickling my neck and the odour of mothballs gently wafting from her cardigan. As the green door closed, its leaded stained-glass panel admitted a little of the street-lamp into the hall where the light was dark, and the air an eiderdown, heavy and enveloping. The front lounge was dominated by cigarette smoke, and warmed by an open fire. Behind a floral-pattern-covered suite, an ancient iron-frame piano sat with candelabra and a hymn book open at *The Day Thou Gavest*. Grandad, inevitably in a three-piece suit, was sagging in his armchair, the London Evening News held high before his nose, his glasses lodged above his eyebrows, the wisps from a *Senior Service Plain* curling round his nose as its ash tumbled down his waistcoat; and on the tall ashtray, a half-crown[1] waited for me.

We would lower ourselves, Mum, Dad and I, into the settee, and talk to Grandad – often about council and town matters – while Granny prepared our supper in the kitchen: a tray of ham-and-egg pie, pickled onions, cucumber sandwiches with sugar sprinkled liberally on the cucumber (Grandad's favourite) custard tarts and lime-green fruit jelly from the pantry under

---

1   2/6 – *two shillings and sixpence; about £5 in today's wages.*

the stairs where it had stood, along with her milk, cheese and butter, on a marble slab in front of the metal gauze window – Granny never did have a refrigerator. This, in turn, was next to her meat safe with Sunday's beef in it, and below shelves of pickles and jams. Occasionally, she would produce one of her infamous bread-puddings whose traditional reputation of solid quality – according to, I believe, my Uncle Alwyn[1] but rarely put to the test – was that it could crack a plate when a slice was dropped from two foot.

Ahead of the pantry and beyond the back door, was the kitchen with a conservatory to the side. It was cold, but was the source of Granny's warmth. A stone sink boasted two taps: one cold mains water and the other also cold but fed from the soft rain-water butt for use in the bricked-in copper with its fireplace underneath. The kitchen steamed alive on Monday when, in her younger days, Granny's Aunt Ruth came to feed the fire and stir the washing while Granny wound the cast-iron mangle in the conservatory, the heavy wooden rollers squeezing the pale grey water out into the pail beneath.

Back in the lounge, tea was poured into china cups with a blackened kettle purring in the hearth, ready to top up the tea pot or to provide hot water for washing up – she had no hot water supply in the kitchen, the only hot-water tap being the geyser[2] in the bathroom. Due to her failing eyesight, she only ever filled our cups to just over half-full. This, in time, became known as a 'Granny full-one'. These being the days of tea leaves, not bags and Granny not using a tea-strainer, a request for a fresh cup meant that Granny deftly twisted her wrist, and flicked the remaining leaves from the cup up the chimney and on to the sloping ledge at the bottom of the vertical flue. They never fell down to sizzle on to the fire.

---

1   *My father's youngest brother.*

2   *A wall-mounted, gas-fired water-heater.*

Granny knew practically nothing about Grandad's work whether at the factory or on the council, save for one occasion when, in 1957 both he and Dad had been at the opening of a new new sewage treatment works on a bitterly cold day. At the small reception afterwards, they had been given coffee laced with rum to warm them up. This in turn had, by the time they both got back to their respective homes, made them both queasy and sick. Granny, always teetotal, commented in a rather self-righteous tone to Mum whilst comparing notes on their respective husbands over the phone:

"You know, I never in all my life thought I'd see Dad the worse for drink!" And therein lies a feature of their generation and upbringing: I never, ever heard her refer to Grandad as 'Ral' – the diminutive of Harold; neither did he ever call her Sarah or Sal(ly) in front of the family. They were always, even to each other, 'Mum' and 'Dad'.

After a couple of hours, my Mum and Dad would make to leave. Grandad would press the half-crown into my hand but I knew I couldn't spend it like Granfy's shilling: this was for savings. As we made our way to the front door, Granny would appear with an egg, carefully wrapped in a small paper bag and would present it to me with the words

"Take home with him, bless him". The which I duly did, having it boiled with soldiers for my breakfast on Sunday morning. I can only think that Granny was still in the austerity mode of the war and immediate post-war years when a fresh egg was something quite valuable. Most cooking had been done with powdered eggs, tins of which had been imported from the USA. The tins bore no paper covering but had their contents printed directly on to the metal container. I certainly remember one remaining – unused – in my mother's kitchen cupboards until well into the seventies!

If Mum and Dad went away for the weekend, Granny and Grandad's was usually where I stayed. The one thing I might do in the evening after supper with Grandad was to play Draughts. He had taught me how to play but it was a game at which I never, ever beat him. Yes, it taught me how to lose gracefully, but it also made me determined to win. After draughts, bath-time at Granny and Grandad's was announced by the explosive kerrumph of the geyser in the bathroom and was a cold, joyless occasion save for the warmth of the abrasive towel granny would have warmed in front of the fire for me while I mounted the thinly carpeted-and-rodded stairs and clambered into the bath, its iron legs sturdy on the wooden floor. She would have filled a stone water bottle with water from the hearth-kettle in the lounge and slipped it under the layers of thick, cotton sheets, blankets and a green-leaf-patterned, ageing eiderdown where the faint smell of mothballs lingered. Later, I would lay my toes against the bed-warmer, curl up under the weight of bedding and dream of the gas masks and Our Keith's[1] Curls kept in the suitcase under the bed. And look forward to the cup of tea and Rich Tea biscuit Grandad would bring me up in the morning.

On Sunday evenings, Granny and Grandad would usually go to Chapel – Strict Ebenezer Baptist or occasionally the Methodist Church on the Square – leaving Granny the whole morning in which to blacken the Sunday lunch. During the week she might have made a thick and heavy steak and kidney suet pudding but on Sundays a large, very singed piece of beef would appear, in the dining room, surrounded in the same dish by a whole sizzling Yorkshire pudding along with piles of vegetables and a thick-crust apple pie with cloves and custard, the whole to be eaten with bone-handled cutlery. In the mornings, Cheryl[2] would have sometimes come over from where she lived in Jeans Way and we'd play together

---

1   (Charles) Keith Parrott, brother no.2.

2   My cousin: daughter of Keith (above) and Dorothy.

indoors, perhaps with Granny's button box and hoping for a toffee from the jar on the window ledge, or in the garden, with Granny pottering around singing hymns to herself – *Tell Me the Old, Old Story, Jesus Wants me for a Sunbeam* and so on. Granny was basically the sweetest, gentlest, most archetypal 'favourite granny' that anyone could ever wish for. And yet she had another, quite hard side to her – as we've already seen (*… into the Beartons and the Parrotts*). At the other end of the scale and in the dining room, where wood and silver biscuit barrels adorned the sideboard, stood a glass cabinet with Granny's ornaments and mementoes. She forbade the both of us to play anywhere near it with a ball, *Although if you did break it, I would still kiss you.* In the same dining room was a door leading out into the garden. 'My Spotty', a cat of uncertain and frequently vicious reactions, guarded it jealously, though seldom ventured through it.

Neither Granny nor Grandad were openly affectionate – indeed, none of my family were – but she would never hear a word said against me and always saw the good rather than the bad or naughty.

Later on, she firstly had trouble remembering names, then lost much more of her memory and also her sight in one eye. It was the same right eye that Dad was to lose the sight in, and his brother Ray went completely blind. My right eye is also the weaker of the two.

Both sets of my grandparents were conventional products of their age and times, but I was fortunate to experience different ways of living and being when I crossed the Luton Road. If I tried to summarise in a nutshell the difference in upbringing and in character between the two pairs, it would be in the fact that, between themselves, Granfy was always 'Len', and Nana 'Eve' or 'Evelyn'. With Granny and Grandad, on the other hand, as I have said elsewhere, they never ever in our earshot referred to each other by their Christian names:

he was always 'Dad' while she was always 'Mother' or 'Mum'. In other respects, Nana and Granfy did not shy from physical contact with me, whereas Granny – and especially Grandad – were often quite arms-length; Nana and Granfy were more relaxed, Granny and Grandad more prim and proper. Len was aspirational, Labour-voting; Harold independent but very conservative. Len was the mains electricity foreman, adept at manual, practical work both in his employment and in his home; Harold was a not-very-successful business man and factory owner, borough councillor and Mayor, the stem of my family name. Both, though, loved gardening. I held them all in undiluted affection and consider myself extremely fortunate to have had grandparents like them.

As I have probably indicated already and elsewhere by my keenness for books and jigsaws, many of my boyhood pleasures were solitary ones. Other than Michael Harwood, any friends I had were purely school-day ones. We tended to see comparatively little of my uncles, aunts and cousins on my father's side, though occasionally, I did spend some time playing with Cheryl[1] – as often as not at Granny and Grandad's as she had moved from Waterloo Road to Jeans Way, on the other side of Luton Road Rec'. Lynn and Diana[2] were both some seven years younger than me and I tended to see them only at family get-togethers.

The occasional visit during holiday weeks by Aunty Eve[3] with my cousins Kevin (4 years younger than me) and Elaine (a further 3 years younger) was always looked forward to and then later regretted, in that Kevin and I always started off playing nicely and then would fall out and fight. On at least

1   *Daughter of father's brother Keith and Dorothy.*
2   *Daughters of father's brothers Ray and Shirley, and Alwyn and Fay, respectively.*
3   *Evelyn Smith, née Estwick, Mum's sister.*

one occasion, Eve brought us both crying indoors, saying to Mum:

"I don't know who started it so I've given 'em both a good clout!"

On occasions, though, I might go out for the day with Kevin and Elaine since Eve and Ray at least had a means of transport. A sign of the late fifties was me at 9 years old on the back pillion seat of Ray's motorbike, my arms round his waist and, like him, without a helmet, while Eve, Kevin and Elaine crammed into the sidecar. One such outing was to Billing Aquadrome to the east of Northampton. After sitting outside a pub on the way back with a bag of cheese-and-onion crisps and a lemonade – children were not then allowed to enter pubs – I threw a bit of a tantrum, refused to ride pillion and insisted on sitting in the sidecar for the (very cramped) journey back to Dunstable. Which I did. Eve's verdict to Mum on our arrival back home was that I had been "a right little bugger!" The best times, though, were spending the occasional Sunday evening at their house watching *Sunday Night at the London Palladium* on ITV. There would be a young Bruce Forsyth and one of the first ever audience-participation games for prizes: *Beat The Clock*, not to mention a whole load of different variety acts – singers, dancers, comedians, magicians, jugglers, along with the Tiller Girls: a high-kicking and stunningly attractive mass of legs and feathers, and the final bow on the revolving stage with all the performers waving. All this would be accompanied by a light supper including a lemon meringue pie which I loved – and still do.

In years to come, however, I found to my advantage that Eve was very easy to talk to: I knew that Kevin's relationship with her was as much a friendship as it was a mother-son relationship and that they could talk about anything. Mum and Dad never talked about relationships or emotions and, as I grew up, it was consequently something I found extremely difficult – with both Mum and Dad, and with others. It always was a pleasantly relaxing evening when Helen[1], my then wife, and I would leave the girls with Mum and Dad, and spend it chatting away with Eve. I certainly used Eve for advice on how to approach Mum and Dad when things were getting very difficult between them and Helen and me. In fact it was to Eve I turned first when Helen and I decided to separate and divorce.

Kev and Elaine were also very different, at least academically. Like me, Kevin passed his 11+ but went to Kingsbury Technical School and later became a librarian, whilst I went to the more academic Grammar School. He certainly inherited his parents' left-wing sympathies, opening his home at Christmas to a local mining family when the miners were on strike during the Thatcher years[2]. School was not for Elaine (she was always teased when, during a Christmas game, she spelt sausage 'sosej') and, after meeting Patrice from Brive, Dunstable's twin-town in France, when she was about 15, she decided that that was where her life lay, left school that year (you could leave at 15 in 1971), worked for a year in *Martins* newsagents and then went off to France where she soon married Patrice and had Céline and then Annie. Unfortunately, Annie was born with tremendous handicaps to which Elaine devoted herself. That, along with their young ages, put a great strain on their relationship and they parted. Elaine has now been with Bernard for many years and happily living in the Dordogne. Céline is married and Elaine a grandmother. Kevin, having also married and divorced quite young, is married to Di and living outside Sheffield. Eve moved up to a home in Sheffield for the last year or so of her life to be much nearer them.

---

1   *Helen née Sinnett, my first wife and mother of Sarah and Heather.*
2   *1979 – 1990, but mainly the early 1980's.*

Carols, Cards and Consequences

Rationing was still in place when I had my first Christmas. A stocking might only have had an orange or tangerine, a small (2oz)[1] bar of chocolate, some nuts and perhaps some orange-and-lemon-slices which would have to be put out for general usage rather than just for me. The idea of Father Christmas as a real, live person did not last beyond my fourth Christmas. School dismissed all such notions as child's play, even though I, along with many, many others, still clung to the idea of a Father Christmas in the same way that we did to Christmas cards, Christmas trees, Christmas cake, Christmas pudding and Christmas crackers: he was an essential part of the general festivities.

But Santa never played a large part in my life, and my last experience of him at the age of four was on a rare trip to London and in, I think, Selfridges. None of the shops in Dunstable ever had a Father Christmas to my memory. My build-up to Christmas was not dominated by interminable lists of wants, though I was rather partial to advent calendars and carol singing in the Priory Church – my favourite was *O Come All Ye Faithful* like Dad, whilst Mum's was *Hark the Herald Angels Sing*. Time was taken in licking and sticking strips of coloured paper to make chains to hang round the ceilings, and in preparing the tree, a gift from Grandad[2] who always supplied his four sons. The type was the only one in those days and began shedding its needles from the day it arrived, thereby greatly offending Mum's sense of house-pride.

We would hold a semi-ceremonial decorating of the tree whereby Dad would first lay the small chain of coloured electric lights out on the carpet. Then, with no lights lighting up, he

---

1   *2 ounces – about 60 grams.*
2   *Harold W Parrott.*

would stomp around, tip of tongue clenched tightly between his teeth in annual frustration, as one of the bulbs must have blown. In those days, if one bulb went, the whole set didn't work, and you had to test each of the lights individually in order to ascertain which was faulty, replace it and then, when they still didn't work, curse silently again as *two* must have gone and the whole procedure started afresh. The lights would then be festooned around the tree, only for Mum then to object to the fact that two red ones were next to each other... Pride of place was given to the decorative glass ball which had survived the war and to the small fairy in a bright yellow gauze dress given by Eve for my first Christmas, and which, every year since, was attached to the top of the tree with an elastic band around her waist. By which time, another of the bulbs had blown...

One thing I detested – almost as much as the Boxing Day ritual of *thank you, it was just what I wanted* letters – was having to paint my own Christmas cards. Mum always bought a dozen for me to do for our nearest and dearest. I was then, and remain, no artist and filling in the spaces with paint, and sticking to within the lines was a chore and a torment bound perennially to end in tears. Whilst I might have done better with crayons, Mum thought they were 'not nice' and felt tips did not then exist. Mum and Dad wrote the rest and would always, but always send them by post[1] – even, I think, to the next-door neighbours, such was their insistence on the tradition of receiving cards by post. Tradition did not, however, extend to attending Church apart from the odd carol service in the run-up to Christmas.

For two or three years running, I went to the employees' children's Christmas party at George Kent Ltd in Luton where Dad worked. I don't think that Kent's paid for the whole afternoon, since I'm sure Dad had to buy me a ticket to get in.

---

1   *It would then have cost 3d, threepence, or about 70p in today's wages.*

Whatever the arrangements, I always enjoyed the afternoon which gave me my first-ever sensory memory of the odour of grease, oil and dust on a factory floor as we made our way to the large canteen hall. There, we focused on three main activities: watching cartoon films – invariably *Tom and Jerry*, having tea – lots of white bread sandwiches, tiny pieces of sponge cake with jam, a mince pie and brightly coloured fruit jelly in a small bowl – and then being given a decent present to take home. Since this was the mid- to late-1950s, political correctness or even sensitivity did not play a part in the presents. One year, I was given a plastic gun which fired rubber-suckered darts. The idea was to hit the large, red, shiny nose above the thick, red lips and below the black, fuzzy hair of a darkest-African 'Ubangi Warrior' – the name of the 'game'. If successful, his head would fly off. Not exactly 'woke', was it? There again, I have no recollection of other colours and ethnicities in Dunstable in my boyhood and certainly not at Ashton School or even later at the Grammar School where, to my memory, we only had a couple of Polish boys. I have difficulty also in remembering what my own attitudes were in this respect – if, indeed, I had any. Trying to put myself back some sixty-five years, I suppose in my ignorance I looked on people of colour, of other races, as curious, very different and possibly dangerous, rather to be feared like the 'Indians', now 'native Americans' in the western adventures shown on television and in the cinema.

My preference for presents, as oft stated to aunts and uncles and grandparents was for "books and jigsaws" and the occasional board game. The books were most frequently the *Regent Classics* editions of such as *King Arthur and His Knights of the Round Table*, *The Black Tulip* or *Treasure Island*, with the occasional addition of a (much more exciting) *Biggles* adventure. Ordinary toys were always made of painted metal – like Karel Hackl's crane from *Hamleys* – or wood, and it was rare to find plastic, save for the gun used to shoot the

Ubangi Warrior! Another common present popular at the time and, for the fifties, still quite new, was the selection box in which you would find several different bars of chocolate such as *Cadbury's*, *Crunchie*, *Fry's Turkish Delight* and *Cream Bar*, *Mars*, and *Bounty*, along with tubes of sweets such as *Fruit Pastilles*, *Wine Gums* and *Smarties*, though Mum and Dad forbade chewing gum and gob-stoppers. Yes, we were warned about sweets not being any good for our teeth, but there was little if anything about weight problems and obesity, probably because of the privations of the still-recent war.

Grandad, having given us all trees, would then give (rather disappointingly, in fact!) each grandchild or pair thereof a box of crackers – or *bonbons*[1] as he used to call them. I started with the standard Christmas stocking of small, clearly post-war gifts and graduated to a pillowcase tied to the end of my bed. Early on Christmas morning I would be pinching and feeling all its contents, tearing the corner of the paper off to see if I could tell what was inside. I rarely appreciated presents from Mum and Dad of new pyjamas or a dressing-gown: that wasn't Christmas to me. Once, though, it was a 1500-piece jigsaw puzzle of Queen Elizabeth I – that was much better! If I have one regret, it is that I never had a train set. Perhaps I never asked for one and perhaps it is only now that I can look back at model train sets and layouts and wish that I, too, could have run one all

---

1   *Tom Smith of London invented crackers in 1847. He created the crackers as a development of his bon-bon sweets, which he sold in a twist of paper (the origins of the traditional sweet-wrapper). As sales of bonbons slumped, Smith began to come up with new promotional ideas. He added the "crackle" element when he heard the crackle of a log he had just put on a fire. The sweet itself was eventually dropped to be replaced by a trinket; fans, jewellery and other substantial items. The other elements of the modern cracker – the gifts, paper hats and varied designs were all introduced by his son, Walter, to differentiate his product from the rival cracker manufacturers which had suddenly sprung up.*

over my bedroom. But then Mum would have complained that she was not able to hoover and clean efficiently...

Christmases were always a time for family and invariably extended over three days. Anything I had been given and had opened on Christmas morning would have to be worn or carried with me to show the givers how much it really had been *just what I wanted.* Christmas Day and Boxing Day were family days and always alternated between 28 Kingscroft Avenue, my home, and 45 Hillcroft, home of Aunty Eve[1] and Uncle Ray, Kevin and Elaine. One year, Christmas Day would be at our house and Boxing Day at at Eve's; the next year, we would reverse it. Granfy would be there with Nana (when I was very young), and Aunty Dor[2]. Occasionally, Ray's mother, brother and sister-in-law, and Aunt Emily would join us later in the afternoon.

Christmas Dinner never varied. Everyone – every lady, that is – knew their role in helping to bring all this to fruition. Mum would help Eve in the kitchen and Aunty would always do the brussels in a bowl on her lap in front of the fire. Turkey or chicken took centre place along with all the traditional trimmings of brussels sprouts, roast potatoes, stuffing, bread sauce, carrots and parsnips, followed by a flaming Christmas pudding – not forgetting the lucky sixpenny bit which lay buried in its depths – and mince pies, both served with custard and brandy butter. Wine was a treat, a luxury, served for the first time in 1958. *Mateus Rose* it was called: a Portuguese wine from the Douro Valley which was, for a short time, probably the most popular wine from the local off-licence – no supermarkets then in Dunstable. In keeping with its special status, only one bottle was served, shared between the adults:

---

1   *Mum's sister, Eve, née Estwick.*
2   *Leonard and Evelyn Estwick, and Doris Child, sister of Evelyn.*

one small glass each. More often, there was only water and beer. It was after the dinner that I (along with Kevin and Elaine) would be very disgruntled when packed off to bed for a nap, *so that you'll be awake for the evening*, when all I wanted to do was to play with my presents.

The evening began at around five o'clock with Christmas-tree presents for everyone: small, unpretentious items which invariably engendered greater excitement than the largely anticipated morning presents. Granfy had, throughout the year, saved his threepenny bits and had divided them between Kevin and Elaine and me: we each received a tobacco tin with about 30 threepenny ('thrupenny') bits (seven shillings and sixpence[1]) inside. This was followed by tea – a full high tea, that is with a cold joint of ham, some cheese and some pickles, with bread and butter, more mince-pies and Christmas cake. Then everyone would gather in a large semi-circle round the fire, drinks would be served – I would be allowed a very small glass of ginger wine (Stones' at first, later Crabbies' green) – a bowl of mixed nuts (with nutcracker) would be passed round along with the Turkish Delight, Newberry Fruits, Orange and Lemon Slices, and dried Figs and Dates.

Then the games would begin: Granfy would lead us in various verses of *I'll Sell my Bat and I'll Sell my Ball* wherein we had to imitate playing various instruments, though he was always the drummer. *Fish, Fruit and Flower, Consequences* and *Last Will and Testament* were word games, whilst *Adverts* and *Faces*[2] perforce took a deal of preparation by the host and inevitably took a long time for everyone to get through all 20 adverts or faces etc. And yes, you're right: there was no telly. But by far the best was one year when Aunt Emily was present. Dressed in severe mourning-matronly black and

---

1   *Thirty 3d's = 7/6 = 38p but was worth about £18 in todays' wages.*

2   *See appendix for explanations of the various games.*

with her white hair pulled back in a roll, she announced out of the blue that she had a game for us all to play and that she would come round to each of us in turn and whisper the name of a bird in our ear. Mine was 'crow' but under no circumstances were we to say what bird she had whispered and we all went along with it because that was the spirit in which we played all these games. Then she said that if she called out our bird, we should get up and run out the room as quickly as possible. We all sat there, all twelve of us on the edges of our seats, expectantly, legs twisted round ready to escape, waiting for our robin, sparrow, tit, blackbird whatever. Aunt Emily drew breath, looked round the room and called out: "Crow!" Whereupon all twelve bottoms left their seats in a mad, tumbling rush to the door while she just sat there and laughed. It was inevitable, I suppose, that Aunt Emily became known in the family as 'the Old Crow'.

Occasionally, on 27th December, the Parrott family would gather at Granny and Grandad's, 103 Luton Road. I say family, though Keith and Dorothy (and Cheryl) were not over fond of such gatherings and attended but rarely. Having prepared her usual spread of cold meats, pork pies, pickled onions, cucumber-and-sugar sandwiches, sausage rolls, bread pudding and jellies along with large catering pots of tea topped up by the black kettle kept in the hearth by the fire, Granny would sit in her armchair and beam beatifically on her surrounding brood: she just loved having everyone together. Grandad, who just sat in the armchair on the opposite side of the fire and puffed away on his Senior Service Plain, liked it too, I'm sure, but was probably equally happy when the house was quiet again after we all left. His contribution to the event was something he loved: a collection of indoor fireworks. These were very small imitations of their more fiery external cousins, which smoked, sparked and generally disintegrated within the bounds of the hearth – hopefully!

Granny and Grandad had no television until well into the 60's so there had to be games in those days and, especially with Ray and Alwyn there, the louder, the more boisterous the better! *Charades* were always on the menu and I remember particularly how the word 'domestic' was conveyed in three syllables with the three brothers, Ray, Alwyn and Haydn, my father, making great and rather rude play on the 'mess' syllable. Then there was *Come and Sit in My Chair* in which we thwacked with rolled-up newspapers those members of the family who sat in the wrong seat. Some measure of restraint was insisted on, however, and I was only ever given about five sheets to roll up, never a whole paper. What can you really 'thwack' with only five sheets?

These early Christmases gave me a lasting love for Christmas as a time at which families should get together – though it does perhaps become more and more difficult the more families are split by distance or by divorce and separation, and with the consequent multiplicity of ties and tugs on everyone's time, not to mention the on-going problems of Covid19 as I write. Regardless of problems, though, I cannot help but feel that households, eyes glued to the television or the smartphone and with the relative demise of the nuclear family, are nowadays missing out on the togetherness that games brought to us.

Books, Board Games and Jigsaws

I've mentioned before how my present list for birthdays and Christmas amounted to just two items: books and jigsaws. The jigsaws grew in size and complexity commensurate with my age – from the smallest and simplest through to – and the only one I can still see in my mind's eye – the one which pictured the might and glory of the Tudor Elizabethan era and which had 1500 pieces. I cannot remember what happened to it, save for the memory of losing a piece on about its sixth reincarnation – and that is the point at which a puzzle becomes fit only for the dustbin. Neither were jigsaws for sharing as Mum and Dad soon realised: the satisfaction that came from their organisation, compilation and completion had to be entirely mine. I have to admit straight away that jigsaws are still an abiding interest and relaxation of mine. I can lose myself completely in a puzzle and whatever the cares of the day happen to be I can forget them in a jiffy in the attempt to find all the straight-edges, to collect the red-stripey bits, or to assemble the line where building and trees join the sky. Size is only limited by the sheer space available, with 3000 pieces being the absolute limit. Complexity now has given way to the desire for just a really interesting – but still challenging – picture. I have never liked the 'chocolate box' type pictures, nor those with masses of sky; neither do I revel any longer in a puzzle which is nothing but a two-sided, turned-through-90 degrees pile of brussels sprouts! Very often it will be a classical painting which attracts and challenges me in equal measure.

So far as books are concerned, I can remember most that I read – or at least the series, if not the individual titles. My reading was essentially classical and traditional with no element of modernity whatsoever – not even the slightest hint even of Enid Blyton's *The Famous Five* or *The Secret Seven*. I suppose that books existed essentially to create another world for me and one I could not hope to inhabit – and that is how they remain: an evocation of place, of plot, and of person to which I have little real aspiration. And yet – and this may appear contradictory – I am no fan of science fiction. My parents had a liking for the 'Regent Classics' editions and they came in red hardback with brightly coloured, if thin and fragile, covers. The paper was, as Alan Bennett remembered *mealy, slightly freckled*

and looked not unlike the texture of the ice cream of the period.
Ben Hur I read avidly and enjoyed greatly, as I did *Oliver Twist*,
but failed to complete *Kidnapped* and found *Treasure Island*
rather laborious – likewise with the Mark Twain books of
Tom Sawyer and Huckleberry Finn whose American culture
meant little to me. Jules Verne, on the other hand, was a page-
turner writer whose characters immediately appealed to me at
the age of nine or ten and – with hindsight – I would say it
was because they had some depth. Character depth was not an
issue in the total fantasy tales of *King Arthur and His Knights*
of the Round Table and *Robin Hood*, the adventures of whom
prepared me for my adventure favourite, *Biggles*.

Capt. WE Johns' flying hero was, along with his companions
Algy, Ginger and Lord Bertie, ageless: between his Sopwith
Camel of the First World War and his Spitfire of the Second,
he appeared not the least diminished, and belonged much
more to the days of Empire, rather than in the fifties' days of
Britain's declining power when I was reading him. Still, it was
pure escapism from a conventional existence and one story in
particular, *Biggles Fails to Return* set in World War II, aroused
my abiding interest in and love for the south of France and
for its language. Johns' description of Monaco and the Alpes
Maritimes with its orange, and lemon trees, its olives, figs and
grape-vines, the sun-baked slopes, the three Corniches[1], the
Mediterranean Sea glistening in the moonlight, and the little
town of Eze *perched upon a pinnacle of rock*. Then there was
Lord Bertie Lissie, who spoke French – like a native of course
– who, having arrived in Monte Carlo from La Turbie stopped
in a café to eat. How I envied him his language, how he could
blend in and the way he effortlessly ordered *la soupe* as he

---

1   *The three cliff roads connecting Nice and Monaco. The Grande Corniche*
    runs through mountain foothills,, the Moyenne Corniche is lower, and it is
    The Basse Corniche which is closest to the coast and which carries the heavy
    traffic.

knew that that was all they served. This was all so inspiringly other-worldly for a Dunstable boy, and fitted in perfectly as an antidote to the drabness of post-war Britain – as indeed later did Ian Fleming's *James Bond* books, offering worlds of excitement, escapism and undreamt-of exoticism.

Although the setting (the1950's) was more modern, I was never really into the Jennings and Derbyshire stories by Anthony Buckeridge, preferring another form of escapism which came with Richmal Crompton's *Just William* books. William Brown did things that I couldn't and wouldn't. He, and his close friends Ginger, Douglas and Henry – the 'Outlaws' – caused havoc in the genteel, well-heeled middle-class English families of the 1920's and 1930s. But this wasn't mugging and drugs, knife-crime and sex. This was 'naughtiness' and mild jokes going wrong, with the worst thing that could happen being the lisping Violet Elizabeth Bott threatening to *thcream and thcream 'til I'm thick.*

Occasionally I was passed on books by other members of my extended family. Through Uncle Stan[1] I had Sir Len Hutton's[2] autobiography and a book about Chelsea which I, being a devoted follower of Manchester United, and it also, being in the wake of the Munich air disaster in 1958, never read. However, Aunty Dorothy stopped him giving me a James Bond book when I was about eleven on the grounds that I wasn't 'old enough'. But it was *The Fifth Form at St.Dominic's* from Uncle Alwyn[3] that I remember best. By Thornton Baines Reed, it was typical of an over-sentimentalised view of public schools and of the friendships between the boys therein. All was very gentlemanly, honour was everything and a rotter was a rotter and a cad a cad – until, of course, they led the cricket

---

1   *Stanley Bearton, Granny's brother, my great Uncle and Godfather.*
2   *Former England Cricket Captain.*
3   *Alwyn Parrott, Dad's youngest brother.*

team to victory against all odds! It was the first Shakespeare quote I ever remembered: one of the leading characters died in the school 'san'[atorium] and his closest friend leant over him and kissed his forehead – something I found very strange at the age of ten – and said, quoting Shakespeare, *After life's fitful fever he sleeps well*[1].

There were some books that made me think. I can remember pondering being alone with minimal possessions and wondering how I would cope – and deciding I probably wouldn't – thanks to Daniel Defoe's *Robinson Crusoe*, published in 1719. *The Wind in the Willows*, by Kenneth Grahame, is one whose depth I sensed even when young and which has stayed with me most, in various ways, including directing the stage play and, in another production, playing Toad in *Toad of Toad Hall*. I was also asked to read and advise on an updated version screenplay set in the violent, drug-ridden inner city, rather than the spiritualised countryside and its 'wild wood'. To my knowledge, it's never been performed.

But there was a lady in Dunstable, not on a par with my lovely teacher, Hope Pratt[2], of course, but still very high in my estimation and affection. Diminutively stocky, with sensible shoes a nice, woollen dress and cardigan, and with her lightly greying hair gathered in buns on either side of her head like modern headphones, Joan Payne was sweetness and gentle help itself. She was in charge of Dunstable Library when I remember it best: in its Victorian schoolhouse-type building next to Chew's House in High Street South[3]. It was there that, with six tickets in my pocket, I would enter past the circulation desk and turn left, up the handful of steps and into the Children's Library. Miss Payne also allowed me to take

---

1 *Macbeth, Act 3, Sc.2.*

2 *See the section on Ashton School.*

3 *The converted building is now The Little Theatre and the home of Dunstable Repertory Company.*

books from the adult section – provided, of course, that they were 'suitable'. It was thus that I developed a liking for Agatha Christie's detective novels. When I wanted to take books out, i.e. borrow them, the reference card that was inside each book would be slipped inside one of my small pocket-like, brown, thin card tickets, which was in turn placed in the wooden rack for that day and a date for the book's return stamped on a printed grid inside each book. This allowed you two weeks to read it, though you could ask for longer if it was for study purposes. I expect Miss Payne served everyone in a similar manner, but the fact that someone whom I only saw but intermittently, and who always remembered my name, meant more to me than she possibly realised.

If it wasn't 'books'n'jigsaws' I was given at Christmas and birthdays, it was games – board games. One thing I was taught by my parents was how to play games – not the big team games which we did at school, but games played round the table or on laps in the lounge. I've always liked the French phrase for such things: *'jeux de société'* and the social aspects and benefits of these games should not, in my view be underestimated. You learn to win generously and to lose gracefully; you learn to share and to enjoy playing for the sake of it – albeit you can still be determined to win! Admittedly there were some games that came my way which could not be tolerated nowadays, such as the *Ubangi Warrior* I mentioned earlier, but my earliest memories are of young children's games like *Snakes and Ladders* where everything is determined by the roll of a die, or *Ludo* where the dice are all important, but a little thought has to go into which piece you move and how your move(s) may affect your opponents' pieces. Of course there were always what I would call pointless games – those which merely occupied a certain amount of time and were of little real value such as *Mr. Potato Head* where, with minimal creativity, you begged

Mum for a potato and then made funny faces by inserting plastic noses, lips, eyes etc. *Bagatelle* was like an early pinball machine: you sprung a ball-bearing or marble into a table with areas marked out with small nails and which scored so many points if you managed to land your sprung ball between those nails. And then there was *Tiddly Winks* – the flicking of plastic counters into a pot – which is still played, I believe, at certain august academic institutions and at international level between England and the USA!

My two grandfathers were responsible for teaching me dominoes and table skittles (Granfy)[1] and draughts (Grandad)[2] – a game at which, to my great frustration, I was never to beat him. But that was, in a way, the point. I had to learn how to lose as well as to win – and I was never *allowed* to win. So much so that consequently, when I did (at other games!), I was indeed elated. There again, neither did I ever, in future years, willingly let my own daughters beat me, nor my grandchildren, whichever game we played from cards to draughts and chess to backgammon and Trivial Pursuit. To begin with, I may have avoided certain moves or whatever, so when they did win – and sooner or later they did beat me – oh then it really meant something to them. Dominoes was either straightforward end-to-end, or fives-and-threes (a game in which the joint two end-values of the line of dominoes had to be divisible by 5 or 3; table skittles was, like dominoes, more of a pub game, but Granfy and I played it on the dining room table. Chess, I taught myself later and in readiness for the Chess Club at the Grammar School where many boys would also have the little pocket chess sets which were popular forty or fifty years before smartphones and their apps were invented.

---

1   *Leonard Estwick.*
2   *Harold Parrott.*

The equipment for all ages was and remains a pack of playing cards. Of course we had *Happy Families* which easily introduced me to grouping and classifying my cards, and to searching for various types, but of the real card games I remember one in particular: *Sevens*, whereby, the four 7's are laid out, the players are dealt seven cards each and you take it in turns to add to the four 7's, in suit and in sequence, or take another card from the pile. Easy to play, simple to grasp. *Snap!* was generally derided and ignored in favour of *Pairs* or *Pelmanism* – the favourite for my parents and me – in which the whole pack is placed face down and separately on the table, and with the aim being to turn up two at a time, in order to collect pairs of cards and to remember where they are when non-pairs are replaced face down. Of course, finding myself alone – not an uncommon occurrence for an only child – there was always *Patience*: various forms of *Solitaire* now played in myriad ways thanks to modern technology. In my late teens and young adulthood – I would move on to *Gin Rummy*, *Whist*, *Pontoon*, *Brag* and *Poker* – for 1d[1] stakes. Later still, in adulthood, I would take up *Bridge*. *Monopoly* and *Cluedo* only figured much later, along with *Trivial Pursuit*. But there was also the growth in games based on popular television shows, especially those from the commercial channel, ITV, such as *Double Your Money*, *The Army Game*, *Wagon Train* and, from the BBC, *Spycatcher*. I think Mum and Dad thought those slightly beneath me as in their place I was given quiz books. General knowledge was at a premium in our house – and they enjoyed the questions and answers far more than games in which your progress depended on the role of a die. If I have any regrets about the games I played or the toys I had, it was that I never had *Meccano* – which just might have encouraged me to turn out a tad more practically technical than I am – or

---

1   *1d = 1 penny or 1/240th of a pound. About 10p nowadays.*

a train set: though my joy in later life has been to travel First Class from London to Cannes on the railways.

But there is one game whose name I have completely forgotten and of whose board I have but a dim, but lasting memory. It was one of those many and varied games where the roll of the die determined whether you advanced, went back, missed a turn or doubled your score. I cannot remember its design save for a faded recollection of a cross-country, through-woods journey, but have a feeling that it came to me second-hand as, in my mind's eye, it has left a rather agèd impression. What has stayed with me – and vividly so to this day – is the arrangement of its numbers. Give me a number between 1 and 100 and I immediately picture that number in one particular position on an uneven pathway from the left of the folding board, up and down and round to the bottom right.

Entertaining Ourselves

My listening to the wireless (radio) at home was limited to *Children's Favourites* with *Uncle Mac*[1] on a Saturday morning on the Light Programme, *Two-Way Family Favourites* on Sunday lunchtimes, also on the Light programme, and both music-request programmes. The latter, designed to link families in the UK with those serving in the forces in West Germany and overseas in general also introduced me to things such as BFPO[2] numbers and place names like Akrotiri, Belize and Osnabrück. [3]

---

1   *Derek McCulloch.*

2   *British Forces Post Office numbers – never the full address for security reasons.*

3   *In Greek Cyprus, North-East Central America and (West) Germany respectively.*

Although Granfy[1] had bought a television to watch the coronation in 1953, we did not have a set until I was nine in 1958. Radio Rentals, the shop where you could rent radios and televisions rather than buy, supplied us with a black-and-white set which stood in a shiny wooden cabinet on four spindly legs. It possessed the only two channels available: BBC and ITV and the screen was more or less the size of a small, modern laptop and even then, in the late fifties, reception and the resultant picture quality were quite poor. Dad justified renting on the grounds that any repairs needed were also covered, and that valves (the main driving force inside the TV) were so expensive! The first programme I ever watched was a cartoon featuring the diminutive Popeye the Sailor-man who could produce a tin of spinach from his sleeve, swallow it down without removing the pipe firmly clenched between his teeth and then use the enormous strength it gave him to fight and beat Bluto the big, brutal, bearded bully, and win his tall, beanpole of a sweetheart, Olive Oyl, from his clutches. I don't think I was terribly impressed as, even during the relatively short cartoon, my attention wandered and Mum even told me off for not watching the telly "now we've got it".

The sounds of the high-pitched *Weeeed!* and much lower *Flobalob* were imitated with great glee thanks to *Bill and Ben the Flower Pot Men. Sooty and Sweep* and *Muffin the Mule* I treated with only mild interest though I can also remember hiding behind the settee, scared that Looby Lou was creeping up on *Andy Pandy.* However, I found the slapstick comedy of *Mr. Pastry* stupid and the public school pranks of *Billy Bunter* ridiculous. I always preferred the BBC's *Crackerjack* to ITV's *Playbox*, but wasn't a great fan of *Blue Peter*[2] – perhaps because I was just hopeless at making nuclear power stations

---

1   *Leonard Estwick*
2   *This began in 1958 and is still running.*

out of cardboard loo rolls and sticky-back plastic. Apart from that, I think Mum also had little faith in my dexterity as she never retained these essential items in the home. But my main viewing, and that which I remember best were those programmes we watched together as a family, with parents or grandparents and which were essentially totally beyond my narrow experience. I loved the original cowboy hero *The Lone Ranger* (Clayton Moore) with his Indian (Native American) side-kick, Tonto, (Jay Silverheels). That *tonto* means 'fool' in Spanish and his, Tonto's, name of endearment for the Lone Ranger was *kemosabe*, which, it seems, means 'soggy shrub' in Navajo, was not then known, it being the days before political correctness and Wikipedia. A joke at the time maintained that a truly cultured person would know a piece of music as the overture to the opera *William Tell* by Rossini, not as the opening theme tune to *The Lone Ranger*. Other western heroes were a young Clint Eastwood as Rowdy Yates in *Rawhide*, and Dale Robertson as Jim Hardie in *Wells Fargo*, but the battles between Conrad Phillips as the Swiss folklore hero *William Tell* and Willoughby Goddard as the grossly dictatorial Austrian overlord, Gessler, were just as stirring. Then there was the reassuring, avuncular and, I have to say now with hindsight, unreal portrayal of the police, *Dixon of Dock Green*[1] on the BBC, *The Billy Cotton Band Show*, and the all-singing, all-dancing, all-laughing ITV show *Sunday Night at the London Palladium*, not to mention the BBC's *Black and White Minstrel Show*, extremely popular at the time but which was later to be dropped[2] never to be revived on grounds of racism. The days of white men being able to

---

1   *Starring the ageing Jack Warner as your very friendly local "bobby", loved and respected by all, and set in the East End of London.*

2   *Dancers and singers would 'black-up' as African-American minstrels, complete with deep-south accents. It began in 1958 and was finally ended in 1978 despite its continuing huge popularity.*

'black up' as, for example, Sir Laurence Olivier had done in the theatre to play Othello, were history.

Other programmes I remember with affection are *Perry Mason*, the American defence lawyer who never failed to free his client and where the prosecution evidence was always "incompetent, irrelevant and immaterial"; *Emergency, Ward 10*, the ITV forerunner to *Casualty*; and Hughie Greene's *Double Your Money*, where contestants had to answer general knowledge questions on a topic of their choice and could double their prize money each round up to £1,000[1]. I especially liked it when my favourite footballer, Bobby Charlton of Manchester United, won the £1,000 answering questions on football – and only a year after the Munich air disaster. There's a list of the programmes I regularly watched in the appendix.

We again gathered around Granfy's TV – updated since the coronation but with only a slightly larger screen – on the day before my 10th birthday in 1959 to watch Luton Town play Nottingham Forest in the FA Cup Final. Luton had beaten Forest 7-1, I think, in an end-of-season game to which I had gone with Dad and I had every confidence in a repeat performance with Luton winning the Cup. Dad was now with his brothers, Ray and Alwyn, at Wembley whilst I had to make do with a homemade black and white (then Luton's colours) rosette which I had painted on a single circle of cardboard and pinned to my shirt with a safety pin sellotaped to its back. Luton lost 2-1, one of the goals against them being scored by Sir Elton John's cousin, Roy Dwight[2], and my rosette lay forlornly ripped in two on the carpet of Granfy's living room.

As I have said elsewhere, Saturdays were full of interest, of town, of grandparents and, I suppose, of being the centre of

---

1   *About £50,000 in today's wages.*
2   *Elton John's real name was Reginald Dwight.*

attention. I would usually find Sundays the most boring day imaginable. It's not that they were not different – they were. It's just that they, well, followed Saturdays, I suppose, and were exactly the same, week in, week out.

Breakfast, having being cereal and toast all week, might change to a boiled egg (from Granny) and – Sunday morning treat! – hot rolls. The mornings would be occupied with Dad doing his gardening or any necessary DIY – from which I was excluded after attempts to chop my finger off (see a previous Saturday) while Mum busied herself with cooking the Sunday lunch plus a cake, some scones or some shortbread for Sunday tea. Church did not figure greatly at any time, even though I went to a church school. Mum and Dad would, however, describe themselves as C-of-E and I would at the age of 12, at their encouragement, be confirmed in the Church of England, in Dunstable's Priory Church by Michael Gresford Jones, then Bishop of St.Albans. I was then glad to attend the earlier communion service, though that may have been due to the fact that there was coffee and hot dogs in the Parish Hall afterwards. Perhaps not the most spiritual of reasons for attending Church.

There was at home, however, a ritual with the Sunday Express general knowledge crossword. Dad would go through the questions over breakfast without entering the answers in the grid – that would be saved for coffee time at about 10:45 when we would all three of us sit down and attempt to complete the crossword over our elevenses. I have always had a good general knowledge and possessed at the time books of questions which we would "play", either the three of us or Mum and I at bath time: "Let's play 'Capitals'" I'd suggest and Mum would then sit there and ask me, wallowing in the bath, what the capitals of Australia or Colombia or Libya were. Anyway, the questions in the Sunday Express would usually be completed, all bar half a dozen or so, and I would then spend the next hour ploughing through an atlas, dictionaries, the *Pears* encyclopaedia (given to me at Christmas by my parents so that I could solve their crosswords), or *Enquire Within* which was a compendium of topic based information about everything from American presidents to how to deal with wasp stings. Of course, these were the days long before computers, *Google* and *Wikipedia*. Personal computers and Tim Berners-Lee's WorldWide Web would not be in most homes for another forty-five years at least!

Soon it would be time for my contribution to the Sunday lunch: setting the table, including the serviettes each in a personal silver ring: mine was a different style to those of my parents and Mum distinguished hers from my by some sewing thread tied discreetly in the silver filigree work. Then I would make either the mustard sauce (for the beef), mint sauce (lamb) or apple sauce (pork) since those joints were rotated on a three-week cycle. I also would help with the cake-making, graduating from licking the bowl out, to stirring, to following a recipe – something which would stand me in good stead for the future. For pudding there would be, always with custard, of course, the inevitable pie or crumble: apple – sometimes with the early-autumn variation of blackberries which I had picked in 'The Jungle'[1] or up on Dunstable Downs, or with the addition of cloves and other spices – or plum, or gooseberry depending on the season. Then there were the tinned pie fillings for when fresh fruit was not available.

After lunch and when I was a bit older, I would listen to *Beyond our Ken* and its later incarnation *Round the Horne* on the Light programme, with (mainly) Kenneth Horne, Bill Pertwee, Betty Marsden and Kenneth Williams. These programmes followed on from *The Goon Show* in terms of ground-breaking comedy and were laced with double-entendres and sexual innuendo, a brief example of which is in the following song

---

1   *The nearby bush-and-scrub land – see an earlier story.*

lines from a countryfied character known as Rambling Syd Rumpo, played by Kenneth Williams:

In Hackney Wick there lives a lass,
Whose grommets would I woggle,
Her gander-parts none can surpass
And her posset makes me boggle!

As Kenneth Horne himself once said "It's all in the mind of the beholder!" I also recollect listening occasionally to comedies such as *The Navy Lark*, with Leslie Philips or *Hancock's Half Hour* with Tony Hancock. As I have already implied, visual humour has never particularly appealed to me. Verbal humour, on the other hand has always seemed to be on a totally different, if not higher, plane and reaches the spot in me that other humour does not.

But then would begin the stultifying boredom of Sunday afternoons during which the world and his wife went to sleep and I would read, do a jigsaw, make a half-hearted attempt to do my weekend's homework (when later at the Grammar School), or just sit there wishing and praying that the phone would ring and that it would result in someone visiting us for tea, or in us going there, or in us going out in the evening to, say, Aunty Eve[1] and Uncle Ray's – anything to change the routine. Once or twice a year Mum and Dad would entertain such as Uncle Stan and Aunty Dorothy[2] for lunch, but Mum hated entertaining as she was always afraid things would go wrong. They never did (except when Uncle Stan broke one of the set of six dinner plates and Mum was heart-broken). I was never allowed out to play on Sundays, not in the road (*never in*

---

1   *Mum's sister, Evelyn Smith, née Estwick.*
2   *Stan (Sarah Smith/Bearton, Granny's brother) and Dorothy Bearton.*
     Uncle Stan was also my Godfather and someone I looked up to tremendously.

the road!) nor in the Park. The most I could normally expect to go out was in the garden or maybe, just maybe, a walk – but that would only have been if we had been invited out to tea with someone.

So mostly we stayed in and, at about five o'clock, Mum would present our regular Sunday 'tea' all the while watching the Sunday serialisation of literature classics on BBC television – *Treasure Island*, *The Secret Garden*, *The Silver Sword*, *Oliver Twist*. Those would then be followed by perhaps a game of Ludo or Snakes and Ladders in my younger days, or *Scrabble* later on (but after *Songs of Praise!*). Word games were also the thing: either choosing a word and then seeing how many other words you could make from its letters – *Anagrams*, I used to call it – within a given time frame, say, five or ten minutes. Three-letter combinations such as *ate, eat* and *tea*, or *rat, tar* and *art* were always popular! But then Scrabble came along and my parents were hooked – as was I – for the rest of their lives, playing regularly and keeping their score cards over months, if not years.

Later, when I was older, there would be serials like *The Brothers* or *The Onedin Line* which became compulsory viewing at 7:30 in the days before VCR recorders.

As much as I have always enjoyed a good Sunday lunch and can still listen with fondness to archive editions of *Round the Horne*, I always remember Sundays as a weekly low point of dull routine, occasionally lifted only by the good grace of others.

I have the impression that many performers of all types including actors were, at some early stage in their youth and following a visit to the theatre or the cinema, imbued and impassioned with the stage or screen as a career. I have to admit to no such experience and my own enthusiasm for the stage came from my primary school and Mrs. Hope Pratt – but more of that later. My first visit to the cinema – the local *Union*, later the *ABC*, was in 1957, for *Man of the Moment*. This starred Norman Wisdom, an English actor, comedian, and singer-songwriter best known for a series of comedy films produced between 1953 and 1966. They featured his hapless and helpless, rather Chaplin-esque on-screen character, Norman Pitkin, with his expressive face, ill-fitting suit, turned-up cap peak and trip-up-and-stumble, and his battles with the authority figure of "Mr. Grimsdale". These battles – and ultimate victories – of the ordinary man against a corporate, capitalist figure meant that Wisdom's films remained the only western films ever to be shown in the ultra-Maoist state of Albania right up to the fall of its ruler, Enver Hoxha, in the mid 1980's.

My second visit was to *Davy Crockett and the River Pirates* starring Fess Parker, an eminently forgettable feature film. The ABC Cinema in High Street North, Dunstable, seemed the grandest building in the town, though, with red, plush curtains and gold-painted columns. Of course there was only the one screen, unlike modern cinema complexes, and you could always pay a little more for the privilege of sitting in 'The Circle', the upstairs level. I sat there only once and that was for free as Mum, Dad and I were guests of the cinema for the first showing in Dunstable of *The Guns of Navarone* in 1962 when Dad was Mayor – he, replete in his chain of office, even had a small 'guard' of uniformed local cadets to inspect! But I, at 13, liked having drinks in the manager's office!

Occasionally, when I was about 10 or 11, I was allowed to go to the ABC Minors: 6d bought you Saturday morning in the cinema: a couple of cartoons and a B-movie western; another 3d[1] might get you an ice-cream. A- and B- movies or films were then typical of a cinema's programme, with the A

---

1   *6d, would be about £1.20 in today's wages, and 3d about 60p.*

films being the bigger, usually more popular features, with the B films of lesser value – artistically and financially. The former Hollywood actor, Ronald Reagan, US President from 1981 to 1989, was often disparaged as being *nothing more than a B-movie actor*. In between the two features, we were treated to The News. These were the days before 24-hour news coverage and even before mass ownership of televisions. It was provided mainly by *Pathé News*, which began with a cock crowing loudly amidst a fanfare of trumpets, but also by *Gaumont British News* and *British Movietone News*. One thing, though, was rapidly dying: and that was standing for the National Anthem at the end of the evening as the last film finished. The playing of the anthem in cinemas was to die out completely in the 1960s.

I think my only trip to the theatre proper was when Mum and Dad took me in 1960 to the Victoria Palace Theatre near Victoria Station in London to see *Young At Heart*, a variety show and one of the last performances of a group known as The Crazy Gang: Bud Flanagan and Chesney Allen, Jimmy Nervo and Teddy Knox, Charlie Naughton and Jimmy Gold and sometimes 'Monsewer' Eddie Gray. I cannot say that I remember anything at all about the show save for a dim visual image of them all walking and singing across the stage in a single line, upstage hand on upstage shoulder, with Flanagan, in his trademark fur coat and hat with a broken and up-turned brim, bringing the house down with *Underneath the Arches*.

That I went to see Bertram Mills' Circus at Olympia when I was about 7 is a matter of fact, but left me with no particular memories whatsoever. I oohed and aahed, laughed and clapped along with everyone else but any residual impressions quickly died. My second visit to the Circus – and my last – was over thirty years later in what was then called Leningrad, now St. Petersburg. I was one of five staff accompanying forty pupils from Pershore High School visiting the then Soviet Union, now Russia. This circus visit was memorable for one thing:

at the beginning of the second half and when the cages were lowered, heralding the arrival of the big cats, some of our students quietly stood up, walked out and sat in the foyer in protest against the use of animals. The look of horror on our Intourist's guide's face was as if we had desecrated Lenin's tomb. When we explained the sensitivities of our students to her, you sensed that the lady wanted to be totally outraged – you didn't do that sort of thing in the Soviet Union where circus was one of the great art forms – but she was overwhelmingly perplexed and so did nothing. Neither Olympia nor Leningrad – indeed circus as a whole – made the slightest lasting impact upon my consciousness.

That my musical interests were centred on the light classical is due largely to the tastes and interests of Dad and of Grandad, his father. Dad would take me to, for instance, the Luton Choral Society's annual. where I would follow the score that Grandad had given me. This gave me an abiding love for the work which I was to sing many times in later life in Hagley with the Haybridge High School, in the Royal Albert Hall, and with the Worcester Festival choir. Grandad himself had formed and run the Dunstable Girls' Choir and loved music, particularly brass bands For many years, he and a small group of close friends would go to London for the National Brass Band Championships. And for two or three years running, from the age of about eleven, I accompanied him – which I loved not just for the event itself, but also for being with him. We'd arrive at the Royal Albert Hall in Kensington to find that vast hall's stage set out in readiness for the twenty-four bands due to play. In the arena just in front of them was a long, locked cabin where sat the judges – and they weren't allowed out until every band had played. This was so they would not know which band was playing and judge each one purely on how they interpreted the test piece. Grandad would check the programme an.. ..rarlge our coffee, lunch and tea breaks so that we wouldn't miss the best bands (e.g. Grimethorpe Colliery, CWS Manchester, Black Dyke Mills, Fairey Aviation, GUS Footwear – bands were usually from factories and other companies). Lunch was always taken at *Daquise*, a small, rather dingy Polish restaurant in South Kensington which is still there today, though much modernised. We'd hear probably 14 or 16 of the 24 bands – I'd be following the score he always bought me – and then we'd stay for the results and the massed band concert before catching the train back to Luton. The epitome of excitement it was not. But I can honestly say that I used to look forward to that yearly visit with Grandad which, in terms of brass band music, score-reading and general musical appreciation was to prove a milestone in my love of music.

Away Days and Holidays

In the late fifties, travel possibilities were improving with the first package holidays arranged on the Costa Blanca in Spain in 1957 and mass jet travel becoming common with, in 1958 and for the first time, more travellers going to the USA from the UK by plane than by ship. Closer to home, the first motorway, known as the Preston Bypass, opened in 1958, while much closer to home, the real first motorway, the M1 (its first phase was from London (Watford) to Rugby), opened in 1959. The previous year had also seen the first parking meter, but all this passed me by as though none of it had ever happened: Mum and Dad were not interested in mass jet travel or foreign holidays, and never owned a car, never bothered to learn to drive. What you never have, you never miss. So they say.

Now I was getting older – and perhaps less of a handful – we took our holidays just the three of us, rather than with either set of grandparents. Dad took two weeks holiday in what was then called the "works' fortnight" in July, but we only went away for one week, Dad insisting that he wanted to give Mum a complete break from housework. This, in terms of what he could afford, meant that we went full-board to a small hotel in such places as Paignton, the Isle of Wight, Bournemouth and Folkestone.

In the mornings, Dad and I would be up around seven – it gave Mum a lie-in – and I would accompany him on a walk along the front, firstly to a newsagent where he could buy his *Telegraph* and then to one of the tea-bars along the promenade and on the edge of the beach for a large, thick china cup of tea. Those around us were mainly males, often on the early-morning dog walk and I felt older than my years to be out with my father and with them. Back at the hotel, we'd sit down to cornflakes, followed by a full English and then toast and marmalade, with the only real choice, as with lunch and dinner, 'take it or leave it'. These were not the days – indeed, these were not the hotels – of the fruit juices, the multiple varieties of tea and coffee, the croissants, the fruit, the cheese and the cold meats so common nowadays.

Usually half of every day was spent on the beach with an occasional treat such as a ride on a donkey, or – something I really liked – eating pears: heaven knows why! The other half would be a walk along the cliffs or through some gardens, a game of crazy golf, a wander round the town, a local museum, church or castle. On occasions, we would take a bus ride to a neighbouring town – though with my inability to journey very far without getting travel sick, that was not very frequent. Wherever we went, we always had to be back at our hotel for luncheon as it was called then, invariably salad with ham or cheese. If the morning had been spent on the beach, it would mean me going through the changing of beachwear, washing and redressing, albeit it in just a summer shirt, shorts and sandals. Once, we did manage to have one 'luncheon' which required our Sunday best on a Saturday though. We were on our way to the Isle of Wight and Dad, thanks to his work as an export clerk, had managed to get the three of us luncheon on one of the ships of the Union Castle Line in Southampton docks. The size of the ship and the 'poshness' of the hospitality was quite overwhelming for this eight-year old.

In the evening, dinner – still in many places called 'tea' – was a traditional English hot meal of roasts, stews or the likes of shepherd's pie. However, it was expected that one "dressed for dinner". This was in no way black tie – not in the modest little places in which we stayed – but rather collar, tie and jacket for us males and the ladies always wore a dress or suit and blouse, with nylons – never a bare leg for dinner! The one thing Mum and Dad always insisted on, whether at home or away, was on being "correct" and they were terrified of being found not doing or saying the proper thing – and that extended to me. When once a waitress asked me if I'd like another helping of the apple pie dessert which had been served with a spoonful of thick cream on its crust, I replied,

"Yes, please." (Good – polite response, correct, tick.) and then added "With a *dob* of cream, please." (Bad – impolite slang, wrong, cross) And they were: very cross. "You don't say *that!*" Forget the *please* at the end: my informal, slang use of *dob* had broken their conventions of what was acceptable. I had quite plainly let them down and it was something they did not let me forget for a long, long time!

Evenings would invariably be occupied by a stroll, usually along the front. If television were required, then it had to be viewed in "the television lounge" as a set in your room was only available in luxury hotels in those days. But this was holiday, and holiday meant a holiday from the dreaded goggle-box too. Once in a blue-moon, we might go to the local theatre. I certainly remember going to a performance of Agatha Christie's *Ten Little N*****s* – yes, you could still call it that in 1958, though it changed later to *Ten Little Indians* and then to *And Then There were None*. My principal memory of seeing this dramatisation of what is often considered Christie's best novel is that I had nightmares, usually focused on the image of the Judge with a bullet through his forehead, though – spoiler alert! – it turned out that it was the Judge himself who faked his own death and was slowly murdering the other nine guests at this island hotel.

With the advent of smart phones and social media, one holiday tradition which has declined in recent years is that of the holiday postcard, whether the deeply coloured and highly complimentary views of the town and beach, or the rather rude cartoons of busty blonds and hen-pecked husbands. We always used to send postcards from wherever we went, each one matched to the recipient: that saucy one for Uncle Ray; Granny and Grandad would like the one of the church, and so on. Perhaps the popularity of postcards with my parents was due to the fact that they did not own a camera until, several years later, I bought them a slim rectangular one that would slip into a pocket or hand bag. At the age of nine, they bought me a Kodak 127, a very basic camera which used roles of paper film and produced small black-and-white photographs no bigger than the roll of paper film itself. Later, and with the money that Granfy[1] had left me, I was to buy myself a Kodak Retinette 1A which took 35mm celluloid film although Mum and Dad only ever wanted me to take slides not pictures. We would hang a sheet up in the lounge and display them to all and sundry via a small projector, something they found more to their taste than everyone trying to gather round an album, looking at different photos over two pages at different times.

Back home, Mum and Dad would always try to take the

---

1   *Leonard Estwick d.1965.*

occasional day out, probably in London. These were the days when entrance fees to St.Paul's and Westminster Abbey were only voluntary and my father would refuse point blank to pay an entrance fee saying that no-one was going to charge him for entering *the House of [his] Maker*. And they didn't. He always made a contribution, though, on his way out. They also encouraged me to collect the Pitkin *Pride of Britain* series of guide books to the famous buildings and cathedrals that we visited in various parts of England, so they gave me pocket money but then directed my spending!

Nevertheless, I always felt a certain sense of adventure on these expeditions. Dunstable held pride of place as my home town, but exciting it was not. Anywhere with a mighty cathedral, castle, museum or mediaeval walls just had to be great, to be important, and London, via a bus to Luton and a train to Saint Pancras, with Tower Bridge, the Houses of Parliament, Buckingham Palace and its many museums, was – and is still – simply the greatest. In London's Madame Tussaud's, I was duly fooled by my father into asking a wax model of a commissionaire for directions. I was sick on a boat on the Thames on my way to the Tower of London from which I brought home a painted model of a Beefeater – a model made of lead and painted in lead-based paint: no 'elf 'n' safety'; in the late 1950s!

These special days out, whether from Dunstable or whilst on holiday in Scarborough, Bournemouth or Folkestone, imbued in this young boy, inevitably but not overtly, a sense of belonging to a great country with a fascinating history.

Trips to London were also facilitated by Uncle Stan[1]. My godfather, who was my granny's brother, my father's uncle and hence my great-uncle, was a successful business man who had risen from an ordinary milk roundsman to become Managing

---

1   *Stanley Bearton, husband of Dorothy and father of Jennifer.*

Director of Lea Valley Dairies. I loved going to his and Aunty Dorothy's house at 4, Woodlands, North Harrow, if for no other reason than the fact that he always seemed to treat me as a young man rather than as a boy. He was always interested in my school work, in my future and exercised his status as godfather with great care and interest – not to mention the postal orders at Christmas and for my birthday, usually for 10/-[1] – but he was also to insist when I had reached the age of eleven on allowing me to drink a small 'mixed Martini' before Sunday lunch, something which really made me feel grown-up! In 1957, he took us to the Battersea Fair which had been part of the 1951 Festival of Britain[2]. I went on its main attraction, a wooden-construction rollercoaster called *The Big Dipper*, hated it, and swore never to venture on such a thing again! It was closed some fifteen years later after an accident in which five children were killed.

Then there was Karel Hackl. Through his work at George Kent, my father came into contact with this Czech business man at a time when business with Czechoslovakia[3], was often difficult due to it being part of the Eastern (Europe) bloc and one of the Soviet Union's satellite states. Although my father was quite lowly in position at Kent's, this Czech took a shine to him and to us and invited us annually to London for the day. He would entertain us to lunch in his house in Cricklewood, where his lounge was large enough to host a dais in a massive bay window, complete with grand piano and room for an ensemble for him to indulge his passion for live chamber music. Then we would go into the West End where on one occasion we had tea in Harrods only for me to be scared that we would

1   10/- or ten shillings (50p), the equivalent of about £30 in today's wages.
2   The exhibits introduced new styles of pottery, ceramics, fabrics and furniture made from new materials – fibreglass, plywood, formica and plastics, and was designed to show Britain was getting back on her feet after the War.
3   Now the Czech Republic and the Republic of Slovakia.

be locked in for the night when the announcement came that the shop would be closing *in one hour's time*. On another trip, he took us – me in particular – to Hamley's in Regent Street where, in one department, he asked me what I would like. I looked around and saw some red, painted metal cranes with a string-and-hook hoist, wound by a small handle in the side.

"May I have a red crane, please?" I said politely. Karel Hackl turned to the shop assistant,

"I vornt biggest red cren you hev!" And I carried it proudly out of the shop and all the way home.

From the Jungle to the Parks

Moving house had meant that I had to leave Miss Spraggins and the cosy confines of Chiltern Road Infants School. My new school was the Ashton Voluntary Aided Primary School in Church Street which was to provide me with my favourite teacher of all time and, thanks to her, an introduction to a future career. Our new abode also meant that I could go the few yards to the end of Kingscroft Avenue and look out on to seemingly vast areas of wild fields which ran all the way past the tall hedge which delineated Grove House Gardens Park, and up to the railway line in front of Vauxhall Motors and its massive water tower that dominated the horizon. To this six-year old boy, gone was the slope of Waterlow Road and our postage-stamp of a back garden – and Dad wasn't that keen on me playing in our new back garden for fear I damage his roses – and a whole new world of open, green spaces in which to play presented itself. Across the field and set in a tall hedge was a gateway into Grove House Gardens Park. This was for swings and slides, conkers and cricket. However, it was another area of land which proved even more exciting: The Jungle. It was an area about fifteen yards wide and a hundred long: a waste land of bushes, trees and shrubs which was home – to me – to dens and to every adventure hero then on television or at the cinema. It led up towards High Street South and the Fire Station which still had its wooden siren tower, used during the war to signal the approach of enemy aircraft – though Dunstable itself was never bombed. It also ran past some dilapidated, disused pre-fabs which had been erected to ease the initial post-war housing problem. Now, even though the park is still there – though in a much diminished state – all the land is given over to roads, to carparks, to an Asda (which replaced the Queensway Hall), Dunstable College, a court house, an ambulance depot, a leisure centre, theatre and library.

Having started at Ashton School in April 1955, I was fortunate to have found a friend with whom I would stay close for about six years until the streaming at the Grammar School and his family's move of house, separated us. This was Michael Harwood who lived just round the corner in Dorchester Close. He had a sister Janice and a younger brother Robert. His father, Frank, was a site foreman for Wimpey's and worked hard for the local Scout movement, while his mother Joan would say in an embarrassed tone when she heard one of us fart "Who wants to go to the toilet then?" Michael and I not only went to school together but also to the 3rd St.Peter Cubs, attached to the Priory Church, and later the Scouts where I sadly remember giving him a really hard time when he didn't fan my patrol's campfire quickly enough and it went out.

Our usual venue for playing together was The Jungle. There, Michael and I acted out our American cowboy heroes such as the Lone Ranger or Davy Crockett, and fired small cap guns at enemies as well as each other, though I have to say that I always bagged the leading part: he was Tonto to my Lone Ranger and Georgie Russell to my Davy Crockett… well,

Mum had made me a black mask and I also had the imitation racoon-skin hat complete with furry tail!

We'd gallop through The Jungle and up to the High Street, past the Fire Station with its shiny red monsters crouching in their lairs, as far as *Foster Bros Men's and Boys' Wear*, full of school uniforms and what Dad said looked like 'Utility' suits[1] Then we'd ride back, in and out of the pre-fabs and down and across into The Jungle. This was where the US Cavalry defeated the Indians, where Davy Crockett and Georgie Russell fought the Mexicans, and in which the Lone Ranger and Tonto hunted down outlaws – that is, until The Enemy called us in for tea.

It was also home to a tramp called Coal-Black Charlie, though Grandad[2] always called him Mr. Smith when he saw him in the town. He also saw him when he made his regular appearance in the Magistrates' Court a few days before Christmas, having committed some minor crime in order to get himself sent down for a decent Christmas lunch.

One day, we arrived in time to see some smoke rising from the middle: Indian smoke signals – must be some Cheyenne nearby. Our horses we left in the clearing and crawled through the bushes to where the Cheyenne was sleeping next to his fire, a half-empty bottle of fire-water cradled in his arms. I suggested we tie him up and capture him.

"What with, Davy?" said George. "I ain't got no string – have you?

"Let's do a war dance round him and the fire." I said, shedding the Davy Crockett hat and tying a hanky round my head (you always carried a handkerchief in your trouser pocket in those days).

---

1   *Suits made during and after the War using government approved designs and cloth and invariably of poor quality.*

2   *Harold W.Parrott JP.*

"Yeah. Put some more wood on the fire first, though. Mind Coal-Black don't wake up."

"Cheyenne!" I corrected him, "We're Apaches and I'm Geronimo." Yes, I bagged the leadership again.

On went some twigs and the dry bits of some dumped off-cuts, and soon the fire was blazing. Forgetting that the Cheyenne was sleeping, we leapt around in the Jungle, whooping and screeching for all we were worth.

Suddenly, the Cheyenne awoke, fuddled confusion on his grime-brown face, daubed with blackberry juice war-paint.

"Wha' the f…?" He staggered to his feet, forgetting his bottle was open and the fire-water splashed down the front of his coat and on to the fire. The flames licked greedily at the rags as the Cheyenne lurched towards us.

"Liddle bastards…!"

Having quickly regained our horses in the clearing, we left the Cheyenne busily flacking the flames from his coat and galloped off across the prairie meadow, past the prefabs and towards the small gate in the large hedge which went into the Park. Sometimes, switching from Davy Crockett or Geronimo to a game of cricket just seemed like a good idea…

Occasionally we would vary the venue – though rarely in each other's house or garden: more likely the land around the bowling green at the top of Dorchester Close and between some flats and Ashton Primary School (where we both went). I am reminded of this every time I put my socks on as one day I fell and cut my shin open on the edge of the wooden surround to the bowling green: the scar is still there to this day.

Of course, Dunstable was blessed – and still is – with four good parks or 'recs'[1] which were around in my day. My 'local', as explained above, was Grove House Gardens, site of air-

---

1   *Recreation Grounds.*

raid shelters during the war, the lawns of outdoor Mayoral receptions[1], VE and VJ[2] celebrations, the Coronation children's tea, and the annual 'Old Folks' summer fete. Above all, it was the pride of Mr. Fred Cundy, the Parks Superintendent for the Borough Council, who, with his staff, maintained the flower beds in such an excellent way that could not nowadays be afforded or envisaged. Its gardens and borders were pristine and colourful, its lawns neatly clipped and very green, its conker trees plentifully fruitful; the Bandstand, a large three-sided and roofed stage was only used occasionally; its tennis courts and putting course more so, while its swings and slides and rocking horse, and its open play areas for football and cricket were all used extensively by me and by plenty of others.

From a narrow beginning on the High Street next to Grove House, aka the Council Offices, the park widened to include a greenhouse area which not only supplied the plants for Grove House Gardens, but also for other Council amenities. With the large bandstand towards the left, you were confronted by a row of holly trees, whose gaps gave access to the play area. There were the conker trees: beautiful, massive horse-chestnuts, each showering its autumnal presents to us eagerly waiting boys. Did girls play conkers? I don't remember any. Recipes for the hardening of conkers were muttered from lip to ear or boasted about in secretive terms. There were personal preferences for stringing, for soaking in liquids such as vinegar – supposedly a hardener – and for tactics and for how to swing, and how to strike your opponent's conker in vulnerable points. But beyond the conker season, it was football and cricket which filled the grasslands beyond the conker trees. Occasionally in the summer months, and while Mum shopped on a Saturday

---

1   *The large room with the big bay windows and doors was the Mayor's Parlour, or office, and is now the room used for conducting civil weddings.*

2   *Victory in Europe (8th May 1945), and Victory over Japan (14/15th August 1945) celebrations.*

174

morning, Dad and I would cross into Grove House Gardens and go behind the tennis courts to the putting course . For 6d[1] each, we would play a round of 18 putting holes with putters, balls and score cards provided by the 'parkie' or Park Keeper, a man of some authority who was often openly mocked and ridiculed. Despite enjoying these occasional rounds, I have to say neither Dad nor I was ever tempted to take up golf as a sport.

The park officially ended with a wire netting fence beyond which one could only gaze at the mammoth water tower that was Vauxhall's, separated from the fields by the railway line heading to Dunstable North Station up High Street North from Dunstable Town in Church Street – yes, two stations! You can tell when this was as, thanks to a certain Dr. Beeching[2], we lost both in 1963.

The Park fronted High Street North with ironwork gates between large columns and with the 'Council Offices' to the right which was where the main work of the Borough Council was conducted, and rates (now 'Council Tax') were paid: Grove House[3] itself. For meetings of the council and its various committees, Dad and Grandad would go to the rather dark and fusty back rooms of the Town Hall further along High Street North towards the crossroads. To the left of the entrance to Grove House Gardens stood the former ambulance depot which, in the sixties, became the Civil Defence headquarters where, in preparation for my Duke Of Edinburgh's Silver Award, I would follow a course in how to

---

1   *6 pence or 2½p, which in today's wages would be worth about £1.25.*

2   *Chairman of British Railways, he produced the 1963 report on The Reshaping of British Railways, known as "The Beeching Report", leading to far-reaching changes in the railway network, cutting over 4000 miles of lines and a host of stations including the line Luton-Dunstable-Leighton Buzzard.*

3   *The late 16th century building, formerly the Duke of Bedford's Arms inn.*

bunker my family and myself in a cupboard under the stairs in the case of a nuclear attack. So optimistic! So helpful! At the rear and husbanded by a Mr. Fred West, a round, jovial man who also served the Council as chauffeur to the Mayor, was the town's mortuary. Between that and the park ran Dog Kennel Lane which, passing by the public conveniences behind the mortuary, led between the park and the Grammar School grounds, past open fields, over the railway line with Vauxhall Motors to its right, all the way to Houghton Regis. It was a route I was later to detest in that it formed part of the cross-country practices at the Grammar School.

Another central park, Priory Gardens, behind Priory House and to the south of the Priory Church was in two parts: the formal flower beds which led to the town's War memorial, and then the much bigger area to the side of the Church, an open space which originally housed the Augustinian priory and which was the site of Dunstable's Pageant in 1963. This pageant was to celebrate the 750th Anniversary of the consecration of the Priory Church and the centenary of the town's borough status as incorporated in a Royal Charter, and was performed by over 1,000 people. From the earliest days through to the modern, the town's history was re-enacted by the various clubs and societies of the town, though at 14 years old, I was not a member of any. Yes, I took part in plays at school, but for some reason not known to me, Dunstable Grammar School played no formal part in the Pageant. I do remember, though, going to the end-of-pageant-week celebration to the music of Kenny Ball and his Jazzmen.

The area was also used by Ashton Primary School and Britain Street Secondary as their sports' area, though I have no memory of any personal involvement. Perhaps it was only during the Pageant that those in Priory Gardens really gave much thought to the fact that they were being entertained over the graves of the monks who had at one time been an intrinsic part of an Augustinian Priory. Now, the Parish Church is the sole remaining element of that Priory which, in 1540, Henry VIII 'dissolved' – a word which seems unfortunately to equate the destruction of a religious community with the stirring of sugar into tea.

Standing between the Luton Road to the north and, to the south, Jeans Way, the railway to Luton (until Dr. Beeching) and Blows Downs, (hills on to which I rarely ventured, though they had been popular with my Uncles Ray and Alwyn[1] when young as an area relatively undisturbed by adults...) Luton Road Rec. was quite simply for me through a gate at the end of Granny and Grandad's[2] garden. It boasted a children's play area (swings, a slide and a roundabout, all metal and on solid tarmac, unlike today's more safety-conscious materials), sports fields for football and cricket, and a fenced-off bowls club. It was also where Granny would take Cheryl[3] and me to play – to get us out of the house, I suppose. On one occasion, I rushed to get to a swing before Cheryl did, and got banged on the nose by a swing already in use. Amidst the blood and tears I could hear Granny saying that that "served [me] right". On another day Granny was quick to take us back indoors when the language in a football match, refereed by my father, became a little too ripe for her Baptist ears. It was also where I would later bring Pip, Granfy's Yorkshire terrier which he got following the death of his wife, my Nana[4]. Never was a dog so obedient or could run faster – at least, that's what I thought at the age of 9.

A similar park or rec., though perhaps slightly less well-

1   *Raymond and Alwyn Parrott, 3rd and 4th of Harold and Sarah's sons and my father's youngest brothers.*

2   *Harold and Sarah Parrott at 103 Luton Road.*

3   *Cousin; daughter of Keith and Dorothy Parrott.*

4   *Leonard and Evelyn Estwick.*

loved, at least by me, was Bennett's Rec. to the south-west corner of the town. This was primarily in my memory, a sports' ground and one I attended but rarely, save for my one excursion in Ashton School's football team one freezing cold, bleak, mid-winter, Saturday morning with the ground as hard as iron, as the carol tells us. That was both the beginning and the end of any pretence I may have had to play football.

To get to the fifth one required a little effort on my part. These were the days when drinks came in glass bottles, not cans and every bottle you bought required a deposit – perhaps 2d or 3d[1]. Michael Harwood and I would gather Corona, Tizer, assorted beer and other bottles from bins and from the fields and take them back to the various shops to collect the deposits on them all. We would then spend that money on buying two children's return tickets to Luton – at the cost of a shilling[2] each. We'd sit in an individual carriage with string netting luggage racks, romanticised pictures of Beds., Bucks., and Herts[3]. above us and a large leather strap with holes in on the door whereby we could lower the window, stick our heads out and get a face-full of grey smoke from the engine, despite the signs warning us that to do so was dangerous. In Luton, we'd then spend the afternoon in Wardown Park which had a lake and sports facilities.

And as well as all these parks, of course, there were The Downs, the Chiltern Hills, further west on which was situated Whipsnade Zoo and, from the top of the hill known as Pascombe Pit, where the Orange Rolling took place, you could look down on to the London Gliding Club and watch the old biplanes as they towed the gliders up, up into the currents of rising air, amply facilitated by the hills themselves. But it

---

1   *Tuppence and thruppence: somewhere between 30p and 50p in today's wages.*

2   *1/- = 5p or about £2.40 in today's wages.*

3   *Bedfordshire, Buckinghamshire and Hertfordshire.*

was on the Downs that kites could be flown – that is, with the exception of the one my father tried to make me out of bamboo and bits of old sheeting he'd used as dust-covers for his decorating and which were splashed with pastel shades of paint. Dad also tried to make me a toboggan out of a pallet he'd had delivered from Kent's. He separated all the planks and then fashioned runners and a surface which he then covered with a piece of old carpet. But it was so heavy and took all my strength to drag it anywhere, let alone up the Downs. He had many skills, did my father, but handicraft was just not one of them. But it was on the Downs that you could just walk in the (very) fresh air or go blackberry picking in August, perhaps disturbing the odd couple who had sought privacy amongst the bushes or, more likely, getting your arms scratched until they bled. Also to the west of Dunstable and opposite the Downs on the other side of West Street there was Green Lanes, too, where Mum had worked in the war in the Meteorological Office: a long green pathway lined with bushes and shrubs leading down towards the Maiden Bower hill fort archæological site and into Totternhoe. This was an area I loved then, but was to loathe later when we used it for the annual inter-house cross-country race at the Grammar School.

In all these areas, from Jungle to Green Lanes, you grew to know your alder from your elder and how red-spotted dock leaves could soothe nettle stings. You distinguished your hips from your haws, coped with briars and their blackberries, and soon recognised oaks from sycamores and horse chestnut (conker trees) from sweet (edible) chestnut. Summer was when the sun shone on dandelion seeds floating gently in the warmly scented air, while cabbage white, tortoiseshell and red admirals fluttered by, in and out of the shrubs and bushes. You learned which sticks could do for swords and which woods did not make bows and arrows

It is difficult now to imagine how much freer was the life

that I had as a child compared to that which primary school children have now. I was free to roam over open fields and parks and in The Jungle. There seemed to be more open, public spaces and you were free not only to enjoy yourselves but you were also free to make mistakes. Sometimes those mistakes were painful if you hurt yourself or fell. But you learned, hopefully, how to put them right and/or how to avoid the problem in the future. There was less traffic around then than there is nowadays and perhaps there were fewer dubious types, unless the media is such nowadays that we just hear more about them. But I was not allowed to play outside on Sundays: not because Mum and Dad were particularly religious but because they felt that it wasn't 'done', that it was not a correct or proper thing to do. After all, what would the neighbours say… ?

Dyb, Dyb, Dyb

Apart from school, the occasional couple of hours with cousins[1], and playing with Michael Harwood in the fields and in The Jungle, peer social life existed in my membership of my local Wolf Cub Pack, and later of the Scouts. In fact, Michael joined too, and his father, Frank, was to become one of the leading lights in the local scouting area. Looking back, I think participating in an organisation was important to me not only as a way of learning, doing and expressing, but from the acceptance and the sense of belonging that went along with it. There were things I couldn't do – like a forward roll on a mat on the floor, or swim – but many I could. And for those I won approval, evidenced in the badges I sported on the arm of my jersey.

The 3rd St Peter's Pack in turn 'belonged' to the Priory

---

1   *Probably Kevin and Elaine, or Cheryl.*

Church and had their meetings in the Parish Hall, a perpendicular-windowed, Victorian edifice with a small stage at one end. On a Friday evening, I attended this hall, resplendent in my green cap with yellow braiding, my maroon neckerchief, the St.Peter's badge at the back in the V shape, a leather woggle, my rough green top with the itchy neck, short grey trousers and a steadily increasing number of badges for such important life-skills as the lashing together of poles, the application of a sling, or the cooking of custard. These in turn, plus an increasing superiority in years meant that, by 1959 and at the age of 10, I, along with Michael, became a Sixer, able to boss around a team (six Cubs, obviously) junior in years. We were all led by Akela, Baloo and Bagheera[1]: three redoubtable ladies of varying ages, sizes, talents, attitudes and jolliness. Our evenings from 6:00 to 7:30 consisted of practicalities to do with tents, ropes, poles, flags, pots, pans and bandages; team games designed to run off energy were played and there were exercises to increase our mental acuity and observational abilities – such as "*Kim's Game*" where objects were placed on a tray, shown for a minute, then covered and we had to write down as many as we could remember. Then there was the ritual of the Promise to do our duty to God and the Queen and to keep the Wolf Cub Law. After that there came a "DYB DYB DYB!" from Akela, to which our response was "A-KE-LA! We'll DOB DOB DOB"[2] ending with the final 'V' salute to the side of the head – making sure it was the right way round, of course[3]. Being an only child and in such an organisation also brought me much more into the realms of team-work, of sharing and of responsibility.

The one thing the Cubs left me with, though, was a dislike for cocoa. I attended the annual Camp in my last year: a

---

1   *From Rudyard Kipling's "The Jungle Book": Akela is the Mother Wolf, Baloo the Bear and Bagheera the Black Panther.*

2   *Do Your Best and Do Our Best.*

3   *With the palm-side of the hand facing forward.*

weekend in a field somewhere where we all slept in smelly, old, canvas tents supported by large wooden poles, and kept upright by rope guy lines staked out with wooden pegs thumped into the ground with massive mallets. The sides had to be rolled up in the morning, though that did little to air the canvas and rid it of the impregnated odours: a mixture of sweat, unwashed bodies, damp, mud and wood-smoke. For most, it was their first night away from home or from close family. Not all took to the idea straightaway: there were those who silently cried themselves to sleep, and the odd one who was not silent; there were a few who were only too glad to get away, but I was one of the great majority who regretted leaving home but were determined not to let it show. Mum and Dad had bought me a groundsheet and I had an old sleeping bag, given to me by Dad's cousin, Jennifer,[1] who had been in the Guides. These, along with spare clothing and washing stuff, were packed into Dad's old RAF kitbag he had hauled out of the loft. This was the first time Mum taught me how to pack and how clothes would stay looking reasonably good if you rolled rather than folded them flat, especially in something like a kit bag, or nowadays in the ubiquitous hold-all. We had to go equipped also with unbreakables: an enamelled metal mug, an enamelled metal plate, and a knife, fork and spoon which could be clipped together. Our food was cooked for us – it was not until we were in the Scouts that we had to prepare our own and cook it over a camp fire. Our days were filled with activities from the militaristic setting out of our kit in the approved pattern on our groundsheets, neatly ready for inspection first thing in the mornings, to the tying of knots and the lashing of poles, and from team sports to individual badge work. Toilets became 'latrines' in the woods surrounding our site and consisted of a

---

1   *Daughter of Stanley (brother of Granny, Sarah Parrott) and Dorothy Bearton.*

hole in the ground covered with a wooden seat and surrounded by more yards of canvas held up by poles and ropes and stakes. In the evenings, we draped ourselves each in our own 'Camp Fire Blanket'[1] and sat round the camp fire for the narration of heroic parables from *The Jungle Book*, and the singing of jolly ditties. On one occasion, we must have been too involved since Akela, Baloo or Bagheera forgot the dixie with the cocoa in it and burned its bottom. I must have been given one of the last tin mugfuls: it tasted foul.

Frank Harwood gave my kit-bag and me a lift to Kingscroft Avenue when we arrived back at the Parish Hall. Mum emerged from the house delighted to see me home in one piece only to cringe with embarrassment when, getting out of Frank's car, I announced in full voice to her and to any listening neighbour:

"... and I haven't washed once!"

Oranges, the Statty and the Shops

How many times can you hear someone say *Of course, in my day, you could go into town and always meet someone you knew.* Perhaps that's not necessarily the case in a seething metropolis like London where I now live, but every shopping trip we made in Dunstable took an age as it was punctuated by conversations with friends and acquaintances. In that sense, Dunstable was just as much a part of my life as any member of my family. With my father and grandfather both on the borough council, the political and social life of the town was ever present in my family, and especially, of course, the year when my father was Mayor – but more of that later. I loved the small-town pomp and ceremony of the annual mayor-making in the Town Hall,

---

1   *A blanket covered in Cub and later Scout 'memorabilia' – badges, patrol colours etc: a great symbol of status and one-upmanship.*

the civic church services and the Remembrance Day parades, the fêtes and the fair. I loved the feeling that we were very much part of the town and was proud of our involvement, though saddened when, in 1974 after local government reorganisation, Dunstable and its council were relegated from the status of a borough to that of a town with all the consequential diminution of powers and responsibilities. Its continuing motto, *Justitia Omnibus Fiet* (Let Justice be Done to All), has always appealed nonetheless to my sense of fairness.

The town's traditions were few but honoured regularly and one of them brought my father on to early evening television. Since the middle of the eighteenth century, an unusual and unique tradition was practised on the slopes of Dunstable Downs leading to Pascombe Pit and towards the London Gliding Club. Every Good Friday, the people of Dunstable and its neighbouring villages would gather at the top of the Downs, originally to chase oranges rolled down the hill, attempting to grab them! Later, things became more of a scramble and the Mayor would need a strong throwing-arm to launch them high into the air so that they had some chance of being caught by an ever-ascending crowd of youngsters. Although there are similar traditions in other parts of the country of rolling items such as eggs down hills, said to symbolise the rolling of the stone away from the tomb of Christ, only Dunstable Downs has been recorded as using oranges. And on Good Friday too – two days early, so hardly the most appropriate day from a Christian perspective! The Second World War was to bring the first break from this tradition, as by 1941 the fruit was in short supply owing to rationing and the German U-boat menace in the Atlantic supply lanes. Post-war, the Dunstable Chamber of Trade moved to bring back the event and it was in 1964 that my father was filmed for television hurling – no longer rolling – oranges down the slope. But due to a lack of support from local traders and concerns from the "'elf'n'Safety'[1] merchants of doom (someone might get hurt by a deadly hunk of citrus!), it was decided in 1968 to put an end to the custom. One good thing that came from the filming of the orange rolling was that a letter arrived at the Council Offices addressed to Bill Parrott, an unknown. It did not take long for the letter to be passed on to my father. It was from Jack Thornton and his wife Dorothy, then residing in Bradford. They had seen the programme and Jack thought he recognised the man throwing oranges. He had been with my father in New Delhi 1945-46 and were to resume their friendship again after a break of nearly twenty years.

Another tradition dear to me was the Statty Fair. After Dunstable became a Borough incorporated by Royal Charter in 1864, the council initiated a statute (hence 'Statty') whereby a pleasure fair would be held on the fourth Monday of September. It began with swing boats, side shows and a boxing booth in 1871, but changed to add dodgems (1935) and other rides which were quite tame by today's theme park standards. The boxing booth had disappeared by the time I started going in the mid-fifties. With thruppenny bits, tanners and bobs[2] from parents and grandparents alike jingling in my pocket, it was the one evening of the year when Dunstable came alive with a blend of people, music, lights and games on The Square. There were toffee apples which pulled your teeth out, candy floss which went up your nose, 'spit-rock'[3] (lovely name!), dodgems where you didn't dodge but tried to ram others (always my favourite) hoop-la (I never won a goldfish swimming forlornly

---

1 *"Health and Safety" concern and subsequent regulation have increased greatly in recent years – and not always in a manner thought sensible!*

2 *3d pieces, sixpences and shillings – or approximately 50p, £1 and £2 in today's wages.*

3 *So called because the makers of the rock would spit on their hands before handling the hot sugar.*

in a plastic bag), fishing for ducks with a ring dangling from a cane, the rifle-range with air guns whose sights were always set so you'd miss – or so we reckoned – swing-boats that made you sick, and roundabouts that went up and down and round about in constant dizziness. The Statty had them all, – all, that is, for the fifties and sixties. Grandad would move slowly round with Granny clinging to his arm: Grandad because it was a council affair and his family was there, and Granny because the fuzzy whirl of excitement, people and her grandchildren amused and bemused her. My cousins Cheryl, Lynn and Diana were usually there along with my aunts and uncles: it was both a civic and a family tradition. Now it does still exist but, it has to be said, much changed and, I think, somewhat diminished from its less common-place, more glorious days, by the advent of massive theme parks with their bigger, wilder, more daring rides and attractions than could ever be assembled for one night on the fourth Monday of September on The Square in Dunstable.

Dunstable in the 1950s was provincially conservative in the foods that were available; equally, those foods were determined by seasonal availability. There was no way Mum could buy January strawberries grown in polythene tunnels in Spain and transported in refrigerated conditions. Strawberries were grown in England and she bought them only when they were available: in summer. She did provide tropical fruits (peaches, apricots, pineapple), but they came only in tins and swimming in thick syrup. Apples, pears, gooseberries and plums were home-grown, the first two needing careful, cool storing in outdoor sheds (or in a former air-raid shelter such as my Granfy[1] had dug) if we were to continue to enjoy them into the winter months. Mum often cooked plums and gooseberries

---

1   *Leonard Estwick, Mum's father.*

and stored them in airtight *Kilner* jars. Salads were on her shopping list only from May to September. Of the things I take for granted these days: blueberries and cranberries, rocket salad and broccoli, sweet potato and traffic-light-coloured peppers, avocados and aubergines, chillis and courgettes, root ginger and garlic – none were available to Mum in Barney Green's fruit and veg shop in Dunstable's High Street North.

Of course, rationing was a thing of the past by the time of my primary years, but old shopping habits died hard. Mum usually went to the shops with whom she had been registered for rationing, queues were still common as everyone seemed to take their time and shopkeepers were well-known to their regular customers, as indeed were their customers to them. With shopping taking place often every day, Mum would go from shop to shop having conversations with the grocer, with the greengrocer, with the butcher, the baker and the candlestick-maker[1], asking their opinion as to what was best at the moment or indeed even what they *had* at that moment. Fortunately, I was spared most of this queuing and chatting as I was firmly ensconced in my primary school.

I was not in Dunstable by the time Tesco, its first supermarket, (though no bigger than a Tesco Metro now), opened its doors on 28th September 1971 at 71-77 High Street North, well away from the main shopping area and opposite Grove House Gardens. But that, in itself, is an important date as it signifies that, in the shops in Dunstable prior to September 1971, Mum was still served by a human being, invariably behind a counter. Even in Woolworths – which, in its design and aisle-layout was as close to a supermarket as we could get before Tesco arrived – you were served by an assistant who would

---

1   From the rhyme "Rub-a-dub-dub, Three Maids/Men in a Tub" and meaning people of various trades.

find, weigh and package or brown-paper-bag your purchases; much, even things like sugar and biscuits, was sold loose. They would then take your money, ring it up on a till, and give you your change – save, perhaps for the Co-op stores near the old fire station in High Street North, where, in the words of Dylan Thomas, *the change hum[med] on wires*[1]. This was where the assistant put your money along with a bill into a tube. A triggering mechanism would then be activated and the tube would zip along the wires round the ceiling of the shop and up into the cashier's office, from whence your change, in the same tube, would eventually whirr back. It was indeed a sight for this young boy to stand and watch with amazement.

In those days, of course, we always shopped locally. It was rare indeed for Mum and Dad to go over to Luton, Dunstable's much larger neighbour who, like a large conglomerate, seemed constantly threatening to take over its smaller, sometimes bullied neighbour in what could only be described as a power-driven land grab. It never succeeded. Mum wouldn't normally have gone to Luton during the week – it was a half-hour bus-ride away – even while I was at school, and Dad positively refused to go back on a Saturday as he'd already travelled to and from Luton the five days of his working week. Anyway, as some used to say: *The best thing to come out of Luton is the road to Dunstable*.

Of course, these were also the days long before shops could open on a Sunday. Dunstable shops also closed on a Thursday afternoon ('half-day closing') while Luton shops closed on Wednesday afternoons.

In addition to the shops I've mentioned previously (Barney Green's greengrocery, Tom Cowper's grocery – from where Mum was later to have her weekly order delivered – and Don

---

1   *Mog Edwards, proprietor of Manchester House, a drapery, in "Under Milk Wood".*

Janes' news-agency from where Dad's *Telegraph* and *Sunday Express* would come), Mum always liked to shop for her clothes at Fred *Moore's* in High Street South, one of the longest-standing retailers in the Town and provincially up-market, while Dad went just across the road to the always-well-dressed Phillip Buckle in *EJ Buckle and Son* in Middle Row for his clothing, though it would have been *Wilds* in earlier years for his referee's outfit. My school uniform, though, was supplied by *Andersons* and by *Foster Bros. Mens and Boys Wear*. It was invariably Ken Imms at *Elite Decorations* in Albion Street (near Don Janes) who supplied us with wallpapers and paints, and Beverley Stott with furniture, while Joan and Peter Allen were the hosts at *The Old Sugar Loaf.* This was a former coaching inn with its archway and stables and in my youth Dunstable's foremost central hotel, restaurant and banqueting venue and where, at an Operatic Society dinner, I was to be introduced to the delights of a red wine which has remained a favourite: Bordeaux St.Emilion. These were the years long prior to today's café culture and there was consequently no more than a handful of refreshment places in the town centre. Our preferred haunts of a Saturday morning were firstly the *Noah's Ark* on The Square and, before 1955, immediately adjoining – appropriately enough – the cattle market. Later, we moved to the 'coffee morning' at the Methodist Church, also on The Square, and only very occasionally, the *Post Horn Tea Rooms* in Albion Street. We never, to my memory, patronised either the *Whipsiddery* or the *Central* cafés. Nails and screws and other hardware items could be bought from a former Mayor of the town, Walter Robinson in his tiny shop in High Street North. If you only wanted six 1½ 8's countersunk screws, then that's all you bought – and they were weighed and then priced: no pre-packaged polythene bags with far more – or one less – than you needed. When we got around to having a television set, Dad rented it from *Radio Rentals*, believing it was cheaper in the long run and probably not trusting the new-fangled technology, though he did later patronise Arthur Chattell who had the town's central wireless and television business in High Street North near the Old Sugar Loaf Hotel. Arthur, a dapper, little moustachioed man and Emily, his larger-than-life and full of fun wife, would invariably join them, frequently with the equally larger-than-life Ken Ball from *Connell's* estate agency, on the same charity-wine-and-cheese circuits popular in the 60's.

A favourite haunt of mine was *Charlie Cole's* cycle and toy shop just down High Street North from the cross-roads, from *Barclays* and *Lloyds* banks and *Gibbard's Grain and Seed (Corn Merchants)* shop where we would occasionally buy eggs. Mum was furious with me one day when she'd sent me up into town to *Gibbards* to buy half a dozen eggs – presumably to be carried home in a brown paper bag – and I had spent the rest of the half-crown[1] she'd given me (and damaged her weekly economy) on a plastic egg box as I thought I would carry them more safely like that. Charlie Cole was a racing cyclist, riding still into his 80's, and the penny-farthing mounted high above his doorway was a well-known local landmark. One year, I even joined his 'Christmas Club' to try and save a little money for Christmas presents – a somewhat futile exercise as the account book yielded no interest whatsoever but in doing so, I do remember feeling that little bit more grown up and a little bit more responsible as it was *my* initiative and not Mum and Dad's.

I think it worth emphasising here that these were days of relatively individual towns each with their own character and well before the chain stores and charity shops that fill – some would say 'blight' – our high streets today. Dunstable then had

---

1   *2/6 – two shillings and sixpence or just over £5 in today's wages.*

but a handful of the shops likely to be seen in other towns: Woolworths, the Co-op, Freeman Hardy & Willis, Home and Colonial. Nowadays, our high streets are full of such as Boots, WH Smith, Starbucks (and other café chains), Next, Marks & Spencer, Dyas, Holland & Barrett, TK Maxx, H&M, Tesco (to name but one of the big supermarkets) plus of course a host of charity shops. And one high street can look remarkably like any other...

Neighbours and Fireworks

Kingscroft Avenue proved a happy place for Mum and Dad and, by extension, for me, even if life in general was still not easy. Recovering from ravages of the Second World War, Britain was virtually bankrupt and in massive economic debt to America who had, after much cajoling by Churchill[1], funded our war effort and supplied much of the equipment needed to fight such a conflict. Nevertheless, there was still great camaraderie and pride in ones country. You knew your neighbours and had a sense of belonging, of community. People were trusting: doors were left unlocked, if not open. To our left at number 26 we had the Raithbys, soon replaced by a jolly, bubbly, rotund couple, two of the first Polish migration into Dunstable, Janet and Ramon Barylak. Her hair had turned white almost overnight on smelling the body incinerators in Nazi-occupied Danzig, or Gdansk, her native home. Here in England, Ramon survived a scaffolding pole falling on his head on a local building site in the days before helmets were compulsory. They would go back to Poland, then still a Soviet Union-dominated state behind the Iron Curtain, loaded with clothes (some from Mum and Dad) for their friends and

---

1   *Winston Churchill, then Prime Minister.*

family there, and bring back gifts of Polish crystal, some of which I still have. To our right were Olive and Roy Walker with their daughter Julie, a year or so younger than me. Roy was a carpenter with Robinson and White, a local building firm which also featured my Uncle Ray[1] as one of its rising employees and future director, while Olive was an upholsterer. They were the best of neighbours with Mum and Dad, but only for a chat over the fence or when each was needed – they were never in and out of each other's houses as some can be. In fact, they only ever socialised formally: on New Year's Eve, taking it in turn to host each other.

Belongings were modest – from a wartime 'make do and mend' mentality and post-war utility furniture. In the fifties, I experienced no peer pressures to grow up any quicker than nature intended, or to conform. Childhood for me was very carefree, very certain in its safety. Socially though, apart from School, the Cubs and from playing with Michael, my interaction with others was always with those much older than myself, whether they were relatives or family friends. I found I always got on well with 'oldies', and could engage with them. In general, we – my peers and I – had respect for our elders, for figures of authority. In my boyhood certain people were still accorded, for the most part, an automatic respect for their authority purely for their office, their age or their experience: teachers, police officers, public servants, councillors, – even the Park Keeper, a much maligned character whom we loved to hate for their often quite dictatorial manner and, basically, the way they would always spoil our fun. Nazi salutes along with a *Sieg heil!* were not uncommon.

Opposite our house, at no.33, lived Maurice and Ethel Lewin and there was a time – probably no more than for six

---

1   *Ray Parrott.*

months – when Saturday mornings were for Esperanto[1]. Both were Jewish and had lost their entire families in the Nazi gas chambers during the war. They were ardent supporters of the United Nations, but would have nothing whatsoever to do with anyone or anything German. Both highly educated, polyglot people, they thought, nonetheless, that the world would be a better place in terms of international understanding if we all spoke the same language. Michael Harwood[2] and I were therefore invited to spend half an hour with Maurice every Saturday morning, in what I remember as a rather fusty, airless house with little light and full of heavy, dark wooden furniture, learning basic Esperanto. It didn't last long. One remnant of Esperanto is still with me, however – I'll leave you to guess why two young boys remembered these words:

"*Kiel vi fartis?*" "*Mi fartis bene, dankon.*"[3]

Next to the Lewins' house was some waste land leading to allotments and the High Street. From the beginning of October each year, Michael and I would collect all the rough wood we could find, begging occasionally for redundant delivery pallets and build a ginormous bonfire in readiness for 5th November and the guys we had both made. Other neighbours from Kingscroft Avenue and Dorchester Close joined in, each with their own children and fireworks. Those were the days before "elf 'n'safety"[4], and fireworks – which we had been collecting assiduously for weeks – were let off more or less at random as there was no formal display. Penny bangers were the thing – twelve for a shilling[5] of course – and grandparents and parents had been tapped for ample funds on the run up to Bonfire

1   *A 'universal' language, mostly based in general on European languages, formulated by a Dr.Zamenhof.*

2   *My Primary School friend.*

3   *How are you? I am well, thank you.*

4   *Health and Safety.*

5   *About £2.50 nowadays, or just over 20p per banger.*

Night. My savings went on bangers, Jumping Jacks, Helicopters and, if I had enough, a Mine, reputed to be the loudest bang you could get. Dad's contribution would be the 'pretty' ones like rockets, Catherine wheels, Roman candles and, at Mum's insistence 'a nice packet of Sparklers' – and yes, I suppose we did get some pleasure out of drawing shapes in the dark night air with the sparklers, but I still preferred my bangers. We got all our supplies from Don Janes' news agency in Albion Street. Don was a cousin of Granny's[1] and had been a prisoner of the Japanese during the war but never, ever spoke of it. For Michael and me, both because our close friendship was fading and because the land had been sold for re-development, our last bonfire was in 1962, and one to which, by formal letter in our best handwriting addressed to the Mayor's Parlour, The Council Offices, Grove House Gardens, we invited the Mayor of Dunstable. And he came but didn't wear his chain of office. We forgave him all the same – it was only Dad, after all.

Rules and Breaking Them

I was born into an age in which this automatic respect for authority to which I have already referred, and with it the natural politenesses of social behaviour, was starting to decline. Nevertheless, my parents clung to a great middle-class conventionality, as evidenced in their refusal to let me play in the street – Kingscroft Avenue was more upmarket that Waterlow Road and there were more cars around – and certainly never outside on Sundays. This was nothing to do with religious observance. Whatever I pleaded, their standard, conventional response was *Whatever would the neighbours say?* To be honest, I don't think the neighbours would have minded that much if

---

1   *Sarah Parrott, née Smith/Bearton and wife of Harold.*

they had been asked, though these were times in which, in the post-war Britain of the 1950s and with youth culture changing, the middle class clung even more tightly to its views of what was proper and correct and still viewed National Service in the Army, Navy or Air Force[1] as a jolly good correctional for any disaffected youth. Things were changing, though, and especially for the young, for adolescents, for that 'disaffected youth', with the advent of a youth culture in music and fashion, and the start of the Rock'n'Roll era. Not that Bill Haley and the Comets, and the young Elvis Presley had any impact whatsoever on this particular youth who was much more interested, like his parents, in the light classical music of the sort to be found on *Your Hundred Best Tunes* on the Light Programme[2] of the BBC on a Sunday evening, hosted by Alan Keith, rather than in *Radio Luxembourg* which played pop music.

Although I have no recollection of seeing them in Dunstable, a young male subculture had grown in the early and mid-fifties – the so called Teddy Boys. Some formed gangs, causing trouble and using violence, but they seemed more confined to the larger cities such as London, Liverpool, Manchester etc. and, though their fashion style – Edwardian 'drape' jackets in bright colours and velvet collars, narrow trousers, 'brothel creepers' or thick, soft soled shoes, and a DA hair style (aka Duck's Arse, whereby the hair would be greased and swept back, leaving a quiff at the front) at least would have inevitably spread to smaller towns such as Dunstable, I cannot remember they and I crossing paths, so to speak.

As a boy, I was invariably well-behaved and polite, but there was a time when I did fall foul of the law. I was nine and wandering round Woolworths at lunchtime probably during

---

1   *Introduced after the Second World War, it came to an end in 1962.*
2   *Now Radio 2.*

the school holidays. There was a product, popular at the time, called *Cremola Foam*. When mixed with water, it produced a fizzy, foaming drink of whatever very synthetic flavour you had chosen. Looking at it on the shelves, something came over me that was determined to have it – though what I would have done with it subsequently or how I would have explained it at home, heaven only knows. I took a tin, the size of a jar of mint sauce, and was about to slip it into my pocket and start to walk towards the exit when suddenly a hand descended on to my left shoulder and gripped it tightly.

"That'll do, sonny. You come with me." Another hand seized my left arm and wheeled me round and began to march me towards a room at the back of the store. There, I was sat down, tears on my cheeks, my mind awhirl with thoughts of panic, family disgrace and shame, while he, my abductor, sought paper and a pencil. That was it: I seized the opportunity and legged it out through the store, running faster and further than I ever had done or was ever to do in my life. I turned right on to High Street South, down Church Street, over the road towards Ashton School, then on towards Kingsway, down left and towards Kingscroft Avenue and home – the instinctive nest of safety and comfort. However, it was also probably the worst place I could have run to, given that I hadn't yet divulged my address to him. Even worse luck: a Police Inspector who lived in Kingsway was just on his way to work after lunch and could not fail to grab the little boy running towards him with a manic Woolworth's employee a hundred yards behind screaming,

"Stop that boy!"

Oh, I denied everything from the moment the Inspector grabbed me. He took me home. Mum and later, Dad, talked endlessly to me, Dad always with the thought of his and the family's reputation being sullied by his son and Harold's grandson being up in court as a shoplifter.

"I was only reading the label." I maintained steadfastly.

"By your pocket?" Mum knew what to ask.

"The writing was small and I could only see it like that", I lied through my teeth. Mum then tried another tack:

"Would you say the same to Mrs. Pratt?" Oh no, not my favourite teacher whom I adored and would have done anything for!

"Yes!"

"Would you say the same to the Rector? Would you swear on the Bible?"

"Yes, yes, yes" And so on and on with me maintaining my total innocence. In the end, Dad and I were summoned to the Police Station where Superintendent Horace Woods, with a knowing smile towards Dad, told me that they were not taking any action this time – the Woolworth employee had, after all, acted too hastily in grabbing me before I had chance to leave the shop – but they might well go further if it were to happen again, which – a meaningful look in my direction – he was sure it wouldn't, would it?

"No, sir." I shook my head. Then he remained certain that I wouldn't see any more of his Police Station and bade Dad and me farewell and we left, Dad typically tight-lipped, the tip of his tongue protruding and clenched firmly between his teeth.

I still do not know to this day why I tried to steal the *Cremola Foam*, other than perhaps some sort of sense of excitement at doing something I wouldn't normally dare and which was so 'other' than my normal rules of behaviour. It shocked Mum and Dad rigid, I think: Mum wondering where she might have gone wrong in my up-bringing, and Dad thinking he might have had to resign from the Council, such would be their perceived shame.

As if that weren't enough, a year later, Mum and Dad found that I had occasionally been helping myself to a few pence of the money Mum used to put aside from her housekeeping into little typewriter-ribbon tins she kept in one of her kitchen cupboards and used to pay occasional bills. Yes, I got a moralistic roasting, of course, but both Mum and Dad realised that perhaps the time had come to give me some regular pocket money. Which they did and, looking back, that seems to me a very enlightened approach. I am pleased to say I stole no more.

On another occasion I managed to embarrass my father possibly even more than visiting the Police Superintendent's office. One day, on my way home from school, I decided that it would be a good joke to move a small, angled wooden ramp that had been placed in the gutter up against the kerb to ease a car on to its drive. Unfortunately I was seen and even more unfortunately had forgotten that the house, no.1 Kingscroft Avenue, belonged to John Wilshire, the Finance Director of George Kent where Dad worked and where he was summoned for 'a word' from his boss.

But there could be a stricter, more punitive side to Mum and Dad. How many of us older people have said *If I'd have spoken to my parents like that, I'd have got a clip round the ear.* Of course, if you gave your child or grandchild a clip round the ear nowadays, Social Services would probably be round at your house, taking away the children before you could Google your way to the Magistrates' Court. But in my childhood days, I had it inculcated in me never to answer back. You would do as you were told because that's how it worked. So far as what Mum and Dad said, *Yes* meant *Yes*, and *No* meant *No* however much I argued or threw a tantrum – though I rarely did since I had been brought up according to certain standards and Mum and Dad were invariably consistent in the application of the rules. Once, though, when my parents and I were at Granny and Grandad's[1] and I had done some minor thing that was wrong, Mum told me off for being naughty.

---

1   *Harold and Sarah Parrott.*

"Oh, he's never naughty, is he?" said Granny indulgently in my direction, whereupon I turned and stuck my tongue out at Mum. The result was a real stinger round my legs along with a "Don't you dare do that!" Dad then lectured his mother on how she was not to interfere with the way Mavis (Mum) dealt with me. My generation of the many children born in the immediate post-war era, the so-called 'baby-boomers', were, by definition, children of parents who had been through the war. The majority of fathers and some of the mothers had been in uniform and had had to become accustomed very quickly to military rules and regulations. There were those who reacted against the rules and regulations – predominantly in the so-called permissive sixties, whilst my parents clearly preferred to cling to a system of some rules and regulations, of right and wrong. And me? Sarah and Heather, my daughters, and those whom I taught, would probably agree that I followed my parents.

If I remember anything about my mother, it was the little sayings she had which she used repeatedly. If I hadn't washed myself thoroughly, I'd only had *a lick and a promise,* or if my tie was crooked, it was *all skew-whiff.* More common, though, if I was really untidy, she would say that it *looks as if you've been dragged through a hedge backwards.* Pull a face and it was *if the wind changes you'll stay like that.* Annoy her greatly and I would hear *oh, I could knock you into the middle of next week!;* after which I might look very unhappy or like *a dying duck in a thunderstorm.*

So what were the rules children like me lived by in the 1950s? It is difficult to be precise, but perhaps the following – and the order is irrelevant – will give some idea of how we behaved, how we reacted, and perhaps to what extent we differed then from young people nowadays. I must also add that I led a very middle-class, ultra-conventional life and that the following may well have varied tremendously in households of different socio-economic and cultural levels.

First of all, table manners were the foundation of being reared correctly. At table, we never started eating until everyone had been served and we always ate together, sitting in the same places every time. I had to hold my knife with my right index finger down the blunt spine of the knife, not in what could be called a pen-grip. I was meant to push vegetables on to the back of the fork not use the tines of the fork like a surrogate spoon. I was never to scrape my knife and fork against each other to clean them, nor to touch my teeth with them. Soup was to be drunk by moving the spoon away from you, tilting the bowl, if necessary, again away from you. You ate with your mouth closed and I could not put my elbows on the table. One of the good things about going on an exchange with a French family in Brive, France, when I was older, was that there I was allowed, indeed encouraged, to clean my plate with bread, something I was never allowed to do at home. In fact there was an advertisement on television showing someone cleaning his plate with a piece of bread and it had the words "*naughty, but nice.*" I could never leave the table without seeking permission first – in fact, I would usually not even bother asking as, in the fifties, we would go to the table together, eat as a family together and leave the table together. Neither was I allowed to be fussy or picky over food, having at least to *try* everything first though, with that proviso, I do remember not liking cream, mushrooms, or the skin on a rice pudding or custard!

Then there was behaviour towards others, of which the essence were the words *please* and *thank you*. These were compulsory and unlike nowadays, if I didn't say it, it wasn't a case of it being ignored or the adult saying what an impolite young child you had been after you'd left: they would tell you face to face. *I want* were two words I wasn't allowed. It had to be *I would like... please* or *Please may I have...?* and never forgetting the *Thank you* when what I had asked for was given.

At school, every teacher was referred to as *Sir* or *Miss/ Ma'am* and upon entry of a teacher into the classroom, everyone would stand. When I wore a cap, I would never wear it indoors, at home or in a shop. I would at least touch it in greeting a lady, if not raise it completely. If I were caught not wearing it on my way to or from the Grammar School, I would be punished by the prefects. *Speak when you're spoken to* is something else you would hear. Although this was declining in importance, I would not normally be expected to make the first comment other than to ask how a person was and would sit politely when we had guests and wait to be spoken to – and that was usually based around what I was doing at school. Mum and Dad did expect me, however, to speak up well for myself and definitely not to be a shrinking violet. I was taught to give up a bus or train seat for a lady or an OAP[1] as we called them, and would always open a door for someone, a woman or any adult and allow them entry or exit before me. Equally, when any adult visitor, except your parents or close relations, entered the room, I would stand up. If I saw a lady struggling with her shopping, I would be expected to offer to help – though I cannot remember that offer ever being taken up!

I'm sure there are many more that those of you who lived in those years could think of! And of course I blotted my copybook on occasions – like asking Aunty[2] when I was four why she had such fat legs, or (when I was twelve) asking my father's cousin Jennifer and Stanley[3], a couple of months after

---

1 *Old Age Pensioner (someone of senior years).*

2 *Aunty Dor[is] Child, sister of Evelyn Estwick (Nana).*

3 *Jennifer (daughter of Stanley & Dorothy Bearton) and Stanley Thompson.*

they were married, when they were going to have a baby. Oh the embarrassment! Oh the upset! Oh the red faces all round – except mine, until Mum laid into me with the usual *You don't say THAT!* If there was one thing, though, which annoyed Mum more regularly than anything it was my reluctance to get up in the mornings. and that has stuck with me throughout my life. It had little to do with sleeping but more, I would maintain, to do with habit and possibly my own body-clock. In adulthood, I found I could read, write and work until midnight, one or two o'clock, but get up early in the mornings – no: that was – and is – anathema to me.

Much of the above would remain for some years to follow, but the main change in youth came about later in the sixties with the advent of teenage culture, especially music and fashion, and with the 'mods' and the 'rockers' nowadays known as 'bikers' – although I must add that the few bikers I've known have all had impeccable manners.

Etiquette and manners were just a part of the fifties lifestyle, particularly in my middle-class upbringing. Life in general was more disciplined: you wouldn't see so much rubbish in the street – there again, there weren't as many snacks, sweets, or cans as there are now and it would be hard to find untidy front gardens. People wanted to show, particularly after the chaos and devastation of the war, that they had things sorted, that they were leading a decent life, that they did the right thing – and children's manners, the way children were brought up, were one way of showing this.

There must be many times, nowadays when people decide that they really can't be bothered to visit, to attend, to take part, to do something they don't want to, so why should they? But my parents instilled in me the sense of doing something not because I wanted to, but because *it gave someone else pleasure.* I try to stick to it; I doubt if I always succeed and only those close to me know if it is still true.

Ashton School[1]

This was 1955 and I was in the maroon-coloured blazer of Ashton Voluntary (Aided) Primary School. I was going to a school whose staff, according to an HMI report[2], formed a *happy, hard-working team* who inculcated a *healthy, purposeful spirit... in a happy environment.* To me on my first day there, the school smelt of stale milk and sick. These were the pre-Maggie-Thatcher-'milk-snatcher' days[3], of course, when we were all given a third of a pint of milk at morning playtime, the drinking of which was compulsory. If left outside in the warm days of summer it would start to go off; in winter's freezing conditions, it was a common sight to see the small crates of milk outside the school with the shiny bottle tops standing proud above the bottles on a column of frozen milk. Of course the only way to defrost the school milk was to place it by or on a radiator, and then we were forced to consume watery, lukewarm milk. And forced we were: *Milk is good for you, child. You WILL drink it all up!* That experience put me off milk as a drink by itself forever. The other early sensory memory of my first day was due to the open area or lobby near the entrance of the school in which lay a pool of sick on to which the caretaker, Mrs. Ashwell, had thrown some sand in order the better to clear it. She hadn't been back to do so and the smell has stayed with me.

I had moved from Mrs. Briggs, Headmistress at Chiltern Road Infants, to Mr. L.H.Cunnington, Headmaster of Ashton School, who had taken over from Miss Mapley in 1944. He was a kindly man but strict, perhaps a tad austere and is forever

---

1   *See also history in the Appendix.*

2   *Her Majesty's Inspectorate, HMSO 04/53.*

3   *In 1971, Margaret Thatcher, then Education Secretary in Edward Heath's Conservative government, did away with free milk for primary schools.*

in my mind a slender elderly gent with thinning, whitish hair, darker eyebrows, and a grey three-piece suit. Mum and Dad always told me off if I ever referred to him as *ol' Cunning'on*. I was put in Miss Pollard's hands, although my sensitivities were hurt when another teacher, one Mrs. Hopwood I think, called me Roger Pa-**rrott**. A good surname it is not, but it is mine and I wanted it pronounced correctly: *like the bird, only with two t's*. It was Miss Pollard who, at the end of my first and only term in her class remarked in my report that I had worked well but that I often spoiled it with my *aggressive attitude towards other children!* That baffles me. I can only, with the advantages of hindsight, put it down to asserting myself in a class which had already been together undisturbed for two terms. But then it was on and into Mrs. Edwards' Class 5 – and no more aggressive behaviour – in which my Scripture was *Good* as were my Arts and Crafts. Reading was *Very Good* while Number was only *Fair* as was my Writing. In Nature, she wrote that I *shew* interest – an old-fashioned spelling of the word.

The playgrounds were at the back of the school and separated into Boys' and Girls'. Games usually included very strenuous sessions of 'tag' with much running between the two end walls involved, and marbles in which you would try to capture your opponent's marbles by flicking your own and hitting theirs. This back yard area was later converted into a new school hall but not during my years there as plans for it were only submitted in 1959, its lack having been noted by the Inspectors in 1953. There again, there had been a summons issued by the council against the Governors in the autumn of 1957 complaining about the *ruinous and dilapidated condition* of at least parts of the school[1]. Indeed, there had been moves to sell off the school for redevelopment. At the time, my father was the council's nominated representative on the board of

---

1   *Dunstable Gazette 01/11/57.*

governors of the school and gave steadfast support to proposed improvements and an extension, inveighing against those who wanted to sell the site for commercial development, describing them as *big business boys against small school boys*. All I knew was that the toilets (outside, of course) were smelly in the summer and freezing cold in the winter. I am reminded that the dinner ladies were the ones to dole out the loo-paper (what happened during the rest of the day?), though one could have been forgiven for thinking that paper was still rationed, they were so mean with it. It was like thick, rough tracing-paper with *Izal* printed on it and a far cry from the soft two-ply tissue commonly used nowadays. I don't remember inside toilets, though Doreen Cove, who was in the year above me, remembers them as the place to which you were immediately taken by 'Nitty Nora', the nit-nurse to have anything she had found dealt with. The nit-nurse used to make regular visits to check for headlice and we would line up to be examined in turn, our hair being combed carefully with a nit comb to see if there were any infestation. This was one of the things I dreaded as I hated having my hair washed with a passion for fear the shampoo entered my eyes and stung them, especially when being washed with *Selsun*, a prescription anti-dandruff shampoo. Even that, though was better than having my hair washed in vinegar, the prescribed anti-nit wash for my mother and her sister back in the 1920's when they had caught them at school. There were also routine eye and hearing tests, and visits from the school dentist, not to mention the infamous *Cough!* command when the nurse or doctor put their hand between boys' legs to make sure that both testicles were in place.

Then there were the vaccinations. Given the arguments over Covid-19 vaccinations raging in some quarters as I write, I cannot remember my childhood ones as being anything other than willingly accepted as a means of avoiding what could be extremely damaging, if not fatal, illnesses and diseases. The polio vaccine was given at school to every child on a sugar lump. We were also jabbed against Diphtheria and Tuberculosis (BCG). Measles, German Measles (Rubella) and Mumps were not vaccinated against; most children contracted these diseases in childhood. Rubella can affect unborn babies in the womb if contracted in pregnancy, and so if a girl in the class was infected, it was not uncommon for her mother to throw a tea party for the rest of the girls so they could also catch the disease. I can remember Mum hearing of a case of mumps in a child not far from where we lived and being very anxious that I should have good contact with him so that I caught it young. I had the contact; I didn't catch it. Chicken pox and measles, yes, but not mumps. Measles was the nuisance in that I had to remain in bed, in a darkened room, doing absolutely nothing: I wasn't even allowed to do either reading or jigsaws as I was told that measles could affect my eyesight.

School class sizes in the 1950s and early 1960s were large: often over 30 children to a class, as these were the 'baby-boomers'. There were no classroom assistants, just the class teacher and discipline was strict. In many schools, it was quite common for a disruptive child to be rapped over the knuckles, on the buttocks or on the palm of the hand with a ruler – and the Headmaster always had the sanction of the cane – though I do not recollect any instance of corporal punishment at Ashton. Apart from the occasional problem, disturbances in classes were absolutely minimal. Yes, any bad behaviour was punished – both at school and then subsequently at home as well as soon as your parents got to hear of it. I have to say that I was probably something of a 'goody-goody', such was the way Mum and Dad had brought me up: I spoke when spoken to, put my hand up to ask questions and tried to do my best even if I didn't always succeed, and I was keen to learn and to do well. Swearing was unknown to me; I respected my teachers – indeed, anyone older than me whether or not they were in authority; and I ate well and handled my cutlery properly at table. I could tie my own shoe laces, and take myself to the lavatory. What more could my teacher want?

Education was very much 'chalk and talk' This meant that you learned what the teacher at the front of the class wrote on the blackboard (supported on an inverted 'V' easel by a couple of pegs) with sticks of chalk while we sat at desks facing him or her, screwing up our faces in mock agony each time the chalk screeched on the board. There was not the wealth of books and materials – and certainly no calculators or computers, of course – you find in school nowadays, and what there were could almost then have been given antique status, such was their age. Books were only ever given out for a particular lesson, not to take home. We sat in twos on a tip-up bench seat at solid wooden desks with iron frames, although the desks themselves had individual lids. The desks and the seats were all stained with the residue of the previous eighty years of boys and girls: ink, milk, powder-paint, papier-maché, glue and what else I dread to think.

Lessons were quite formal with an emphasis on learning things by heart. With very few text books, most things had to be copied off the blackboard into exercise books with, in the early years, pencil and then by about nine or ten, in ink. Not that we had our own pens: we had to use wooden sticks about the size of a pencil with a nib-holder and nib on one end. The two parts of the nib-end would splay after regular usage or increased pressure, leading to much thicker writing and a greater frequency of ink blots! The ink itself was in small ink-wells, filled from a large, gallon-sized bottle and set into the front top of the desk. Reading, [w]Riting and [a]Rithmetic (the Three 'R's) were very important, as was learning by rote. Times-tables were learned by chanting aloud in class, and poetry, such as Wordsworth's *I wandered lonely as a cloud*, would be learned by heart for homework – which was something I could do.

Neat hand writing was seen as very important and practiced daily – and was something I couldn't do and envied my friend, Michael Harwood, his neat, rounded, joined-up letters, all at the same perpendicular, whilst mine, regardless of trying different grips and angles, resembled the proverbial drunken spider crawling across the page. And it's only got worse! History and Geography as individual subjects were not given much space on the timetable and belonged more to the 'topic' category of subjects whereby they blended with, perhaps art, such as the time we learned about the Roman army, and made and painted our own Roman shields. Mine was predominantly purple, a very imperial colour so I was told. Nature study was the only science taught and we were often asked to bring in things such as leaves and seeds to be identified and then we would use them later, but in art-and-craft work.

Indeed, the HMI report had criticised the fact that one class missed these subjects entirely due to swimming lessons. Now that was one area where I was guilty of evading a lesson as much as possible: I couldn't swim, never learned and hated the outdoor pool, the freezing-cold water, the rough towel, indeed the whole idea with a passion. Unless Mum remembered, I 'forgot' as much as possible to take my trunks and towel with me on the appointed day for the trip up to the Downs and the California pool. On the few days I did not manage to escape the pool, we had to change in small, damp, wooden huts on the side. Those who could swim would boast about how warm the water was, while we wimps who could not, stood and shivered in the shallow end, impervious to the exhortations of the teacher. I did eventually learn, but some 55 years later!

As I look back, I am somewhat amazed at the arithmetic we took for granted. Whereas all calculations of length, weight and money[1] are now done in what is called Base 10, i.e. the decimal

---

1   *e.g. 10mm = 1cm, 100cm = 1metre; 100g = 1 kilo; and 100 pence = £1.*

system, in the fifties – and indeed up to 1971, the first twenty-two years of my life – we had possibly the most complicated system in the world! For money we had pounds (*20 shillings or 240 pence (pennies) equalled one pound, £1, a 'quid'*), shillings (*12 pence equalled one shilling, 1/-, s., a 'bob'*) and pennies or pence (*d.*)[1]. Therefore, we would work in base 4 for farthings (*¼ of a penny*), base 2 for halfpennies (*ha'pennies*), base 12 for pennies, base 20 for shillings and base 10 for pounds. There were also guineas (21 shillings) but these were gradually going out of fashion and used only for very formal things like professional fees for solicitors. I think the only place you will see them today is in the name of horse races where the prize money can still be quoted in guineas. Length would be measured in fractions (tenths, eighths and sixteenths) of inches, 12 of which would make one foot (ft), with three feet equalling one yard and 1,760 of those making a mile – I shan't go into rods, poles, perches, chains (the length of a cricket wicket) and furlongs! In weight, 16 ounces (*oz.*) made one pound (*lb.*), 14 pounds were a stone, eight stones were one hundredweight (112 pounds) and 20 of those equalled a ton (2,240 lbs). We would do sums involving the addition, subtraction, multiplication and division of sums of money, lengths and weights, both in writing and in our heads ('mental arithmetic' – something I remain still quite good at) and have to add that we did not have anything resembling a calculator. Yes, there were those who found it difficult, but we were using these calculations day in, day out, and consequently just got on with it.

If you fancy testing your brains, do look at the questions in the appendix (without looking at the answers first!)

The School Broadcasting Council for the United Kingdom

---

1   *£.s.d or L S D came from the Roman money librae, solidii and denarii. Others coins 3d (3 pence), a 'thruppenny bit', 6d (a tanner) 2/- (two shillings) and 2/6 (two shillings and sixpence, half a crown.).*

had been set up in 1947 and the wireless, or radio (no television, of course, and there was only the BBC, no independent or local stations) played a great part in the education of school children in the 1950s. *How Things Began* was a programme I really loved as I remember it involving a 'reporter' observing for instance a group of dinosaurs or some Romans or another episode of ancient- or pre-history. Another such programme was *Singing Together* where the class would sing traditional folk songs and sea shanties such as *Oh Soldier, Soldier, (won't you marry me), A-Roving, Michael Finnegan, The Raggle-Taggle Gypsies* and *Oh No John*. However, when as an adult you examine the content and meaning of some of these old folk songs, it is doubtful that they were indeed suitable or, in today's parlance, *politically correct,* for the under 11s! My own participation in these was strictly limited as I remember being told not to 'sing' so loudly – I then had not one musical note in my body! Indoor PE usually involved the programme *Music and Movement* in which we had to hop, step, jump, stretch, bend and wave arms in time to the music: *Now, children, we are going to sway like trees in the wind.* Then we might change into butterflies, skipping round flapping our 'wings' as we did so. PE outside could involve hoops and balls but, if we had to sit on the ground at all or do forward rolls, we had woven raffia mats. I think the dusty tarmac surface of the playground itself would have been more comfortable! There was no specific 'gym kit' and we usually just removed our outer clothes and did the PE or movement in our vests, underpants and knickers. I, like some others, had plimsolls or pumps – thin soled, light-canvas footwear in either white or black, often bought cheaply from Woolworths. Mum insisted on me having the white as they 'looked better' Some did it in their bare feet. School Sports were held in the green open spaces of Priory Gardens, allowing us to run around above the graves of the monks who once inhabited the Priory.

School dinners were served in the Parish Hall across on the other side of Church Street. They cost 6d (six pence) each and much of Monday morning's registration time was taken up with the collection of the standard 2/6[1] for dinners. But it was not only for school dinners that we crocodiled across Church Street; it was also for church every Wednesday morning. In 1958, the Rev. Canon Christopher MacKonochie had become Rector with James Yates as his curate and it was under MacKonochie that I was later to be confirmed in the Church of England. MacKonochie was, if not in my time then certainly in his later years, slightly eccentric, and it was on one of those Wednesday mornings as he wandered up and down the aisle of the Priory Church, talking to his primary school flock about how we should not expect God to do everything for us, that he said:

"God helps those who help themselves – and that doesn't mean you can pinch things, Roger."

Why me? Perhaps I had my hand up to ask a question; maybe I was one of the few whose names he knew; maybe I wasn't paying attention; possibly it was because he thought I could take a joke. It can't have been anything to do with the Cremola foam. I don't know, but that episode has stuck with me. I did win threepence off his curate, though. I was playing around in school with a monocle – don't ask me where I had got it from – contorting my face to insert it into my eye socket and the Reverend Jimmy Yates, on one of his weekly visits to the school, bet me a thruppenny bit[2] I couldn't do it without pulling a face. No problem.

In July 1957, I received my best report so far with A or A- for all English and Arithmetic sections, although Writing was still only B-. Everything else was B or B+ and with Mr.

---

1 *Two shillings and six pence (about £7.00 in today's wages).*
2 *3d or three pence – not the equivalent, but probably a 20p coin nowadays.*

Oliver (I think) commenting on my *intelligent interest* and my *high standard of work*, I was put up to Class 2, missing Class 3. But my main reward was that I was destined to spend the best two years of my entire education with the wonderful Mrs. Hope Pratt.

Mrs. Hope Pratt

Hope Pratt had joined the school after the war, one of those teachers who were trained urgently in two years, rather than three. She was the teacher for Class 2 and would eventually rise to the post of Deputy Head and a member of the Board of Governors, but that would be after I had left. I also missed out on her being a Cub Mistress at the 3rd St. Peter's pack as I did not join until I was eight and her time was in the late forties and early fifties. Above all, Hope was a leading light at the Priory Church of St.Peter. Husband Phil sang tenor in the choir and, for Hope, her faith was the very bedrock of her existence. They never had children and Hope treated us all as members of her extended family. She was a member of the General Synod from 1980 to 1985 and, when age and infirmity took its toll, she regularly took communion at home. For me, she was also the organiser and leader of the Good Friday three hours for kids held in the Parish Hall, while adults observed the vigil in the Priory Church. We would spend our time, apart from the odd prayer and hymn, doing things like producing a copy of the *Jerusalem Times* with banner headlines about crucifixions and stories about recent events to do with Jesus, palm leaves, donkeys, temples, priests and Romans. I wrote articles and drew pictures and got a gold star from Mrs. Pratt when she found that I knew how to spell 'Caiaphas'. She was also, at the end of the school day, the *Hands together and eyes closed* for the short prayer before we went home.

Around Dunstable, she was a keen member and participant in many organisations from the Citizens' Advice Bureau to the Gardening Club, from the NSPCC to the Women's Institute. But for me she was simply the best teacher I have ever had. Hope taught totally without tears whether we were exploring her love of nature or painting 'Roman' shields, doing mental arithmetic or listening to *How Things Began* on the radio or *Singing Together*. I must have been a right teacher's pet, the number of things she asked me to do which I took to be privileges: ink monitor (filling up the inkwells set in the desks), handing out the pens and the nibs, and reading the lesson in the Church. The last of these had a very practical reason behind it: those were the days before loop systems for the hard of hearing and, even at the tender age of eight or nine, I had a very strong – many would say loud – voice which carried as far as the proverbial deaf-Granny-in-the-back-row. But before I did that and even before I went into Hope's class, I had joined in the activity for which most would remember her: the annual Nativity Play. And thus began what career on the stage I was to have.

Every year, Hope wrote and staged a Nativity Play in the Priory Church. I do not know whether every year was a completely fresh script: I doubt it. But to us it was always new, always just for us in our robes and cloaks, tea-towel headdresses and tin-foil-covered halos. We performed to parents, governors and visitors in front of the chancel screen on a raised platform for just one night only and also for the school on the nearby Wednesday morning visit to the Priory. I began as a page to one of the Three Kings, rose to be an Archangel (my first play with lines!), thence to a King and finally to the best part of all: Herod (the baddie). Looking back, I think I was glad to do the roles I did rather than Joseph, ostensibly the main male part. He always seemed rather too gentle and a bit on the wimpy side of life, though his advantage was that he did get to play opposite Jill Climo as Mary...

Hope also wrote the occasional pantomime which, in my last year, was *Dick Whittington and His Cat* and was performed on the stage of the then Town Hall (later demolished). In true panto tradition, Jill Climo had been cast as Dick, and my best friend, Michael Harwood as the Cat.

And me? Surely my favourite teacher was not going to leave me out? I was no longer in her class, being with Mrs. Calcott in the top class, now, but so were the other two and all the same...

"Roger, my dear, for you I've written a special part. He's called the Demon King..." A baddie! Yes! And my feelings for Mrs. Pratt ascended to new heights. I was dressed in a black cape, heavy eye make-up, purple baggy, shiny pants and, with my body covered in a green wash, I then snarled my lines and leapt around on stage in a far more athletic way than ever I could manage now!

Hope lived to be 100. I had called on her a few years previously on the off chance that she still lived at number 49 Beale Street, Dunstable. She did, and the front door opened to reveal a diminutive, very old lady but one whose eyes immediately lit up when I introduced myself, apologising for the unplanned visit, and whose voice boomed

"Come in! Come in, my dear. Oh it's so lovely to see you again!". That same voice boomed again the day after her 100th birthday when I rang her. Unfortunately, it was muted forever only six months later. People who knew Hope speak of her great energy, her zest for life and for learning, her steadfast faith and, above all, her loyal friendship. Her faith also extended into her gentle humour as in the prayer she wrote and which was quoted at her funeral:

Dear God –
So far today I've done alright:
I haven't gossiped, I haven't lost my temper

I haven't lied or cheated, I haven't been greedy, grumpy, nasty,
selfish or over indulgent.
I'm very thankful for that.
But in a few moments, Lord, I'm going to get out of bed
And from then on I'm probably going to need a lot more help!
Amen

She was everybody's favourite Aunt who would always see the good in you. And in her class, I thrived.

"Now remember, you don't vote for yourself. It's not done." And with those words from Mum in my ears, I went to school in September 1959 to take part in an election for the two School Captains, boys' and girls'. I was now in Mrs. Calcott's Class 1, my last year at Ashton School. That we were to be elected was, I imagine, quite a rare event in primary schools. Of course, the vote could have been rigged by Mr. Cunnington to get the result he wanted. I think not, though. I forget who else was standing with me. In fact, I only remember several names in my class save for my close friend Michael Harwood. There was a blond-haired boy named Martin Streich who was teased for having a German surname some 12 years after the end of World War II, Sylvia Carter (whose father owned the large scrap-metal business in the Luton Road), Susan Ashwell (her mother was the caretaker), Edwina Smith, Anona Maskell, John Tonks, John Venables, John Tandy, Geoffrey Morgan, and Susan Marett. In the election, I did remember my mother's instruction in not voting for myself. But why, on earth should I not have done so? Surely one should have confidence in oneself? But, despite that rare instance of self-deprecation, I was elected along with Jill Clim∩ Being School Captain meant very little in reality other th⌐ ᵥₑaring pinned to my shirt a rectangular badge with b ₃ edging and 'Captain' lettering on an enamelled greeⁿ ₐckground. It meant in practical terms probably no more than doing a few extra tasks for Mr. Cunnington or in the Church for the Rector.

There was one occasion, though, when I took it too seriously. Someone told Mrs. Calcott that they had had something stolen. The poor accused lad was almost certainly 100% innocent but I set to, gathering as much anti-opinion about him as I could before going to Mr. Cunnington's office to tell him all these thoughts and rumours. He listened patiently, thanked me and, with a sadly tolerant look, shooed me out of his office. That was it: I do not remember what happened but the experience did not encourage me to join the CID!

It was probably during my final term at Ashton that I began to realise that girls might be interesting, though that interest never went beyond moderate, and never further than Jill Climo. There was talk in the segregated boys' playground of 'rubber johnnies' along with sniggering giggles which could only mean that they were something to do with girls, though what took me a few more years to realise. At the time, I only had a vague image of some sort of thick, black rubber tubing – rather like the inner tubes on my bike... I clearly had little understanding of things sexual as in the time when I came home from school and announced to Mum I had a new song: *Lady of Spain, I adore you! Lift up your skirts, let me explore you.* Who told it to me I cannot remember, but Mum was understandably horrified. Again, I cannot remember what happened to me as a result, other than a good telling-off.

But of course, Mrs. Calcott's class was, for me, the year of the 11-plus examination which would determine my future secondary school. The 1944 Education Act had established a tripartite system of grammar, technical and secondary modern schools after the age of eleven. This system was selective and all primary school pupils in the top or oldest class sat examination papers in English, mathematics – or arithmetic as we called it then – which was both written (you answered the questions set in the exam paper) and mental (where the teacher read the questions out and you had to do the calculation entirely in your head), and non-verbal reasoning or IQ tests designed to test intelligence through puzzles and problem-solving questions. The range of papers depended on the area or county you were in.

There had already been the beginnings of the comprehensive system (whereby one school accommodated all, regardless of ability) notably in Coventry, though it was rather ironic to see those schools being based on the Public or Independent (Private) School system of 'houses' with pupils having lessons and being cared for pastorally all within the same grouping. The arguments in favour of these schools grew in the late fifties and early sixties until, in 1965, twenty-one years after the Butler Act[1]which introduced the Grammar and Secondary Modern Schools system, Anthony Crosland, then Minister for Education in the Labour Government of Prime Minister Harold Wilson, issued what was called *Circular 10/65* by which all Education Authorities had to introduce plans for the schools in their areas to go comprehensive.

But that was to have no effect on me in 1959/60. Dunstable had three schools for those successful at the 11-plus: Dunstable Grammar School for the boys, Queen Eleanor's Grammar School for Girls, and Kingsbury Technical School (mixed). Word was that the bar – or pass mark – was set lower for Kingsbury than it was for the other two, but I cannot say. If you ended up at one of the Grammar schools it was expected that you would progress through GCE 'O' levels

---

1   *The 1944 Education Act brought in by the Conservative President of the Board of Education in the last year of the Churchill wartime coalition government, R.A.Butler.*

to 'A' levels[1] and thence to university. If you did not pass the 11-plus, then you would attend a secondary modern school – in my case it would have been the Northfield School – where expectations were lower and where a substantial number left school at 15 and went (hopefully) straight into work or an apprenticeship, rather than sit the 'O' level exams. Of course on the one hand the Grammar/Technical Schools helped with social mobility in that an academic education was available on merit even for those from a poor background. On the other hand I, in common with many from a more advantaged or middle class background, had had the material benefits of books, encouragements, support and the parental time and money necessary for all these. Looking back, it is interesting to note that successive British Prime Ministers between 1963 and 1997[2] had all passed through the state Grammar school system rather than the fee-paying public school system[3]. Whether that proves anything or not rather depends on your political viewpoint, I feel.

I cannot remember anything other than my aim being to go to the Grammar School. I expected to go there. I am sure it was equally anticipated by Mum and Dad and by both sets of grandparents that I would get in. Nothing else presented itself as a remote possibility: I don't think I ever considered myself as even possibly heading to Northfield Secondary Modern. I don't think I worked any the harder, but just kept on as I was. However, Ashton VP School was never what people would nowadays call a 'hot-house' of academic learning under Mr. Cunnington. Yes, we were immensely well cared for; yes, we worked quite hard; yes, we had the 11-plus in our sights; but I

---

1   General Certificate of Education 'O' – Ordinary and 'A'- Advanced levels.
2   Harold Wilson, Edward Heath, James Callaghan, Margaret Thatcher and John Major.
3   Unlike those before or those who came after with the exception of Gordon Brown.

really have no memory of being drilled in the type of questions and papers we would face, and urged constantly into doing better. A little practice, perhaps, but I cannot recollect ever being pushed, either at school or at home by Mum and Dad.

Without ever being told, I always felt that I was around the top of my class (main competition was probably Jill Climo) and that Mum and Dad were keen for me to do well as they also put me in for the entrance examination to St.Alban's Cathedral School, a minor public school. How they would have paid for it never occurred to me: I doubt if they could have afforded it just on Dad's very modest salary. Mum could have gone out to work, I suppose, and/or maybe they would have looked around for a grant or two from any charitable trusts, or even sought a scholarship from the school itself. Anyway, other than going to the school one Saturday morning to sit the papers, the only memory I have is of the letter arriving home informing my parents that they didn't want me – probably the first rejection I'd ever had in my life to that point! Dad told me that it had been between me and another boy: we'd been equal in the exam but as he had attended their preparatory school, they felt they should take him in preference to me. This could have been Dad, or St.Albans, softening the blow – not that I remember feeling anything more than mildly disappointed and somewhat embarrassed that I had let them down – but at the time I certainly believed it.

In 1960, I sat the 11-plus in the gymnasium of the boys' Grammar School. I was but one amongst vast numbers (so it seemed) of boys of my age all at single desks in a sort of hall totally alien to my 10-year old mind. We were imprisoned by wooden bars and ropes, and supervised by elderly, grumpy, unsmiling men in flowing black robes who treated us with less respect and less interest than they would have done a pile of library books – after all, they had had to give up part of their weekend to organise this crowd of boys, most of whom they'd would never see again. There were no girls: they almost certainly had gone to a similar hall in the girls' Grammar School. I'm told that in my year, Ashton only had six[1] who passed out of probably 30-32 in Mrs. Calcott's Class 1, though I suppose 20% or so isn't that bad in those days and was more or less the national norm. I cannot remember being nervous; neither did I feel blasé about it. But perhaps Ashton made me too confident? My first term at the Grammar School was to be quite successful – much more so, I have to say, than subsequent terms. If Ashton failed at all, it may well have been in not ensuring that I knew that the essential component to success was hard work...

---

1   *Edwina Smith and Jill Climo went to Queen Eleanor's, Michael Harwood and I to the Grammar School, and I'm told that the other two were Linda Davis and Susan Marett – possibly to Kingsbury Technical School.*

Dunstable Grammar School

1960

1961

1962 with Granny (Sarah Parrott) and Mum (Mavis Parrott, the new Mayoress

1963   1964

SECONDARY YEARS 1960-65

Braving a New World

In moving to the Grammar School, 1960 was not only the start of a new decade, it was a massive new beginning for me. We were in the ninth year of a Conservative government, now with its third Prime Minister[1], Harold Macmillan, and were by and large what Andrew Marr has called *a nation of restraint and decency not yet spoiled by the garish excesses and immorality yet to come*[2]. Britain was a nation which acknowledged authority and kept tidy gardens and well-pressed clothes. It was a leading nation in the world and its cars and motorbikes were sold throughout it – though we had had to wait until November 1959 for our first major motorway[3] to open: the M1, but only then between Watford and Rugby. There had been race riots in London's Notting Hill area and protests were growing, led by the newly organised Campaign for Nuclear Disarmament, against both British and American nuclear weapons stationed here in Britain. 1960 was a year of other new beginnings too: a little known band from Liverpool had just performed their first concert in Hamburg, West Germany, under the name of 'The Beatles'; and the book by DH Lawrence *Lady Chatterley's Lover*, which had hitherto been banned for obscenity, was soon

1   *The others having been Churchill and Eden.*
2   *Andrew Marr: A History of Modern Britain.*
3   *Although the Preston By-Pass opened in 1958, it eventually becoming part of the M6.*

after a trial in court to be published[1]. These were two small events but ones which, in their own way, heralded the whole new world of the sixties, of teen culture, of popular music, and of changing social attitudes and mores. Trust in those who governed us was waning and people were starting to laugh at, to find comedy in, the behaviour of our ruling classes. And in the midst of all this, Thursday 8th September 1960 saw me become a pupil of Dunstable Grammar School. Little comedy in the ruling classes there!

I have to say that I was blissfully unaware of any changes taking place in society or in the way we lived. What was most important to me in my own small world, was the Roneo letter that the Director of Education for Bedfordshire, Mr. T.S.Lucking, had sent to my father (a sign of the times was that my mother was not included) informing him that I had been offered a place as a pupil at Dunstable Grammar School from September *for so long as conduct and progress are satisfactory* – indicating that I could be turfed out into Northfield Secondary Modern School if it were not! The letter went on to say that no tuition fees would be payable (thanks to the '44 Act!) and that my books would be provided on loan throughout my school career.

So, this was where success in the 11+ exam had brought me, and I set off, a new satchel over my shoulder with a fountain pen in my pocket, a bottle of ink in my bag, and pencils, a rubber and sharpener, a ruler and crayons rattling inside a wooden rectangular box with a sliding lid and which swivelled in half, and five shillings for dinners in my pocket. I walked proudly past The Jungle[2], across the fields and through the park, resplendent – in my estimation – in my brown blazer

---

1   *On 10th November.*

2   *The area of rough shrubs and bushes from Kingscroft Avenue up towards the High Street.*

with school badge, brown tie with pale blue stripes and cap to match. My short trousers were regulation grey flannel, my long socks regulation grey and my shirt white (grey was permitted but frowned upon and definitely not for special occasions. Anyway, Mum thought white looked better, more *correct*). All had come from *Foster Bros. (Mens and Boys Wear)* in Dunstable. At home lay two rugby jerseys, one white, one school colours, two white T-shirts, one with my house colour round the neck [1], one pair of rugby boots, one pair of white plimsolls, two pairs of white shorts, one pair of black ASA regulation swimming trucks (*not satin*) and *regulation coloured hose*. Everything I wore bore my name tape: dozens had been ordered from *Cash's Woven Name Tapes* in Coventry, and Mum had spent hours laboriously sewing them into whatever I might be dressed in, underclothes included, as well as all the sportswear – more would be used for cricket-wear a few months later.

After leaving Grove House Gardens and passing the former Ambulance Depot transformed into a Civil Defence Headquarters but still with a mortuary behind – ominous! – I ceased to be alone; for some reason I hadn't even thought of going with my friend, Michael Harwood. I now formed part of a general herd tramping slowly the hundred yards down High Street North towards the entrance to a large, late Victorian pile with a tower, a spire and massive, leaded, church-style windows, the whole set back behind a wall with railings and a holly fence. Trees shrouded the gardens and burly Prefects with five-o'clock shadows and the pale blue stripes of office proudly round the lapels and cuffs of their blazers, guarded the entrance. Only Masters and Prefects were allowed to use the main door; the Common Herd had to access the Quad(rangle) via the staff car park at the northernmost end of the school – a further fifty yards.

---

1   *Yellow for Brown – which sounds strange, but my house was named after a former Head.*

Having reached the Quad – the area between the back of the main building and the lavatories, fives courts, swimming pool and other blocks – I stood there in some trepidation, part of a similarly dressed but unknown herd and feeling physically out of place with my short trousers, knobbly knees and skinny frame. This feeling was to last for at least one long year before I was allowed to shield what Mum had called my *Oxfam advert* skinniness with long trousers. Soon, we were ushered inside by Prefects, crocodiling into the main building, past the communal baths and then to the left out of the Main Hall to wind up the stairs and into D1. So, this was where I was intended to be, where my education had brought me thus far. The truth being that I had never seriously envisaged going anywhere else. Perhaps that childish arrogance was to be the root of the problem...

The school had opened in 1888 as both a boarding and a day school and had been largely funded by the Frances Ashton Foundation. Frances had been the daughter of Thomas Chew, a wealthy London merchant and a well-known, beneficent character in Dunstable. Mr. F.M. 'Tubby' Bancroft (English), in his history of the school written for its 75th anniversary in 1963, records that, in the first term in 1888, there were three boarders and forty-six day boys. By the time I arrived in 1960 there were no boarders, just a three-form intake of about seventy-five to eighty boys who were immediately segregated into three 'Shells'[1] of equal ability A, B and C. I was in the 25-strong Shell C with Mr. J.G.Matthewman, ('Maxy') squat in a blue, striped, double breasted suit, bespectacled and with thinning grey, crinkly hair drawn back. His school books were carried in a small, leather attaché case which had seen better

---

1   *So called because we were meant to 'gestate' into fully-fledged little academics, I suppose.*

days. Maxy was a former head of the Prep. Department, once resident of the ivy-covered Ashton Lodge (a boarding house, though now, in 1960, housing the music department). During the boarding years, he was known for his teas to which, every Sunday, three boys from the Shell would be invited: it was his way of getting to know the boys in his care, though it would probably be treated with suspicion today. To us, he was our English master, teacher of classics such as *A Christmas Carol*, *The Wind in the Willows*, and *Treasure Island*, and wielder of a viciously painful steel ruler. I was fortunate in that the palms of my hands never felt its burning sting. Mr. R.H.Symes ('Slip', Maths and Science) had Shell B and 'Twig', Mr. J.C.Wood (Maths), Shell A.

For an eleven-year old boy nurtured gently by the likes of Mrs. Hope Pratt, the contrast was daunting to say the least. Elderly men in dark suits breasted the breeze that billowed the yards of black 'Batman' cloaks that were their academic gowns. Some wore Bachelor gowns with bell-shaped sleeves, others – and they always walked taller, it seemed – wore Masters' gowns with long, tubular sleeves the full length of the gown itself with the arms passing through a slit at the elbow. Coloured hoods, denoting the subject area studied and the University that awarded their degree, were to hang over their backs on Speech Days and church services. A couple of masters' gowns were decidedly the worse for wear, and one, Mr. J.D. 'Moose' or 'Muss' Milne (Maths), even used the trailing end of its voluminous sleeve to wipe the chalk board! Voices barked, expecting immediate compliance and brooking not the slightest contradiction. I was just a surname – Parrott. Fortunately, I was the only Parrott in the School and therefore had no number attached. Smiths – and there were seven of them, were all numbered, and Smith 6 and Smith 7 were both in my form or Shell (*not* class!) along with Burgess 2 (there was another, somewhere, higher up the School). The appearance and demeanour of these masters (*not* teachers!) was determinedly intimidating, especially for the first term; after which, and when they thought we were trained to a good level of acceptability, a touch of humanity began, very occasionally, to show its more smiling face.

We filed in and up stone stairs, their steps a concave witness to the thousands of feet that had trod them before, down dark corridors and round blind corners. Whoever had designed the School appeared, with hindsight, to have shown little care for emergency exits or even for a sensible classroom layout, the whole building being something of a maze spread over several half-floors. Our form rooms were all former dormitories – Shell C was in 'D1' and inauspiciously next to the Prefects' Study. A smaller room, D5, accessed through D1, down some stairs from us, round a couple of corners and past Maxy's office with its archaeological display cabinet, was, in the mythology of the School, reputed to be haunted as one of the boarders was said to have died in his bed there. We were given our timetables, both lessons and homework – 'Prep', three subjects every evening – this causing looks of panic and despair on some faces, eager anticipation on those of a few – I was part of the former category. We were also given one over-riding instruction, the failure to comply with which would trigger immediate punishment – a caning, even, from the Headmaster, Mr. L.P. Banfield (whose second term it was): any books we were given were to be covered in strong brown paper. Woe betide those who used wallpaper or thin bags from Woolworth's! Many of the textbooks were ancient as there had not been the growth in books that there would be in the seventies, eighties and nineties. Whether an Algebra primer, a Shakespeare play, a volume of post-1814 European history or a slim copy of *Civis Romanus*[1], there would likely be a list

---

1   *Latin text book: "The Roman Citizen".*

of names of previous users on a form glued to the inside – always a challenge to see if you recognised any of them! There might even be some that appeared to have been used by *Mickey Mouse* or *Adolf Hitler*. To say that many books had existed for decades would not be an exaggeration and the dusty depths of Mr. Bancroft's extensive English store on the first floor bore witness not only to the many and varied hands through which the ageing texts had passed but also testified to the protective and preservative qualities of brown paper!

Morning Assembly saw the black-shrouded Masters process from the home of tea, smoke and bridge, otherwise known as the staff-room, near the main entrance. This area of the school always seemed permanently suffused with a lavatorial fragrance – there was just one for the entire staff down in the basement underneath the main entrance (where on earth did Dolly Taylor 'go'?). They then arrayed themselves *en masse* on the stage in the timber-beamed Main Hall with its massive leaded windows. In that first year of mine, there was just the one, solitary female: Miss ('Dolly') Taylor, the long serving art mistress and lone until the arrival of Miss Tabernacle (in 1964) to teach Biology and Marie-Claude Marin (in 1965), the French *assistante* who would later marry Malcolm Woodward (Geography and PE). Small blue *Songs of Praise* hymn books would be handed out as we marched in, shepherded by Prefects. Shells would stand at the front and so on, up and up throughout the school to the tall, almost adult, Sixth Form at the back openly emphasising just how small and insignificant we newbies were. In those days, the few Catholics at the school would go to the Library; I don't remember there being any Jews and there were certainly no Muslims or other faiths. The Head, who had risen to the rank of Major in the army during the war in the Far East, stood tall and upright in his Master's gown, on the dais in the bay window along with the duty Prefect. The Assembly consisted of a short service of a hymn, a prayer from the Head, a reading from the duty prefect, followed by any formal notices, warnings, admonitions or other threats from the Head, and then the prefect would read the notices for the day from an exercise book left available in the main corridor opposite the staff room. Those responsible – staff or pupil – for House activities, clubs and societies would advertise their meetings, rehearsals, and practices. The hymns were led by Mr. Robin 'Acker'[1] Black (Music) on the grand piano. The school later possessed an electronic organ presented by the Parents' Association, but it was disliked intensely by Acker and the fact that he never played it became, I gather, a great bone of contention between him and the Head. I do remember, however, that the hymn *Lord, receive us with Thy blessing* at the start of a new term was never sung as gustily as *Lord dismiss us with Thy blessing* was at the end of term. Just as the staff seemed mainly elderly to us naive eleven-year olds, so the Prefects and sixth formers appeared already adult with booming voices and five-o'clock shadows. The Head Boy – Geoff Mountjoy in my first year – was always referred to formally by the Head as 'Mr'[Mountjoy]. And how come he actually knew my name when, in only the first term, he snapped "Stop talking, Parrott!"?

From the maze of rooms on various floors and in rambling buildings, to a whole school Assembly with the robed masters, the history of the School lettered in the gold names of the Hankey Gold Medal winners[2] and matriculation successes from the twenties and thirties, it was difficult not to feel as

---

1   *Mr. Black had a mop of thick dark hair, giving him, in our eyes, the appearance of a jazz-loving 'Beatnik'. Acker Bilk was a well-known jazz clarinetist.*

2   *Best all-round boy of the year and contributor to school life, usually the Head Boy.*

though I had been fed into a vast machine whose archaic workings and design were mysteries even to the initiated. No wonder several of the staff were Freemasons!

Out of assembly, we were straight into the new world of the designated timetable and subjects I had never done before. Not only that but we had to stand up every time a master entered the room – and remain on our feet until told to sit. I had my form Master, Maxy, for English and History whilst Geography was a Mr. Horwood, along with 'Acker' for Music. Slip had us probably more than he really wanted as we saw him for Maths (then divided into the three areas of Arithmetic, Algebra and Geometry) and for Physics and for Chemistry. Mr. W.N. 'Badger' Brock was a short, stubby Welsh man, bearing close-cut grey hair, and a tweed suit. He taught me French from that most ancient and revered series of textbooks by W.F. Whitmarsh who, it seemed, must have thought *Voici la fenêtre* far more important conversationally than *Où sont les toilettes?*[1]. He frequently arrived at school on his motorcycle and sidecar – a throw-back to his service on the Western Front during the First World War though Mrs Brock was known occasionally to inhabit the sidecar rather than a machine-gunner! From a more classical viewpoint, 'Freddie' Cadle tried but with little success, I fear, to teach us Latin.

My first day also meant an introduction to school dinners. Whereas at Ashton Primary we had trooped across Church Street to the Parish Hall, here at the Grammar, they had their own kitchens, cooks and 'dinner ladies'. It was not long after Assembly had finished that the odour of boiled cabbage would sidle its way upstairs and drift through the beams of D1. Soon after noon and at tables of eight, we stood in anticipatory silence while the Deputy Headmaster, Mr. W.T. ('Fudger') Lack (Physics) wrapped his gown across his girth and mumbled the Latin Grace:

---

1   *"Here is the window" and "Where are the toilets?"*

"Benedictus benedicat[1]"

Supervised in serving and eating by the prefect or sub assigned to the end of the table, soon we would be introduced to the joys of grease-oozing, thick-battered, spam fritters, but that first day, in common with all the other Shells, seven of us from Shell C tackled the rectangular aluminium containers of soggy veg, mashed potato and steak-and-gristle pudding, replete with thick suet crust, and gravy, followed by more aluminium containers, but of steamed jam suet pudding and custard. Little emphasis on healthy diets in those days: filling the stomachs of hungry boys and young men was held to be far more important.

It is difficult to evaluate the enormity of change that the Grammar School represented. For the first time in my life I had a timetable, with different masters in different rooms and different buildings: a total sea-change from the cosy one-room-one-teacher-fits-all of Ashton. We hung around in the Quad where stood the piled crates of the bottles of milk as at Ashton, rather than play in the playground. And there was a Tuck Shop in the window of the front of the New Buildings at which we could buy bags of crisps (plain, Oxo or cheese and onion) chocolate and other snacks at morning break-time (not 'playtime'). Later on, much more pocket money would be spent on the warm jam doughnuts, reminiscent of my teas with Nana and Granfy, which arrived daily from a local baker. It was a new vocabulary that I had to learn which also included gowns, prefects, lines, detention, prep, showers – yes, all naked in together after Games and after PE: not an easy or a happy experience for some perhaps lacking in physical maturity, though after the 'shock-of-the-new', it didn't bother me overly. As daunted as I was, I think I took it all in my stride, accepting

---

1   *May the Blessed One give a blessing.*

that in a new school there would be differences, but never doubting that this was where I was meant to be.

Of course, being in the first year or Shell, we, who had been cocks-of-the-roost in our primary perches, were now the lowest of the low, fit only to be pushed around and generally despised, though my own experience was not of much, indeed any, bullying – other than having our lowly status repeatedly emphasised by such as the remnants of the fagging system whereby junior boys did menial tasks and ran errands for sixth-formers. Gradually throughout the year we would be introduced to the way of life and the rhythms of the school, including its traditions. The whole school would attend a Founder's Day service at the Priory Church to commemorate with thanks such as Mrs. Frances Ashton, the main benefactor. The second Church attendance was the annual Carol Service just before the Christmas holidays. Having only just joined the School, neither Senior nor Junior Prize-givings were for us: they would come later – much later, in my case! I was able, however, to follow a cycling course and to gain my 'Cycling Proficiency' badge, which was allowed to adorn my blazer.

Then there was the ritual of 11th November, Remembrance Day. Misty eyes would sit on the stage among some of the older staff who had joined the School in the 1930s and during the war, and who, some 20 to 25 years later, were still there: Bancroft, Brock, Cadle, Lack, Matthewman, Speke, Symes, Wadsworth: approximately one-third of the staffroom. The Roll of Honour was permanently inscribed in wooden plaques mounted centrally in the School Library, but on Remembrance Day, the names of former pupils none of us had known, but who had been killed in either the First or Second World Wars would be read out to us all.

At one point in my first term, I was chosen by my form to represent them at a meeting with the Headmaster at which he wanted to get the opinions from First Years to Fifth Formers[1] about headwear, namely the much disliked and abused caps. I blanche now at my memory of suggesting to him that we should adopt boaters to replace the caps. He was kindly tolerant; the rest of the boys dismissively incredulous.

Old Dunstablian, Colin Bourne, noted in his *A Dunstable Boyhoood between the Wars* that

> *[Dunstable Grammar School] was not one of the leading schools in the country. It was not expected to be and it never set out to be in the same category as a major public school... It was not one of the topmost grammar schools, although it had been classified early on as a minor public school... But it was a grammar school, a good grammar school and provided a sound all-round education aligned with sporting activities of note. It taught courtesy, politeness and the basic truths of life. And because of the masters over the years and a lot of the boys who went there, it was a character school with a happy atmosphere.*

That is what I found when I went there and, although the future was an unknown quality to me, I was nevertheless, after my first term at Dunstable Grammar School, very pleased to be there.

In my second term, I experienced another School tradition: the school play. This year (1961) it was Jean Anouilh's *The Lark*, his version of the Joan of Arc story. R.J. Foster played Joan and was to go on to play Thomas à Beckett in Eliot's *Murder in the Cathedral* in 1963, my first play on the school stage (as one of the Chorus of Women of Canterbury). Other than that, my abiding memory of the play is of Joan rushing off stage-

---

1   *Year 11, 15-16 yr olds.*

left only to bump into – and rebound from – the entering very corpulent character of Robert de Beaudricourt, amply personified by Nigel Pett.

The House system for internal School competitions made little impact on me as I was not at all sporty and hated all such activities with passion. Nonetheless, I was in Brown; the other Houses were Apthorp, Thring and Thompson, all named after Headmasters and Second Masters going back over fifty years. The new Headmaster was to change both that and our uniform ere long. Saturdays were for team games against other schools, except for one day in the summer: the cricket match at which the School 1st XI played against an Old Boys' team. Compulsory attendance at the sports field in West Parade was exacted, everyone having to sign in with the Prefect allocated to one's form. The following Monday was then retribution day for those who had failed to turn up.

Another instance of a somewhat uncompromising attitude towards the school and its sport was in a story I only heard probably third-hand but which I have reason to believe to be true. A boy was selected to play for the school rugby First XV – a considerable honour to have been earned. However, the boy in question informed Jack Brennan that he could not play as he had a Saturday job at Sainsbury's. Upon hearing this, Banfield picked up the phone and spoke to Sainsbury's manager, informing him that this particular pupil would not be working in future for the shop as he would be representing the school at rugby. End of – as they say.

The annual Sports Day in the summer term was basically athletics, though we were all exhorted to contribute to our House's ultimate points tally by reaching certain standards which were tested during PE lessons: jumping so far or so high, throwing so far, running within certain times etc. Each time you attained a standard, a point was added to your House's score in a complex system invented by Mr. Symes. For me, a roll of drums and a fanfare would have been more appropriate, so rare was any achievement on my part.

The final end-of-year ritual – which varied from year to year according to the ingenuity of those leaving – varied between putting potassium permanganate in the swimming pool, thereby turning the water purple and necessitating its emptying, and in one year painting giant white footsteps over the Quad and the back of the main building. I remember also, I think it must have been in my first year, how a posse of burly sixth-formers managed to lift Mr. Yemm's (Maths) Mini (new off the production line in 1959) and deposit it inside one of the Fives' Courts!

My school work in the first year was something of a curate's egg. I seem to remember getting on well with Maxy[1] and never received either his wheezy wrath or the business end of his steel ruler. Anxious to impress, I nevertheless failed to see the real point of his archaeological display cabinet when I persuaded Granny to let me donate one of her wartime gas-masks. He was clearly not impressed with the gift, but courteous to the keenness that inspired it. His English and History marks for me remained fairly high throughout the year although I appear to have slipped a little in the end-of-year exams in history as his comment was eloquent in what it did not say: *Good work done during term.*

The literature that caught our attention during my first year at the Grammar School was, however, not on any school curriculum or examination syllabus but was, as I have noted earlier, in the daily news during my first term due to its prosecution under the 1959 Obscene Publications Act for content and language deemed in those days to be far too sexual: D.H. Lawrence's *Lady Chatterley's Lover*. The book had been found not be 'obscene' by the court and, having been banned

---

1   *Mr. JG Matthewman.*

since its original publication in 1928, sold more than 200,000 copies in one day! The trial became particularly famous when the prosecution was ridiculed for being out of touch with changing social norms. The chief prosecutor, Mervyn Griffith-Jones, asked if it were the kind of book "... you would wish your wife or servants to read", an attitude redolent of bygone years. How we loved holding a copy of the book by its binding and shaking it gently to find that the paperback opened naturally at the well-thumbed 'best' bits – better than gazing in the School library at the National Geographic magazine's black-and-white pictures of bare-breasted African tribeswomen!

More mundanely, Geography under a Mr. J. Horwood, who remains eminently forgettable to me, was a subject I remember quite liking, but which had also deteriorated to *Not a good term's work* – something of a come-down after *very good and interested* earlier on.

For some strange reason – especially since, four years down the line, I was to fail my 'O' level Music abysmally – the subject remained my best – even more so than French or Latin. I already had the basic understanding of notation that Robin 'Acker' Black was instructing us in, thanks to my self-teaching of the recorder. Given also that the era was the rise of the pop groups in Liverpool and elsewhere, my musical taste was decidedly more classical, which suited Acker and put me at an advantage over much of the form.

In French I retained my 2nd place in the form and *Very good* went up to *Excellent*. Badger[1] was forever trying to sell us home-made string bags for our PE kit at half-a-crown[2] each. It was said that it was these bags that contributed to the mythology of him being a poacher. He did, however, possess the dangerous habit of rocking back in his chair while teaching.

---

1   *Mr. WN Brock.*

2   *2/6; two shillings and sixpence; about £5 now in wages.*

One day in D5 we were working away at some exercise he had set us when there was an almighty crash and all we could see was Badger's size 8 brogues sticking up in the air from behind his desk and a plaintive little Welsh voice saying:

"Well don't just sit there, Chiodini[1]. Come and 'elp me up!

I warmed to French, which quickly became my best subject, particularly when, on leaving D5 one day at the end of a lesson, Badger grabbed my arm and said quietly: "You, know, Parrott, I think we shall make something of you."

I was taught Latin by Mr. 'Freddie' Cadle. My memory of him was as an amiable soul, though mentally I may have substituted 'amiable' for 'ineffective'. I certainly remember that, whenever we had displeased him in some slight way, we were always given the choice between writing out pages of Latin vocabulary or whacks of 'the slipper', a size 10 plimsoll. That was, as we say today, a 'no-brainer' and which resulted in a competition between Terry Pickering and myself to see who could get the most whacks that term. He won with 27 to my 25. Others remember the sting of the pieces of chalk or the painful thud of a board-duster hurled at an unsuspecting head. Nevertheless my end of year results were *Good* and I was 3rd in the form with 78% which may account, at least in part, for the fact that I still remember quite a bit in terms of church Latin and can still conjugate all six active tenses of the verb *amare* (to love). That is even more amazing when you consider that Mr. Alan Baxter, who took over when Freddie retired at the end of our first year, was appalled at how little we knew.

Mr. R.H. 'Slip' Symes was a gentle Maths and Science teacher although with an occasional edge born, I think, of frustration, probably with boys like me who failed to find him

---

1   *Peter Chiodini, at the top of the form, and later a highly esteemed consultant in the Hospital for Tropical Diseases, sitting in the front row of the class at the time.*

in the least inspiring. Science didn't interest me in the slightest. I was intelligent enough to understand the basic concepts of a Bunsen burner and the formation of crystals, but beyond that I lost interest very, very rapidly. Maths was likewise. Whilst I had always had a good head for arithmetic and could usually get my head round problems such as *If it takes 4 hours for 2 men to build a wall 16ft long by 5ft high, how long would it take 3 men...* etc, Algebra remained a string of mumbo-jumbo that I just did not *get* – at least not as quickly as the likes of Peter Chiodini or Keith Sawyer[1]. Once in my first term I was staying for the weekend with Granny and Grandad while Mum and Dad were away. I was doing my homework at about 5:30 pm on the Friday – you can tell it was early on in my school career by that keenness alone – and the Maths homework was a basic exercise in algebraic multiplication: What is 4 times y? Or: What is x multiplied by 2? Of course, the answers were $4y$ and $2x$. But I just sat there with tears in my eyes saying,

"How can I say what 4 times y is when I don't know how much y is?" I wailed to Granny who, peering through her thick lenses at what I was doing, replied, way out of her depth:

"Well, I'm blessed if I know".

But therein lay the problem that was to dog me throughout: Slip never looked at my work (other than to put crosses through it all), never took me on one side or made a concerted effort to explain it all to me as teachers are expected to do nowadays. No: it was expected that all would eventually become apparent as it was deemed *infra dig*[2] to ask for help. Perhaps it did sink in, as I was eventually to give up Maths at the end of the 4th year[3] after getting a grade 6 pass[4] (the lowest) at 'O' level a year

---

1   *Keith Sawyer, Shell C, at the top of the form, and later, post-Oxford, a Roman Catholic priest.*

2   *Undignified, beneath one's dignity.*

3   *Year 10, 14-15.*

4   *'O' levels were then graded from 1 to 6 ('passes') and from 7 to 9 ('fails').*

early. I also failed to see the point of Geometry. Angles and tangents, parallels and Pythagoras all seemed so much useless gobble-de-gook. All the same, by the end of my first year, my Maths remained *Quite good* (Class position up from 14th to 10th) although my Science had slipped from *Good* to *Fair* (down from 9th to 20th)

The kindly but strict Miss "Dolly" Taylor took us for Art in what had originally been temporary buildings of the Portakabin-type opposite the bike-sheds but which, as is the frequently the nature of these things, had become permanent. There, I singularly failed to distinguish myself. In a workshop near the gymnasium and the rifle range, Mr. A.E. Forster tried to teach us woodwork. We thought nothing of using – and frequently wasting – what are today considered valuable hardwoods such as mahogany or walnut and the room often reeked of traditional and very smelly, – made, it was said, from horse bones – wood glue gently simmering on a heater in the corner. I made a toothbrush holder (mortice and tenon joint), a tea-pot stand (cross-lap) and finally a small, table-top book case to our own design (box and through-mortice-and-wedge joints) introducing us also to marking and cutting accurately and using tenon saws and chisels. All of my products were serviceable – just. Indeed, Mum continued to use my tea-pot stand for several years, bless her.

PE and Games was perhaps the one area I detested with all my might and Mr. Jack Brennan was determined, it seemed, to push each of us as far as we could go – which didn't take long in my case. Weakness, fatness and sheer lack of ability soon took their toll of his ambitions for a considerable number of pupils. Games meant rugby in the first term, hockey in the second and cricket and athletics in the summer. Rugby and Hockey were sports I had never experienced. After changing in the New Buildings – the name had stuck, even though they had been constructed in 1924 – we then had a 15-minute walk to the School playing fields at West Parade, clomping on the pavements in our brand new, shiny, studded rugby boots, We then divided into three games on the basis of how fast we could run. Game 1 was those most likely to represent the School for that year, along with the reserves. I was in game 3 – the no-hopers, and with Twig[1] in charge. From being pathetically useless at rugby – for me and it embarrasses me to say so – it was just too rough and tough, I was better at hockey and progressed to Game 2, despite having to play right-handed when I was naturally left-handed (as with a cricket bat). I remember little of cricket save for the fact that which Game we went in was determined by our ability to bowl a ball. My effort went haywire way up in the air and so I was condemned to a lowly status again. My compensation was to follow Uncle Ray on Saturdays and score for Dunstable Town 2nd XI which he captained, my additional reward being the Mann's brown ale to which I would be treated in the bar afterwards. And yes, I was scoring on the day he made 112 not out. It was from the Town's cricket club that, I believe, Ray learned the toast which has since been adopted by the Parrott family:

If Yours and Yours will drink with Ours and Ours,
then Ours and Ours will drink with Yours and Yours
for Hours and Hours and Hours

In the summer term, PE lessons, rather than Games, turned to swimming in the School's own pool. This was a cold, totally cheerless experience for me who was not to learn to swim until my mid-sixties. Brennan was soon only interested in getting those who could swim to swim faster and farther, and we useless ones were left to splash around and shiver in the shallows.

---

1   *Mr. JC Wood.*

As a minor public school and a 'good' grammar school, the existence of a military cadet corps had been only natural and expected in the first half of the 20th century. I arrived, however, just as it was about to be permanently disbanded by the new Headmaster and former army major, Mr. Banfield. The rifle range beyond the Gymnasium remained as testimony to its former existence. Mr. R.F. Broadfoot who taught me Divinity (later to be called RI or Religious Instruction), had captained the CCF, with Jack Brennan as his lieutenant.

It went without saying that a contribution to the life of the school was expected from every boy, whether in the sporting arena or in organisations such as the *Cercle Français*, the Christian Fellowship, the Debating Society, the Geographical Society, the Railway, Radio and Model Aircraft Societies, or the Pyramid Club, the report of which in the Spring 1961 School Magazine informs us that Mr. Black gave a talk on the origins of Christmas Carols, illustrating his talk *by means of a tape-recorder* – high tech' in 1960! Anxious to extend my stage work following my nativity plays and pantomime with Mrs. Pratt, I was disappointed to find that I was not allowed to do anything dramatic until the Third Year[1]. I did join the Chess Club but was invariably beaten. I also dallied with the Christian Fellowship and got a membership badge for my blazer but that was the limit of my religious commitment.

Of course, I failed to figure in the Prize List for the year, the top three in Shell C being Peter Chiodini, Robin Burgess (whom I was to follow to Coventry College of Education) and John Howard who was to be Head Boy in our final year. Perhaps I was just settling in for an easy life…?

On the plus side I was, thanks to my 12th birthday, the proud owner of a brand new silver-grey Raleigh bicycle. Mum and

---

1   *Nowadays, Year 9, 13-14.*

Dad had given me an extremely small, flat wrapped-up parcel, wishing me *Happy birthday*. I had dutifully said my thank-yous and my face only briefly revealed my disappointment when I opened the package to find a key and repeated the thank you. Perhaps I was now considered old enough to have 'The Key to the Door.' At least I was always polite...

"Try the shed," suggested Dad. Which, of course, was where they had locked away my birthday present, bless them.

Were you there?

Ask anyone of the 'baby-boomer' generation, which was their most momentous decade and the vast majority would say *the sixties*. Others would observe that if you remember the sixties, you weren't really there as this was the decade of mind-blowing drugs, of hippiedom, of Timothy Leary's *turn on, tune in and drop out*. In which case, yes, I remember them well as neither of those three states could ever have been applied to me. Neither was I into the music, the groups, the concerts up the 'Cali.'[1] The sixties were the start of my social and political interests, of following the news and elections both local and national and of forming views, some of which would make me blanche and feel quite ashamed these days.

In the first term of my third year (1962) the world was also gripped by the Cuban Missile Crisis in which everyone really felt as though we were on the brink of a Third World – and nuclear – War between the USA and the Soviet Union. Perhaps credit is due to the Head and Staff and the School in that no mention, to my recollection, was ever made of it and that, save for anything being talked about at home – and

---

1   *California Ballroom next to the Pool at the foot of The Downs.*

I can't remember Mum and Dad doing so – we were shielded from the agonising fear that the country – and the world at large – was experiencing. Cuba was in the throes of installing Soviet nuclear missiles which could easily reach many cities in the USA very quickly. John Kennedy,. the American President, faced down his Russian counterpart, Nikita Kruschev with the threat of a nuclear strike. The Soviets backed down and the missiles were withdrawn, as were some American missiles from Turkey.

But it was also thanks to President Kennedy that I began tramping the roads of Bedfordshire well into a May evening. He had inaugurated the idea that every able-bodied citizen should be able to walk fifty miles in twenty-four hours and many organisations and individuals had taken up this challenge not only in the USA but in the UK as well. The Senior Scout troop I was in encouraged it and I set off in my best school shoes, a raincoat and pullover looking a tad conventional against the hiking boots and anoraks of the vast majority. I managed about twenty miles before the blisters began to tell and I dropped out in the early hours of the next morning to be ferried back to Dunstable and home to a relieved Mother. Hardly my greatest achievement.

1963 was, in some respects, the year of tremendous movement in British society. The Conservative government had its application to join the then-Common Market vetoed by Charles de Gaulle, the French President, only later to find its leader, Harold Macmillan, brought down and replaced by Alec Douglas-Home in the wake of the Profumo affair. This affair was the stuff of which my and plenty of other teenage boys' fantasies were made: sex, spies and scandal. The only contribution I remember making, at the time when the Profumo scandal had reached the courts, was when my form-master, Mr. E.H. 'Eddie' Bates, was 'having a word' with me about a report of poor work he had received from another master. My – I thought quick-witted – response was

"Well, he would say that, wouldn't he?"[1] It was just the merest hint of a smile on Eddie's face which saved me, I think, from a punishment far worse than a detention. Harold Macmillan had been the first Prime Minister of whom I was really aware. To me, and from his appearances and utterances on the radio and on television, he always seems the epitome of avuncular, upper-crust Britishness, an impression only furthered when, as the much later Earl of Stockton, he compared Prime Minister Margaret Thatcher's selling-off of state industries to the selling of *the family silver*.

On Friday 22nd November 1963 there were two notable deaths, one of which, thanks to the other, would go unrecognised. Thirty-four years later, I would get to play that man in *Shadowlands*, courtesy of the Lyric Theatre, Belfast: CS Lewis, Oxbridge professor, poet and author of the *Narnia* chronicles, wartime Christian apologist on radio and writer of much, including *The Screwtape Letters* . The reason the death of one of Britain's major writers of the twentieth century went largely ignored was why I entered the lounge at home that same day in the early evening to find Dad in his armchair to the left and Mum in hers to the right, both quite ashen-faced. The television was relaying news of the assassination in Dallas, Texas, of John F. Kennedy, President of the United States. I remember the open-mouthed shock of realising that, although I had heard of President Abraham Lincoln's fateful visit to the theatre nearly 100 years earlier, even the highest in the land, if not the world, were not immune from a violent death. History may tell many stories about JFK, but in

---

1   *The response from Miss Mandy Rice-Davies, a "good time girl", when told in the trial of Stephen Ward who was accused of living off the "immoral earnings" of Mandy and of Christine Keeler, that Lord Astor had denied an affair with her or even having met her – all part of the Profumo scandal.*

1963 he was generally recognised as a beacon of hope in a world which had just stepped back from the brink of nuclear war.

The mid-sixties began to see considerable advances in technology. My own example of this technological revolution had come in the shape of a birthday-present transistor radio: a Phillips, with a metal body inside a black leather case, and with a single ear-piece. This did not appeal to Mr. Martin Hateley, my then French teacher, who found me, ear-piece threaded through the sleeve of my jacket and into my left ear, cupped by my hand, listening to the Test Match during his lesson and relaying surreptitiously to others the falling Australian wickets. But I was safe. 1964 was the year that hanging – capital punishment – was abolished in the United Kingdom. It was also the year that portable televisions went on sale for the first time and, as if to celebrate not only that but also the beginning of BBC 2, *Match of the Day* was first broadcast on that channel.

Two deaths in 1965 were to cast a shadow over me while I was rehearsing a school play: *The Government Inspector* by Nikolai Gogol. The first of national and international importance, was on 24th January of the iconic wartime leader and Prime Minister, Sir Winston Churchill. Many of the older, more senior members of staff were walking round the school with tears in their eyes for several days, such was the impact of Churchill's death. In those days before social media, satellites and 24-hour news coverage, it nevertheless occupied a massive part in the consciousness of the United Kingdom. 321,000 people had filed past his lying-in-state in Westminster Hall and his full State funeral in St Paul's Cathedral was attended by the Queen and by representatives of 112 countries. It is said that Churchill had planned many of the details of his funeral himself, even to the point of insisting that the French President, Charles de Gaulle, a man he had found impossible to work with during the war, arrive via *Waterloo*[1] Station. Watching the funeral on the news on the evening of 30th January, my mind was indelibly printed with the sight of all the cranes in the London docks, so attacked in the war, lowering their jibs in tribute as his coffin travelled on a boat along the Thames.

Later in the year, it was to be the Clown Prince of our then A-level English group, Terry Doughty, who opined that the crowds of people who subsequently visited Churchill's grave at Bladon, Oxfordshire, did so out of *sheer sensationalism.* Mr. F.M. "Tubby" Bancroft, Head of English, i/c the Duke of Edinburgh's Award Scheme, mason and arch-conservative, whose eyes would visibly water as the names of those boys of the School who had died in the wars were read out on Remembrance Day, was, as Doughty spoke, turning a bright shade of red with metaphorical steam issuing from every orifice. When Doughty had finished his mini-peroration, Bancroft exploded.

"Doughty!" he roared, his Welsh background to the fore, "My wife and I went there last Sunday!" Terry was, momentarily at least, subdued.

The second was much, much closer to home. My Granfy, Leonard Estwick, died a few days after his 70th birthday on 12th February. In the early sixties, Granfy had had a serious operation, I think for a lung problem, and went to Esher in Surrey to recuperate. It was there that he met a Welsh nurse named Irene or Rene. Before long – and far too quickly for Mum or Eve's liking – he brought her back to Dunstable and married her. Mum and Eve never took to her, and Granfy couldn't understand why his daughters were so opposed to her. I suppose they just couldn't get used to another woman being where their

---

1   *The site of the final defeat in 1815 of the French army under Napoleon by England and the Duke of Wellington, aided by Blücher's Prussian forces and which, apparently, was omitted from de Gaulle's history of the French army!*

mother had been and, more to the point, that it all seemed so hurried – no sooner had they been introduced to her than she and Granfy were getting married. When Granfy died, Rene was allowed to carry on living at 128 Luton Road and it wasn't until she died several years later that Mum and Eve were able finally to sell the house. The only advantage to me of Rene was that, many years later, I once went to a BBC casting where the part on offer was that of a Welshman in a *Crimewatch File* programme being filmed near Cardiff and Barry. Even though I could do a fair accent, I stretched the truth and told the director, when asked, that part of my family actually came from Bridgend near Cardiff. I got the part – thanks, Rene!

Spring brought forth further smiles – at least to my face – as Manchester United confirmed their return to the top of English football by winning their first League Divison One title since the Munich Air Disaster of 1958. This was shortly before my future Sixth Form courses would be determined by the GCE 'O' level examinations I was sitting in the summer.

The New Look (1)

The Headmaster, Mr. Banfield, and I both returned to School in September 1961 for our Second Year, with the first impact of his arrival a year ago, at least on the school as a whole, evident in my new uniform requirements.

Mum and Dad had exchanged horrified glances when I had brought home the new regulations for a black blazer with a new badge incorporating the Ashton coat of arms, a black cap in similar vein and a black tie with pale blue and brown stripes in it, a reminder of the previous uniform colours. They would not have dreamed of showing any reluctance to provide the new uniform, but their sense of good housekeeping had taken a serious blow when they had to discard a perfectly good, only-a-year-old, big-enough-to-grow-into, brown blazer, tie and cap. But even with all this expense, Mum and Dad still insisted on buying me the superior barathea – some would say 'adult' – blazer, rather than the more down-to-earth wool/synthetic mix that everyone else had. The number of barathea blazers in the school could be counted on the fingers of one hand. But the big improvement was nothing to do with the Head and his new uniform: I now had long trousers! In keeping with my being in the Second Year and having new First Years to look down on and show off to, my new cap began to be perched more towards the back of my head, though Prefects would grab the chance to correct its angle. Failure to wear it at all would always incur punishment, usually in the form of lines: *I must not forget to wear my school cap* written at least one hundred times on lined school quarto paper.

In years gone by, the Prefects were permitted to cane, but Mr. Banfield had wisely removed that sanction. We were later to hear that he also forbade the playing of Bridge in the staff room at lunchtime, as an activity probably 'unbecoming' and perhaps too time-consuming. It has been said, though, that his was quite an arm's-length authority whether over staff or boys and that he was rather remote. Certainly, with his office/study and family accommodation being all at the southern end of the school and the fact that he was rarely seen in the staff room all added to those impressions.

Whilst never having been privy to Banfield's staffing policies, I would say that he quickly sought to replace the older, perhaps less exam-rigorous and weaker-disciplined staff with those he felt more suited to his undoubted drive to improve academic standards. Under his predecessor, Bailey, it is probably fair to say that the school had achieved some success but by no means all of which it should have been capable. Notable appointments were some staff he had known in his previous school in Bromley such as Eddie Bates (Geography) and Brian Duncan (Economics); Alan Baxter (Latin) replaced the rather ineffectual Freddie Cadle and younger blood in the form of Graham Jenner (History) soon made its mark. That is not to say, however, that all his appointments were good ones: R.A.Evans (History), Len Muggeridge (R.E.) (son of Malcolm) being far less than he, Banfield, expected, whilst Wally Allen (French) is said to have been suspended for calling a boy *an idle little bugger*.

Banfield's new look was also apparent in his use of a six-day timetable. This meant that if Day 1 was Monday this week, Friday would be Day 5, next Monday day 6 and the new Day 1 would be on Tuesday…and so on. This was, I assume, instituted to allow greater possibilities of time and balance between the various subjects, though I'm not sure whether it was fully appreciated by the older, more traditional members of staff who were probably as confused as some of the boys actually were – or claimed to be!

Following the emerging wave of pop groups such as the Beatles and the Rolling Stones, Banfield did have more success than Canute in stemming the tide – but of boys wearing their hair longer, and of narrower trousers and Cuban-heeled shoes. Trends were to grow exponentially throughout the decade, though, as young people spent more and more of their money on the latest fashions. For my part, I gave Banfield no problems as I was stuck with a short-back'n'sides, sensible shoes, school uniform and casual clothes that would have suited someone three times my age. I was the epitome of 'square', of strait-laced, old-fashioned conventionalism. It was in March 1963 that I went to the barber's and, for the first time, did not have a short back'n'sides but a 'Boston'[1]. But do not get the wrong idea. This

---

1   *Where the hair is cut straight across the back and round the ears, rather than shaved up the head.*

was to a teenage rebellion what a raindrop is to a thunderstorm. Even with the particularly severe winter of 1962-1963 we were not allowed to wear Wellington boots to school whatever the thickness of the snow. Consequently, many spent the day in wet shoes and socks.

Beyond the railings and the holly hedge of the front of the school, and seemingly in tune with the new look in the Grammar School, Dunstable Borough Council, now representing more than 25,000 inhabitants, felt it high time that the Borough also benefitted from the designer's eye. The sixties were though, for many people myself included, the age of architectural vandalism and 1963 was the year in which it hit Dunstable with some force. The decision had already been taken, despite the impact of the opening of the M1 motorway in 1959, to widen the part of Church Street leading to the crossroads with the A5. That there was a need to do something about the steady increase in traffic was beyond debate, but the widening saw the demolition of the Red Lion, parts of which were over 400 years old, and the White Horse, dating back some six centuries, though there was the token preservation, I believe in the grounds of Beecroft Primary School, of the stone used as a mounting block outside the White Horse. These were old inns where, even in the early sixties you could still see the game hung high to 'ripen'. On the opposite corner, the *Home and Colonial* grocery store where Mum frequently shopped, went too. This was also the start of the ripping out of the central guts of Dunstable in preparation for the development typical of the sixties: the concrete-slab shopping centre, The Quadrant – now, I would argue, a mere ghost of its planners' original but limited aspirations. My father and grandfather must have been part of the council's decision-making but unfortunately I have no evidence of their attitudes or of the position they took in any vote. I hope they would have been torn between conservation and progress; I fear, though, they would have put the commercial needs of the town before the historical.

The silver(-ish) lining to this over-weaning black cloud was, however, the finding by the Manshead Archaeological Society of sufficient Roman remains on the site to prove that the Roman town of Durocobrivis did once stand in the area. At the beginning of the decade, Dunstable gained a ballroom and entertainment centre alongside the California Pool – though my own sense of 'entertainment' only extended to one visit, Downside Primary School – where I was later to teach for a year – Brewers Hill Secondary, and an outstanding Civic – later The Queensway – Hall in which both Mum and Dad, and Grandad[1] were to become deeply involved. While these served the constant growth in the town, national rail policy as evinced by a certain Dr. Beeching only discouraged people from coming to Dunstable by removing its railway links with Luton and Leighton Buzzard and eventually its two stations, Dunstable Town in Church Street and Dunstable North on the A5 Watling Street.

Down and Out (1)

At the end of my primary education I wrote *If Ashton failed at all, it may well have been in not ensuring that I knew that the essential component to success was hard work...*

Now out of Shell C and into the top flight, or stream, 2L (as opposed to 2i or 2ii), we were accorded the honour of what passed at Dunstable Grammar School for a classical education in that we were headed towards 'O' level Latin (hence the 'L'). Sadly, it had been *vale* to Freddie Cadle and his size 10 slipper

---

1   *Harold Parrott was its first Entertainments Officer and Mavis operated the Box Office.*

(retired), and *ave*[1] to a Mr. Alan Baxter whom we were to have for the next four years: a good teacher, but lacking in any great charm. Whilst we continued with Maxy's[2] wheezy, steel-ruled English lessons, we graduated to a new arrival at the school for a form master: Mr. E.H. 'Eddie' Bates, whom I was to know as a Geography master for the next four years with his mantra of such-and-such a place being *an imPORtant PORt for imPORts and exPORts*. Eddie also took a keen interest in the CF (Christian Fellowship) being a member of the West Street Baptist Church. At one point he encouraged me to go on a Christian retreat to Towyn, West Wales, but my parents – wisely, I think now – refused to let me go without saying why. Geography remained one of my better subjects – though as my second year progressed, that was to mean less and less. I appear, though, to have been keen to gain his favour as I volunteered to help record the weather readings. Still, between Eddie and the scouts, I did learn one lasting skill: how to read a map. My sense of direction is dire, but the amount of information you can get from an Ordnance Survey map never ceases to interest and inform me.

Lest it be thought that the Grammar School's staff room was populated solely by strict and dour disciplinarians, a Mr. R.A. 'Ray' Evans joined the staff for the dubious pleasure of teaching history to boys only too ready to exploit a chink in that disciplinary armour. Second Year History lessons involving a mock-up of mediaeval trial-by-ordeal degenerated into farce and the normally, relatively sober attitudes of the top stream assumed a childish magnitude with talking, joking and shouting out reaching epidemic proportions, amidst all of which I invariably played my part.

But I came first in French – at least, in the first term!

---

1   *"Goodbye" and "Hello".*

2   *Mr. JB Matthewman.*

Mr. M.J. Hately commented on *excellent work* and me being *extremely keen and interested*. I mention those now as it was almost certainly the last time in my school career that such glowing epithets would be awarded me. Science was steady, at least to begin with, thanks to Messrs Twig (Physics), Slip[1] (Chemistry) and an R.B. Swift (Biology); and Music with Acker[2] was still *very good* (I came 2nd).

It was, however, Maths in which the slide to academic obscurity began. Mr. Yemm (he of the Mini that had been manhandled into the Fives' Court) took the opportunity to exchange his role with another Commonwealth teacher: in this case a Mr. W.J. Kissick from Canada. Here was a somewhat heavily built and portly, crew-cutted apostle of everything mathematical. My weaknesses continued unchecked and my attitude was only worsened by his proselytising:

"You know, boys, to begin with, I didn't really like Math. [American singular – he couldn't even give it its English name] Then one day my parents left me in the car when they went to do some business. That business took some time and, well, I just got kinda bored and the only book I had with me was my Algebra text book. So I picked it up and began to read. Now, that little book changed my life and I really began to understand what was so beautiful in Algebra…"

It was all I could do to stop myself from vomiting right there and then, and hatred of all things Mathematical sealed itself into my psyche – that is, until now when I find myself actually quite good at tutoring Maths up to lower secondary level. I had sat my eleven plus in just under two years ago in the school gymnasium and I never grew to like it either. I had proved one of those pathetic sports weaklings who could barely clear a low-level vaulting box, couldn't climb a rope, looked

---

1   *Mr. JC Wood and Mr. RH Symes.*
2   *Mr. R Black.*

upon rugby tackling as a suicidal activity, produced regular notes from an easily-conned mother excusing me from all exercise due to a torn calf/stomach/thigh muscle and thought showers an embarrassing waste of time. Jack Brennan, Head of P.E., was not my favourite master and the gymnasium my least favourite space. Alan Bennett[1] described it perfectly as… *the chamber in which one was tortured years ago: here are the long brightly varnished forms, the ropes, the wall bars, the tiered box – always a bad moment when another tier was added – against the unyielding side of which I invariably thumped my crotch.*

In our early days, Brennan had stood Chris (initials CD – "Seedy" – get it?) Smith up against the wall and insisted on bouncing a rugby ball off his rather concave chest in an attempt to encourage him to gather it into that chest when he caught it. That was the only time I was thankful for being able to catch properly and remember feeling quite sorry for Chris. Mr. K.A.'Kad' Davies lent his Welsh fervour to PE and to rugby training, using – and to my cost – the leather-sheathed end of a gym rope to enforce his sense of discipline. Another failure. Nevertheless, Brennan was to remain for the rest of his career with the Head, Philip Banfield, and Graham Jenner, my history master, when 1965 saw the 10/65 circular from the Department of Education and Science (DES) which committed local authorities to adopt a comprehensive system of education. The Ashton School Dunstable, aka Dunstable School, aka Dunstable Grammar School, was doomed and would in 1971 close its doors and transmorph, along with Banfield, Jenner and Brennan, into the comprehensive Manshead Upper School on a new site in the southern extremities of the town.

For some reason unbeknownst to us boys, our form, 2L, was taken over by French teacher, Martin Hately, in the New

---

1   Alan Bennett *"Keeping On Keeping On", Faber & Faber 2016.*

Year (1962). I had managed to maintain a reasonable standard in the Easter term, slipping from 4th in the form to 7th overall. Heaven alone knows what would have been the effect of my joining, had I been old enough, the school play for that year: *She Stoops to Conquer*. But my end-of-year report for July 1962 was ominous: 22nd in the form, only three *goods* and a plethora of *disappointings*, one *weak*, a *very poor* and, to cap it all, two *abysmals* (Biology, and Form), the latter, by Hately, adding that I should be *thoroughly ashamed*. The Headmaster's Study was on the ground floor of the southern end of the school where the above rooms served as his house. My appearance in front of him and with the rest of my form standing behind me in his dark-wood office with its gloriously massive, leaded, bay window giving on to the rose gardens outside and impressive oak desk was not a happy experience.

As, perhaps, a forerunner of any attempts literary on my part, my Third Year at DGS also saw a short story of mine published in the school magazine. *Black Harry* was about a man who has little, gambles it on a horse with long odds, wins big and then gives it all away. Perhaps it was that, more than my day to day work which encouraged Mr. F.M. "Tubby" Bancroft, editor of the Magazine and Head of English, to comment on my *good work* and position of 7th in English. I know I had certainly warmed to his ways. French with Mr. W.A. "Wally" Allen remained *excellent* with a 5th position, whilst all the others ranged from *fair* through *satisfactory* to *extremely disappointing* with my form position at the end of the year a meagre 22nd out of 25. The 'character' who perhaps stood out most in my third year was our R.E. teacher, Mr. Leonard Muggeridge. His discipline was not as chaotic as Ray Evans' was but just as hopeless with several pleas from miscreant boys told to report to the Headmaster, "But Sir, the Bible preaches forgiveness, Sir!" Sometimes it worked, sometimes it didn't.

My fourth year at the Grammar School was again undistinguished – and worryingly so as the 'L' stream were due to take 'O' level English Language, French Language and Maths a year early. With 24 in the class, I was 24th in Maths by Christmas, having failed repeatedly to understand Mr. J.D.B. "Muss" Milne. Muss was getting on in years and behind his tortoiseshell spectacles, watery grey eyes were set in his long, lugubrious face which had all the lines of Clapham Junction deeply etched in a sallow skin on which a grey moustache bore the yellow tint of heavy smoking. His gown's voluminous sleeves hung in shreds due to age and his preference, rather than for the conventional duster, for wiping the chalk boards with them. There was some improvement generally through the year, but *erratic* crops up repeatedly in my reports. Mr. Hendra had a low opinion of my Biology work and kicked me out and into non-GCE Art due to my over-exaggerated drawings of the human reproductive system. I achieved a decent grade in French 'O' level at the end of 1964, but only scraped passes in English Language and Maths, vowing with all my heart never to touch the latter again as long as I lived.

I was, however, the proud recipient of my Duke of Edinburgh's Bronze award having successfully passed various activities including a course in Civil Defence – *Protect and Survive* as the Government's leaflet put it optimistically. Some were to liken it to "Bend down, put your head between your knees and kiss your arse goodbye."

The main 'O' level or fifth year began auspiciously with no Maths! Those who had already passed the exam (my grade 6!) either did Additional Maths at 'AO' level or, as in my case, were allowed to drop it and take up German with the intention of taking it straight to 'A' level in three years. A new master, Mr. Roy Walker, had joined the school and immediately suffered for his large nose being nicknamed 'Conky', or we used the initials 'B.O.' due to his perceived and rather unfortunate, personal hygiene issues. French language gave way to French Literature, as did English to English Literature, both at 'AO' level. Elsewhere, there being now 26 in our form, I came 26th in Chemistry which was to remain my bogey subject throughout the year and occasioned the only visit by my parents, concerned about how I was being treated. Mr. 'Gibbo' Gibbs was the greying epitome of Joseph Stalin, save for the pebble-dash lens in one side of his spectacles. His tactic was short, sharp 'slip' tests (so-called because he would tear up quarto file paper into 12 pieces and dish it out for one-word/formula answers) and, particularly in my case, public humiliation which, at least on one occasion, almost reduced me to tears. After Mum and Dad had discussed it with Mr. Brian 'Taffy' Duncan, who had some responsibility for the Fifth Form, things did ease and I did improve (as did Gibbo) – slightly (in both cases!) – but my 'O' level was by then doomed. Physics was also weak, despite the best efforts of Mr. W.T. 'Fudger' Lack, Deputy Head, JP, erstwhile Mayor and founder of the Dunstable/Brive-la-Gaillarde Exchange for which he had been awarded the OBE. Later on in the year, my 'mock' exam result was only a meagre 33% but Fudger – against all perceived wisdom – still entered me for 'O' level and I am convinced to this day he only did so out of a kindness to my father, a fellow town councillor and former Mayor. French, Latin and Music remained the only beacons almost lost in a murk of *poor, fair* and *not enough effort*.

His Worship the Mayor of Dunstable,
Alderman Haydn W.Parrott J.P.

13th July 1962 and the Queen's
Garden Party

The Mayor and Mayoress of Dunstable
(Alderman Haydn W. Parrott, J.P. and Mrs. Parrott)
request the pleasure of the company of

Master R. V. Parrott

at an

Invitation Ball

to be held at The Halfway House Hotel, Dunstable
on Thursday, 21st February, 1963

Reception 8 to 8-30 p.m.
Dancing 8-30 p.m. to 1 a.m.
Cabaret 11 p.m.

Evening Dress, Uniform or Dinner Jacket
R.S.V.P. to Mayor's Parlour by 31st January, 1963
Tickets £1-10-0 each including Buffet

Thanks are expressed to the Parks Committee and the Parks Superintendent. Mr. P. J. CUNDY, A.I.P.A. for the provision of the floral displays in the Foyer and Ballroom.

BOROUGH OF DUNSTABLE

Mayor's Invitation Ball

HALFWAY HOUSE HOTEL
DUNSTABLE

THURSDAY, 21st FEBRUARY, 1963

Alderman & Mrs. HAYDN W. PARROTT
Mayor and Mayoress

---

8 — 8-30 p.m.
Reception by Mayor and Mayoress

10-30 p.m.
Refreshments will be served in Ballroom

11 p.m.
Cabaret

ALAN SHAXON & ANNE
Conjuring with a difference

GWEN OVERTON & CLIVE STOCK
The Singing Stars from
"Brigadoon" "Oklahoma" "Carousel" etc.

Music for Dancing by
THE JIMMY HARRISON ORCHESTRA

M.C. Mr. H. STEW

PROGRAMME

Snowball Waltz	Quick Step
Quick Step	Barn Dance
Slow Fox Trot	Latin American Medley
Paul Jones	Waltz
Gay Gordons	Quick Step
Waltz	Old Time Medley
Quick Step - Twist	Slow Fox Trot
Waltz	Quick Step - Twist
Quick Step	Last Waltz
Interval Waltz	

1 a.m.
THE QUEEN

Back at the Ranch... (1)

That I remained in the top eight or nine in Shell C probably saw me safe into the 'L' stream. That I later slumped badly brings me no recollection of any reaction from my parents. If someone's performance had so suddenly deteriorated in school nowadays, a good Year Head or Head Teacher would be immediately summoning the parents in for a discussion. But before that downward plunge, passing into my teenage years on 3rd May 1962 had meant my introduction to Chinese restaurants as Mum, and Dad took me to the first one to have opened fairly recently in Luton. Sweet and Sour Pork followed by (tinned) lychees in syrup was the then limit of my new culinary experience, to be followed a couple of weeks later by a visit to Uncle Stan and Aunty Dorothy's[1] where I was handed a Mixed Martini before Sunday lunch in the belief, as Uncle Stan opined, that one should be taught to drink responsibly from an early age and thereby hopefully avoid the abuse of alcohol. It wasn't only for that that I really looked up to Uncle Stan, Granny's brother, my great Uncle and my Godfather. He was what was called a 'self-made man' in that he had started as a milk roundsman and had risen to be Managing Director of the dairy, and a director of Hendon Football Club to boot. Nevertheless, it was these same, forward-thinking people who decided that, at eleven years old, I was too young to have passed on to me a copy of a James Bond novel!

When I look back – albeit with the obvious benefits of hindsight – I have a pretty good idea that not only did I have a natural bent to academic laziness, but that another perhaps ancillary, reason was to be found in a paragraph in the Autumn 1962 Dunstable School Magazine. The occasion was the Annual Founder's Day Service held on 19th July:

---

1   *Stanley and Dorothy Bearton.*

We were honoured by the presence of His Worship the Mayor of Dunstable, Alderman H. Parrott, and the Mayoress. They later attended the School Swimming Sports, when Mrs. Parrott presented the prizes.

My father had joined the Borough Council in 1952, elected as an Independent for Dunstable's Park Ward. He was the council's nominated representative on the board of governors of my primary school, Ashton and gave steadfast support to its proposed improvements and extension, inveighing against those who wanted to sell the site for commercial development, describing them as "big business boys against small school boys". More recently he had been Chairman – described as *wise* by a report in the Gazette – of the Housing Committee which had just completed its 1000th house. Furthermore he had supported the necessity of the proposed new Civic Hall and had given his backing to the pageant to celebrate the centenary of the borough's charter and the 750th anniversary of the Priory Church. He was now to emulate his father who had been Mayor of Dunstable for the final war years, 1943-1946. These were still the days when great respect was accorded automatically to the borough's chief citizen, whose attendance at a fête, garden party, dinner, charity ball, church service, jumble sale, hospital, factory, school, cheese-and-wine evening or coffee morning was symbolic of its importance. Such was the deference in those days that Grandad, even when he rang Dad, his own son, would always greet him with "Good morning, Mr. Mayor." In becoming – or in being 'made' – Mayor, Dad had had to get permission from his employers, George Kent Ltd in Luton, to have time off where necessary to fulfil his mayoral duties. This, Kent's gave willingly and on full salary, too, as these were also the days before any financial remuneration for councillors. I do remember Dad saying that he had a fund of £1,000 (about £20,000+ nowadays) for his expenses during the year which included funding his official reception, donations to charity and clothing for him and Mum – hence his first-ever dinner suit. Many events – from chairing council meetings to white-tie balls – were in the evening; many such as fêtes, garden parties and church services were at weekends. But there were also various events during the day time, particularly those involving charity organisations, local welfare groups and greeting important visitors to the town.

Being Mayor suited well Dad's sense of service to the town and his own discipline, like his father's, of putting duty before everything else. Whether it was Christmas Day or New Year, Dad (with Mum, of course) would be there at the crib service in the church or with the newly born in the maternity clinic. He had been successful in getting him and me balloted tickets for the First Night of the Proms, but then he was asked to attend yet another charity cheese-and-wine evening and immediately decided that that was where his duty lay and gave his ticket to Maurice Hinchcliffe, a friend of his, with whom I went instead. He had a rule to which he stuck: first come first served. If calling the numbers at a pensioner's bingo evening was already in his diary, then that took priority over a black-tie do for some big commercial entity whose invitation came later. Weekend engagements, especially fêtes of which in the summer there would be at least one every Saturday, would see me there, too. One such annual occasion was the 'Old People's Fête' held in Grove House Gardens to benefit organisations that cared for the elderly. In the year of Dad's Mayoralty, it was opened by the actress, Gwen Berryman, who was famous as Doris Archer in the radio serial, *The Archers*. Mum, always attired for official occasions complete with hat and gloves, bought the cookbook she had recently published and was promoting. Granny bought the chocolate cake I had made for the cake stall – but there again, I always made a cake for the cake stall and Granny always bought it.

One evening event I remember clearly was the formal screening at the ABC Cinema of the newly-released *The Guns of Navarone*, a World War II adventure, to which the Manager invited Mum and Dad. And me too. A Guard of Honour, made up of local Territorial Army personnel, was also laid on, as were drinks in the Manager's office. Other than that, I was deemed old enough at 13 to be left at home without any form of sitter, save for late evening engagements when I would go and stay with Granny and Grandad, Granfy and Aunty[1], the Hinchcliffes, or Lou and Cherry Palmer (friends, and a former Mayor himself).

Fred West was the rotundly jolly Mayoral chauffeur – and part-time mortuary attendant. It was his job to collect the Mayor's and Mayoress' chains of office from the safe in the Council Offices and to bring them round to our house prior to taking them to an engagement. In the winter, and if Mum was wearing an evening dress with little on her shoulders, Fred would hold her chain of office in front of the fire to warm it up before placing it decorously round her neck. With my father's chain, he would be careful to position it so that the hooks would fit into the loops my mother had carefully sewn into the jacket, thus minimising any damage to the material. All this done, they would sally forth into the black Humber Hawk, YWK880, with the Dunstable crest on the front of its bonnet and Dad always ready to acknowledge the salute of any police officer they passed. Fred would wait throughout the event – often several hours – and enjoyed being invited to *get his feet under the table* – meaning that he, probably along with other chauffeurs, had been fed and watered, too.

I suppose I got a vicarious sense of importance, hearing about the various events to which my parents had been invited, especially when it came from Buckingham Palace for one of

---

1   *Sarah and Harold Parrott; Leonard Estwick and Doris Child.*

the Queen's garden parties and I watched them leave, Dad resplendent in hired morning dress (tails and a grey topper hat) and Mum in her new hat, gloves and outfit. Every Mayor was expected to nominate a charity for his or her year that might benefit from various Mayoral events. My father had chosen the Freedom From Hunger Campaign and I remember being tremendously impressed when he said he was due to share the platform at a fund-raising meeting in the Town Hall with "Miss Essex". Fancy – a real beauty queen on stage with Dad! Imagine then, my disappointment when I saw the photograph in the next Dunstable Gazette of Dad and the 'beauty queen', Miss Rosamund Essex, sixty if she was a day, plumpishly rounded, and complete with knitted woollen hat and cardigan over a tweed skirt, thick support stockings and brogues.

At least I got the opportunity to sport my first-ever, hired dinner suit when, much to my surprise, Mum and Dad announced as they were getting ready themselves for the end-of-year charity ball, that I didn't have to wear my school uniform after all. Once I had got over the relief of not having to wear what I had already worn at school – I didn't possess a suit in those days – I spent the next half-hour Brylcreeming my hair and then donning my shiny satin-lapelled dinner suit and black bowtie. My cousin Cheryl, in a yellow, three-quarter length gown, was allocated to be my partner for the evening and we were taken to the Halfway House in style by the Mayoral car, which then returned to collect Mum and Dad. It was probably from this point that I realised that dancing and I were not natural partners. During the days leading up to the Ball, Mum tried to teach me to waltz. 1-2-3, 1-2-3… Provided I could have walked my partner straight across the dance floor, stopped, turned round and gone back again, I might have been all right, but doing a circuit of the floor was way beyond my ability. And so it remained for the rest of my life – musical, yes, rhythmic, yes, but surrendering my body movements to music and remembering which limb went where and when: definitely not.

On a more ordinary note, the mayoralty did bring us a washing tub! Within the past few years, Dad had taken it upon himself to take our washing to the Launderette up High Street North on a Saturday morning, sit there, read his paper, and then be home with washing done and dried by about 10:30 ready to go into town for our normal Saturday trip round the shops with coffee at the Methodist Church on The Square. I suppose many would have opted for a service or 'bag' wash, but the thought of letting someone else see your dirty washing was not something that Mum would have liked. Mayor of Dunstable was a role Mum thought did not sit easily with sitting in a Launderette and persuaded Dad to buy her a washing tub. This small machine was connected by a hose to the tap of the kitchen sink water supply, the washing put in the top with the powder and the lid closed and locked. The machine then began to go round one way, then back again, then up and down and so on, accompanied by suitable whines and whooshes, for a set period of time after which the water was let out into a bowl, and the washing was extracted and put through the mangle. Later, we added a spin drier and did away with the mangle! Washing day had gone back to Mondays...

Dad's Mayoralty lasted until May 1963 by which time I was well through my third year at DGS and beginning to show signs at least of not being totally abysmal. But had that year been in some way the cause of my academic decline? Many youngsters nowadays suffer from parents too bound up in their work and careers to spend even a little time on what their offspring are doing at school. I have to say that Mum and Dad were very 'hands-off' when it came to such things as, for instance, my homework – Mum had paid far more attention to trying to teach me how to waltz than to my history essays. But I feel sure this hands-off approach was exacerbated by the Mayoral year in which their minds and energies were clearly elsewhere. And, I suppose, so were mine, too. I remain inordinately proud of what both my Father and my Grandfather contributed to the town in their years on the Council. Yes, it was thought that I should have followed in their footsteps, but that was not to be.

And if that all sounds like a lack of fun or excitement, then so be it, for my upbringing, whilst loving and caring, safe and secure, interesting and improving, had, on reflection, little real fun in it. In the family, Uncles Ray, Alwyn and Aunties Eve and Fay[1] could guarantee fun by their sense of humour, their irreverence, and their lack of middle-class correctness that my parents so valued. It was not until I became involved in School plays that I feel I began to develop my own personal sense of fun and enjoyment.

Christmas 1963 did bring me though, at long, long last, a means of recording and playing music. Mum and Dad gave me a Grundig reel-to-reel tape recorder. I think they got the idea from Ray who, another, earlier Christmas, had, unbeknownst to us all, brought a tape recorder to a Christmas family get-together. We all had no idea of what he had or what was to happen. We had to leave the room and then go back in, blindfolded, and do something like recite a poem, say a nursery rhyme or sing a song or Christmas Carol. Afterwards, and much to our horror, we were all brought back in and had for the first time in our lives to listen to our own voices – in my case, singing. I was only about 11 or 12 years old, perhaps slightly older I don't know, but singing was one thing I certainly could not do – as the recording showed me. My tape-recorder, however, enabled me to record my own favourites from radio programmes like *Your Hundred Best Tunes* and 'conduct' them with Mum's knitting needle over and over. The Grundig had a small, stubby microphone which

---

1   *Dad's youngest brothers and Mum's sister and Alwyn's wife.*

I could either hold in my hand or rest in a plastic stand close to the speaker of the radio to record favourite pieces. The last thing I wanted then was for Mum to burst into the room in mid-*Finlandia* and ask in a voice loud enough to drown out the orchestra, if I wanted a cup of tea.

Looking at my two 'O' level years, I have to say that I cannot remember either Mum or Dad ever putting any real pressure on me to work, whether generally or at specific times or on specific subjects. They might ask me if I'd done my homework; they might occasionally express surprise at how little time it seemed to have taken, but they never bothered to look at my books, to take me to task for a poor report, or to use carrot-and-stick tactics to encourage the proximity of my nose to the grind-stone, so to speak. This was not because they were not interested, neither because they did not care or were not supportive. The contrary is true – witness my trials and tribulations with Gibbo (see *Down and Out 1*) Firstly it was, I believe, because they knew and feared that the work I was doing was beyond their ken, neither having been formally educated beyond the age of 15. Secondly, their discipline of me came from unstated expectation, from reason, from conventional middle-class morality, which wondered what the neighbours would say and which felt that arguments were best avoided. I don't remember them, at any stage, ever putting me under real pressure to improve, seemingly content to let the school do its job. And yet it wasn't that they weren't interested – far from it – I even wonder at times if they were almost afraid of pushing me or of any confrontation that might engender. Thirdly, they had lives that did not necessarily always revolve around me. Yes, I was an only child, but Mum had health problems, had worked as a volunteer on the local Family Planning Association round at the Health centre near where we lived and had given up in protest at the Pill being given to unmarried women, sold tickets for Queensway Hall events and was soon to start a small part-time job at the Court House; Dad worked full-time, was still on the council and was soon to be made a Magistrate (JP) in his own right; they also worked hard in organising the Dunstable Amateur Operatic Society, featured regularly at charity events and had a routine of life at home that brooked little variation. That's not to say that I was free to come and go as I pleased. Far from it. I had little to get me out of the house as I had relinquished (at last!) the violin (see later) and also the Scouts – or, by this stage, the Senior Scouts.

One small element of teen culture I had imbibed, though, was smoking. My first cigarette had been won while in the scouts two years previously at an Eastbourne Pier slot machine and by now I was a regular smoker and from my trip to West Germany and West Berlin at the end of the fifth year (see *Beyond the School*), was keen to bring home with me 200 Stuyvesant at duty-free prices (yes – no membership of theEU in those days). Earlier, Mum had commented on how yellow the index finger on my right hand was. Chemistry, I lied, some chemicals we used. Dad had given up the year he became Mayor of Dunstable, though Mum still smoked a little (*Weights*) and I reasoned that she would be so relieved to see me home safe and sound that that would overcome the inevitable disappointment when I told her and Dad that I had started smoking. I was right. It worked! It was a good time to bury bad news.

Back to the Future (1)

But at the Grammar School I was about to revisit what was to be – thanks originally to Mrs. Hope Pratt at Ashton School – an abiding interest and love, not mention future career for me. The School did not take part in the *Pageant*, the celebration of

Dunstable's history, the centenary of its royal charter and the 750th anniversary of the consecration of the Priory Church to be enacted in Priory Gardens in the summer of 1963 by the various organisations in the town, each having its own episode. I remember watching the performance with a mixture of awe and excitement – not only an historical cavalcade of my own town, but also with real horses too! Having missed out on joining this, and on the earlier school productions of *The Lark* and *She Stoops to Conquer*, I was now rising fourteen and, Third Year that I was, eligible to join the cast of the next school play and hopefully justify Mrs. Pratt's confidence in me. March 1963 was to see *Murder in the Cathedral*, a verse drama by TS Eliot about the assassination of Archbishop Thomas Beckett in Canterbury Cathedral in the year 1170 by four knights anxious to curry favour with King Henry II, and I was to join five other boys, including Graham Lippiatt and Michael Griffin from 3L in the Chorus of Women of Canterbury. The play was to be directed by Mr. B.C. "Chin" Arthur, the Head of Modern Languages, assisted by a newcomer to the staff, Mr. P.D. "Pete" Lawman. Clad in long robes and with wimples covering our heads, we walked up the central aisle through the audience on 3rd April 1963, thus making our entrance and starting the play:

Here let us stand, close by the Cathedral. / Here let us wait...

All went well until the second night of the three when, whilst mounting the small steps up to the stage, Michael Griffin put his foot through a poorly constructed tread and a muted but unmistakable addition to the Eliot verse was heard:

... Are we drawn by danger? Is it the knowledge of safety that draws our feet / Towards the (Oh shit!) *Cathedral.*

We not only spoke in chorus, but had individual lines as well, holding our breaths in performance, too, when another of the 'Women', a boy called Barrington, had the solo line:

One year the plums are lacking. He had said it once in

rehearsal in a broad Yorkshire accent causing us to corpse with laughter:

Woon yee-er the plooms are lackin'. Fortunately, he did not repeat it in performance.

Murder in the Cathedral saw not only the beginning of my secondary school acting career, but also the beginning of close friendships – with Graham (who was to enter the Immigration Service and latterly become part of the Government's COBRA[1] team) and with Michael who went from a Woman of Canterbury to Lady Macbeth the following year and who is now Father Griffin, a retired Catholic priest. I would do more with both Messrs Arthur and Lawman, the former also helping with my Duke of Edinburgh's Award (Bronze and Silver – I didn't make it to Gold) and the latter with my (unsuccessful) audition for the RADA[2].

That small stage occupying one end of the school hall became my second home in terms of school plays, one-act evenings and the House Drama competition. Costume was hired in and was of a good standard; and Mrs. 'Dolly' Taylor was at her more imaginative when it came to painting the backdrop or wing flats. The lighting was primitive but the most was made of the limited facilities of some floods and a handful of spots and fresnels, controlled by massive *Strand* rheostats with up-and-down sliding dimmers and wooden bars with which the lights were all dimmed or raised together. Make-up was always done in the School library: lots of *Leichner* no.5 (cream) and no.9 (reddish-brown) grease-sticks, along with the maroon Lake for character or ageing lines and massive powder puffs in tins of pink talc – not to mention copious volumes of 'liquid paraffin' and cold cream

---

1   *Cabinet Office Briefing Room A – where emergencies and crises are discussed.*

2   *Royal Academy of Dramatic Art – for which I was to revisit Murder in the Cathedral with the speech by Becket "Now is my way clear…".*

to clean it all off afterwards – heaven knows what that all did for the many acne'd complexions!

But I think it was the time between the end of school and the start of preparations for the evening's performance that I liked so much. It was almost as though the school had become ours. It was anticipation. It was no longer a question of aged, stuffed gowns parading up there on the stage for all to see, it was to be me, us; and people – friends and family – were paying to come and see us perform and hopefully entertain them. By the time the VI form days arrived, it was more a question of nipping over to *The Bull* opposite after the show, especially if our uniforms were well-covered...

As was sports day to an athlete, so too were my appearances on the school stage: the highlight of the year. The end of the Christmas term of the Fourth Year saw me as Ergasilus, 'a parasite' in a one-act play by Titus Maccius Plautus called *The Captives*; this was followed in March as the First Witch of the three in *Macbeth*. Loads of make-up, putty noses, severed and bloodied papier-mâché heads, lighting and smoke effects, along with cackling laughter and 'horror' voices way over-the-top, and Richard Thornton, James Mentor, the other two witches, and I were in our element.

One new experience for me, though, was being in a 'film'. The school's PTA had bought a cine camera for use by the pupils. This seemed to be in the hands of sixth formers who had devised some type of screenplay for which I was chosen to be the boy who is hypnotised by a swinging light (in one of the classrooms of the New Buildings) and who has some sort of fantasy adventure in the park (Grove House Gardens). Looking back, I can remember not being at all concerned about where the camera was or what it was doing, and left that all to the cameraman/director, just doing what was asked of me. Wish I'd done that more later in life! More than that I cannot remember except to say that the film itself was not memorable!

Moving into the 'O' level year, perhaps the last thing I should have been doing was spending hours rehearsing. Still, the Christmas term did end on a high with an evening of one-act plays, the second half of which was entirely taken up by the first act of *Topaze*, by Marcel Pagnol. Topaze (me) is a French teacher desperate to be awarded his *palmes académiques*[1] while also being in love with Mademoiselle Muche (Keith Sawyer, a future Catholic priest), daughter of Monsieur Muche, the Headmaster (Terry Cosgrove, a future Chemistry professor). The write-up in the school magazine noted the lengthy part of Topaze *would have daunted many boys had it been in English, never mind French*. Terry and I, still close friends some fifty-plus years later, were accorded the 'acting honours'. The reviewer had missed the point, however, when Terry, forgetting his lines, had improvised remarkably well what was vaguely French-sounding gibberish and I, fortunately, knew what came next and our scene continued unabated.

While the slow, unremitting grind of exam work was taking its course, I was able to find some sense of purpose and achievement in rehearsals for the next school play: *The Government Inspector*, by Nikolai Gogol. Some would argue that my part in this – and the one I was to play in the Lower Sixth, Private Bamforth in Willis Hall's *The Long and the Short and the Tall*, were typical me. This latter was the role of a stroppy, anti-authority, barrack-room lawyer, whilst Khlestakov in Gogol's play is an artful civil servant who is mistaken for a high-placed Government official and sucked-up to by the town he is passing through – the reviewer called him an *effervescent nincompoop* whose name means *torrents of fine talk*. Type-casting? Maybe, but Khlestakov was my first leading role. For

---

1 *An award to teachers of skill, knowledge and experience.*

some strange reason unbeknownst to me, the director, Mr. B.C. 'Chin' Arthur, the Head of Modern Languages, insisted on colouring my light brown hair black, using some sort of soot-like powder. This drove my mother mad as she insisted on washing my hair for me every night – and there were five of them including the dress rehearsal – for fear I discolour her pillows. Still, the reviewer felt that I *looked the part, had the right voice for it, lied theatrically and passionately with an abandon full of nervous cadences and came as near to making the fellow likeable as Gogol permits – a most creditable performance in every sense.* This was a far better 'notice' than many I have received and I was beginning to entertain thoughts of a career on stage...

Beyond the School (1)

Meanwhile, Mum and Dad had encouraged me to take up an instrument and, through a friend, Dad had secured the loan of a Maggini violin and found a teacher, one Leslie Dawson at 10/- for half an hour.[1] For two years I was to learn the violin with him, first at his house, a bus journey just beyond the Dunstable/Luton boundary and then later I had to go to a room he'd rented above the Milk Bar in central Luton. I never did like it. I got to Grade 4, but it was just not for me. The other thing was that the sixties were not the age for being seen with a violin under your arm: I used to try and hide it under my coat when in the street. Acker Black did persuade me to play it in a school concert once – but never again! It wasn't that I lacked musicality – far from it. I think it was just that the violin was not my instrument. perhaps if had learned the piano things might have been different. I did try later on in life (in my forties) but lacked a piano and gave up. I was, however,

---

1   *Ten shillings would be about £20.00 in today's wages.*

delighted when Sarah did so well on the clarinet and Heather tried her best with the flute.

In the meantime, I had drifted apart from my primary school friend, Michael Harwood. Friendships were largely determined by which class you were in or by joint activities and interests. He had joined Shell B and had not made it into the L stream. In any case, he had moved from nearby Dorchester Close to Great Northern Road and we had also lost our main play area, The Jungle, which, along with the fields and fire station made way for a massive car park surrounding the new Civic (later Queensway) Hall and a Library, all glistening concrete and glass. I had not yet linked up with anyone I could consider a close friend. Sport was anathema to me, save for the occasional attendance at the Table Tennis Club; academic work failed to entice: there were those who had a natural talent for hard work, for keeping their noses to the grind-stone as 'twere, and I was never one of them.

Out of school, my only activity was with the Scouts. I had joined the Cubs in the fifties and went through to the Scouts until about 14 and then was briefly in the Senior Scouts. Bob-a-Job week came round annually: a week of shoe-cleaning, weeding and sweeping in return for a shilling – hopefully more – for scout funds by tapping friends, neighbours and relatives. I'd been made a Patrol Leader, but never really looked forward to camping and all its 'woodcraft'. I've never liked 'roughing it', hated the hastily dug tented latrines and, even though I was reasonably competent with camp fires, cooking and kit inspection, I only really looked forward to our Wednesday off when we were allowed to go out for the day to a nearby town. I remember going to Eastbourne and, through a penny-slot machine on the pier, winning my first cigarette, a Woodbine, which I smoked and coughed my way through a gale-force wind walking towards the end of the pier. Occasionally there would be rumours of terrible rites of passage known as "Camp

Christenings" but these in my experience were no more than just anecdotal myths handed down by older boys in an attempt to prove their virility. We all sang jolly songs round the fire and envied the 'campfire blankets' of older boys with their badges and memorabilia of countless other camps sewn on to them. At an official scout camp site you could get your leather scout belt branded with the insignia of the site itself – another sign of one-upmanship. But I was not always a respectable goody-goody. Roger Norman, the "Skip" or leader of the 3rd St Peter Troop, once put me on dixie and billycan cleaning duties for leading the singing of obscene songs in the tent at night.

Later in 1963 and at the age of fourteen, I was to graduate to the Senior Scouts. We met in the large shack at the bottom of Arthur Buck's garden in Friar's Walk. David Buck had been through the senior scouts and into the Rovers and Arthur himself was the local Scout Commissioner. I remember little of what we did save for a night exercise during which we had to carry an aspidistra up to the top of Ivinghoe Beacon by midnight in competition with other Senior Scout troops and prizes would be awarded for the most inventive way of carrying the said aspidistra. Ours was in a 'litter' of lashed-together scout poles and improvised curtains. We didn't win. I was very nearly stopped from going all together when Mum looked out of the window and decided the weather wasn't very good. If I was going to go, then I should wear my raincoat. A raincoat?! On a scout expedition? Unheard of. But I didn't have an anorak then. Yes, I wore my raincoat, but I pinned it short with safety pins so it looked shorter. Like an anorak. It must have looked absolutely ridiculous but I was desperate not to be teased for wearing a *raincoat*. The night was spent in the scout hut at Studham to which we returned from Ivinghoe Beacon. There we were entertained by one of our older members showing us what a *one-pole tent* looked like using his sleeping bag and…

well, never mind. I never enjoyed this more macho side of adolescence. I was skinny, I wasn't as muscular as others and I was mocked for having *thin wrists*. Neither was I ever to own a parka or a Lambretta scooter like several of my contemporaries during the rise of the Mods (scooters and parkas) and Rockers (motorbikes and leathers) – the new trend in the early sixties.

However, this year was to see my khaki Scout shirt with its assortment of colourful badges and patrol tabs blighted by a black armband as I attended the first funeral of my life. John Wilshere was the 12-year old son of my father's boss at George Kent Ltd and lived in the same road as us; he was also at the Grammar School and in our Scout Troop. On holiday with his family in Liechtenstein, he jumped into the hotel swimming pool at the end of a hot day and died immediately of a heart attack. I remember little of the service except for being rather bemused at the rites and rituals... Anyway, I was there to represent the Scouts, not as a relative or friend. I had been forced to miss my Nana[1]'s funeral as I was deemed too young at the time. I still wonder why I was, to my memory, devoid of emotion at what was undoubtedly a very sad occasion. Later on in life, especially when I was doing more acting and then when I was at drama school, I would bemoan the fact that I could not cry as easily as some. I know that it is not that I cannot feel sad. Occasionally, I can think myself into a sad situation and begin to feel tearful – but then, of course, I stop myself. I can also become quite emotional with certain stimuli – a TV programme or a film, for instance. I remember reading through *Shadowlands*, the stage play, before a casting (a successful one!) for the role of CS Lewis. I was sat in a sunny Regent's Park in London after buying a copy of the play at Samuel French's. Towards the end, when Lewis' wife, Joy, has

---

1   *Evelyn Estwick, Leonard's wife*

died of cancer and Lewis begins to talk for what seems the first time in his life in a very personal way to her son, I found myself, on a park bench amidst many happy people, with tears streaming down my face – I couldn't help it. As a young man I was never very demonstrative in my affections – something which I believe came from my parents and which caused my first wife to 'comment' – let's leave it at that! My affair in my early forties with someone thirteen years my junior was to cause something of a revolution in my powers of expression, even to being accused of "wearing my heart on my sleeve".

Still looking for something in which to get really interested, however, I swapped my rather poor stamp collection – a few early 20th century British with a load of brightly coloured, pretty ones from outposts of Empire and African states whose names have long since changed: Basutoland, Swaziland, Tanganyika, Rhodesia, Nyasaland and Bechuanaland[1] – for a fishing rod and reel. John Hinchcliffe, son of Maurice and Jean, friends of Mum and Dad, and in the year below me at school, was the dubious beneficiary. Mum even seemed prepared to let me cycle the eight miles to the Grand Union Canal by myself, something her nerves would not have dreamt of letting me do ten years later! On my bike, my rod and tackle strapped to the cross bar between my legs and a duffel bag over my shoulders containing my bait – a bag of maggots from Pedders in Dunstable – Mum's sandwiches and a flask of Heinz Tomato Soup, I would make several sorties to the canal at Cheddington or Leighton Buzzard. For a short while, I even had the weekly Angling Times delivered, such was my commitment – but I rarely caught anything other than a couple of tiny gudgeon. Although my interest eventually waned completely, I still remember sitting

---

1   *Now Lesotho, eSwatini, Tanzania, Zimbabwe and Zambia, Malawi and Botswana.*

on the canal bank, rod in hand and gazing at my bright orange float, willing it to disappear into the water, a sign that a fish had taken the bait. Time passed, quickly and peacefully.

The summer holidays in 1964 were then to prove to me that one idea I had had for a future career was not to be my destiny. For some time, I had nurtured thoughts and aspirations in the direction of cheffing – cooking for a living. Mum had always encouraged me to help her and, starting very young with making the accompaniments such as mint sauce for Sunday lunch, eventually taught me to follow a recipe, to make cakes, and to decorate and ice them. This, I still do, making celebration cakes for Mum and Dad's Ruby and Golden wedding anniversaries, birthday cakes for Sarah and Heather when they were young, making the wedding cake (3 tiers) for Veronica and me, two wedding cakes for Sarah, and the occasional speciality cake for other birthdays ranging from an MG racing car in British racing green colours to a Schnauzer dog.

The Old Sugar Loaf Hotel was one of the two top places to eat and to stay in Dunstable. It had been a popular coaching inn ever since the 17th Century, in the days of stage coaches and highwaymen, and still had its archway and courtyard stables (now store-rooms). Thanks to the kindness of Joan and Peter Allen, the proprietors, I spent about four weeks of my summer holiday washing up and occasionally being allowed to prepare simple plates such as a green salad. If the endless swilling and scouring of copper saucepans with liquid sand alone did not convince me that this was not my future career, or my initial failing to please the exacting standards of Chef Roger Dover put me off, then it was one memorable day that the stock pot did the trick. It radiated the remains of meat dishes, their bones and their fat which had all been left to congeal in a warm, damp atmosphere for days. It was all I could do to stop myself from adding the contents of my stomach to the mix and cleaned it as quickly as I possibly could.

I was not part of the Beatlemania that began in Britain in 1962 and that became a greater phenomenon with the group's tour to the USA in 1964. This was the year of consecutive album number ones, along with three Top Ten singles number ones. But I did not own a record player – not even the most basic *Dansette*[1] – though I did occasionally tune into *Pick of the Pops* on a Sunday afternoon as a refuge from homework! In truth, I was stuck firmly in the light classical zone of *Your Hundred Best Tunes* with Alan Keith on the BBC Light Programme of a Sunday evening and *Friday Night is Music Night*. The only link between them all was a gold-coloured pair of my mother's knitting needles. These served two purposes. The *Hallelujah Chorus*, Beethoven's Fifth, Rossini's overture *William Tell*, or Tchaikovsky's *1812 Overture* were all conducted *con brio* by yours truly, knitting needle beating time and left hand bringing in the horns or the tenors as necessary. The knitting needles were also used as putative drum-sticks, either on my knees or on the felted-table, imagining myself to be the Ringo Starr or the Dave Clark I never would be. Later, at the age of 17, I would get my chance to pay a real set of drums at Graham Lippiatt's house while he played the piano and made up songs to well-known tunes. He was great; I was rubbish.

After the Munich air disaster of 6th February 1958 in which half the team was wiped out, Matt Busby's Manchester United, a team dear to my heart since that day, won their first major trophy in May 1963, the FA Cup, and signalled their return to the top flight of English football. In the summer, though, I went on a Scout camp in woods near the appropriately named Forest Row, in Sussex. Sat on my kit bag in Victoria Station, London, on 8th August, I couldn't help but notice the newspaper billboards proclaiming a large robbery from a train in Buckinghamshire – after all it was then the largest theft that

---

1   *The most common/popular brand of boxed record player.*

had ever taken place, some £2.6 million[1]. It turned out that the Great Train Robbery, as it became known, had taken place at Ledburn outside Leighton Buzzard, not far from Cheddington where I would go fishing on the Grand Union Canal. But then we all trooped on to the train and I had to catch up with the details as they unfolded after my return from camp.

All this time, I was an onlooker rather than a participant as The Sixties 'happened'. The music, the youth culture, the breaking of social mores, the sex, the drugs, the rock and roll were all rapidly passing by my own, personal rut. My hair, my clothes, my friend(s), my socialising all reeked of 'squareness', of conventionality. On one occasion in particular, it was my shirt, a brown nylon sort of long-sleeved t-shirt, that reeked in more ways than one. In August that year – and before the 'O' level results came out, Roy Walker the German teacher took four of us (Neil Parr, Mick Cheshire, John Mawson and me) and a male friend of his, whom we promptly christened "Rosebud" (though it was unclear what their relationship was), to West Germany. Our accommodation was in rooms of three and my peers were pushing for me to share with Conky and Rosebud. That was definitely not to my taste and after some moments of 'discussion', Neil volunteered to share with me and Conky, while Mick and John tolerated Rosebud. We spent three nights in Cologne, visiting Bonn and Königswinter before taking the train through the Eastern sector to West Berlin for four nights where twice we entered East Berlin through *Checkpoint Charlie*, a gateway in the Berlin Wall which had been built by communist East Germany to halt, with concrete, mines and machine guns, what had been the relentless flow of people from them to the far more liberated and economically affluent West. With the inestimable value of hindsight, I'm not sure

---

1   *About £140 million in today's wages!*

whether, at the age of 16, I understood fully how the people of East Berlin had felt when they were summarily prevented from ever seeing their friends and relations again, although the occasional memorial to someone who had been killed whilst trying to cross the wall, did help to bring it all home. On a corner near Checkpoint Charlie, a museum had already been established to record the history of The Wall and of those who had escaped and lived to tell the tale as well as of those who died in the attempt. *Es Geschah an der Mauer* – 'It Happened at the Wall' – was still there, albeit much enlarged, some fifty years later when I revisited the city. The difference between the two parts of the same city, though, has never left me: the lights, life and richness of the West in stark contrast with the drabness, dark and abject poverty of the East.

But back to my brown nylon shirt. When I looked at what Mum had packed for me, it was an East-West contrast in fashion and style between me and the other three. I felt embarrassed and ashamed. The one and only item I possessed of any style whatsoever was the long-sleeved brown nylon shirt, and I wore it. Every day. For a week. It drew comments, and a few nose-twitches but I persisted, refusing to dress in shirts I would normally wear in school.

1967   1966

1965, DGS "The Long and the Short and the Tall" by Willis Hall
Graham Lippiatt, Richard Thornton, Mr A. Goodwin, Mr B.C.Arthur,
Terry Sycamore, Terry Cosgrove, Michael Griffin
Roger Parrott, Michael Bannister, Bruce Royan

THE SIXTH FORM AND AFTER
1965-1968

Sweet Sixteen and never...

So there I was at the age of sixteen, a few very average 'O' levels under my belt[1] – I'd failed Physics and Chemistry, Music and History completely. I knew my Music theory but couldn't be bothered to learn all about the various symphony and sonata forms[2], did not revise the Corn Laws and the Great Reform Act, remained eternally poor at science and was about to start the Sixth Form doing English, French and German to 'A' level. These were the subjects I had wanted to do, although few other opportunities presented themselves save, perhaps, for Geography. These were the days when Sixth Forms were segregated into Arts and Sciences and ne'er the twain did meet, save perhaps for Economics bridging the gap between Geography and Maths.

In school, and thanks mainly to the uniform we had to wear, fashion trends could not be adhered to, and so I fitted in with the general crowd. I had to have what Mum called 'sensible' shoes and she had studiously avoided any suggestion of mine to buy some of the fashions of the early sixties: winkle-

---

1   *English Language, English Literature, French language, French Literature, Latin, Maths, Geography.*

2   *'O' levels were graded from 1 to 6 (pass) and 7 to 9 (fail). These last 4 were all grade 8.*

pickers, cuban heels, or drain-pipe trousers. For weekend or casual wear it was clothes which were basically smaller sizes than Dad wore: a tweed 'hacking' jacket, a 'nice' tartan-pattern tie – a present from a Mum-and-Dad holiday in Scotland – useful, multi-purpose, multi-seasonal shirts to ensure I got maximum wear out of them, a cardigan or 'club jacket', a v-neck sweater knitted by Aunty[1], Airtex vests and pants and grossly synthetic socks or more that Aunty had knitted. I had been allowed to have a pair of 'hipsters' – trousers which were fitted round the hip rather than the waist and with a wide belt – but this was a rare surrender on Mum's part.

Social life revolved around Mum and Dad's activities: a cheese and wine for the Cheshire Home at Ampthill; occasional couples from the Operatic Society – never a proper party except for after the umpteenth Gilbert and Sullivan show or some such musical theatre offering; and the Old Peoples' Fête – all very calm, genteel and respectable. I knew that other lives existed, that there were other ways of going out, of being with other people, but I had no experience of them and was, I suppose, reasonably content with what I had.

And, just as I had started smoking regularly, cigarette advertising was banned on British television, leading to no more *You're never alone with a Strand* or *Consulate* which was *as cool as a mountain stream*. Amongst my fellow smokers there was definitely a tobacco class-system with *Benson and Hedges* ('B&H'), *Stuyvesant* ('Stevies') and *Rothmans* at the top, with *Embassy* in the middle and *No.6* "Is that all you've got?" at the bottom. Smoking was still advertised before 1st August as being sociable, combatting loneliness, sexy and alluring. I was soon to move on to French brands – but that's another story.

I was, by now, telling Jack Barber in High Street North opposite the Old Sugar Loaf – yes, his name was his occupation

---

1   *Aunty Dor – Doris Child, Mum's Aunty and my Great-Aunt.*

– that I wanted a 'Boston' which was where the hair was cut in a neat line at the back and round the ears, rather than being shaved in the conventional "short-back-and-sides" so beloved of my father. This allowed your hair to grow more in keeping – to my conventional eyes, anyway – with the mop-tops of The Beatles and with the shaggier look of The Rolling Stones. The added attraction of going to the barber's was soon becoming the other things they stocked, ancillary to, but far removed from, haircuts. Girlie magazines – pretty 'soft' by today's standards – or so I'm told, of course – were starting to be left casually on the table by the waiting chairs. Then, "Anything for the weekend, sir?", especially at Ellis's in West Street, was not an invitation to a splash of after-shave but rather to the purchase of what was generally known as 'a packet of three'. I believe the price of the ordinary or standard *Durex* was 3/6, whereas the posher, more 'sensitive' *Featherlite* was 5/-[1]. Sex was topical, though, in more ways than one. Ian Brady and Myra Hindley had been charged with what became known as The Moors Murders, burying the bodies of their child victims on Saddleworth Moor near Oldham in Lancashire. Then on 13th November the word 'fuck' was spoken for the first time on British television by the theatre critic Kenneth Tynan. This brought the redoubtable Mary Whitehouse to prominence some two weeks later when she founded the National Viewers' and Listeners' Association with the aim of combatting what she saw as the degeneration of moral standards on radio and on television.

That leads on, of course, to talk of the opposite sex of which I have so far said nothing. But, despite the enthusiasm of the barber, that is perhaps not surprising, given my somewhat sheltered existence and my attendance at a boys' grammar school. Sex was the subject of Lady Chatterley's Lover; sex was

---

1 *3/6 – three shillings and sixpence now about £6 in wages; 5/- five shillings, likewise about £9.*

what went on at some of the weekend parties. Having It gave one kudos; getting It regularly gave serious status and maturity beyond ones years. Me, I could only dream and secrete on standby my packet of three *Durex Featherlite* where I thought my parents would never find it.

If I were to say that during my first term in the Sixth Form I also had my first girlfriend, I would have to add that that was not 'had' in the Biblical sense as the *Featherlite* packet remained, like its owner, in virgin condition. I cannot remember how I met L. – though it was probably at one of the the first parties I happened to attend – just that she was a very attractive girl with everything – well, a couple of big points you might say – that would attract a male from fifty paces. She had an elder sister, J., who had a massive reputation for generosity with her body, though none of it ever came my way save for one evening at a party when it walked past me on the landing upstairs in all its natural glory! Still, my ardour for L. cooled rapidly and very much for the good when I found out that she was only 12. And the daughter of – shall we say a prominent senior authority figure in Dunstable? Later and as part of the French exchange visit to Dunstable from Brive, I took one Magali Devaux to the cinema and later started to write to her, but any interest there might have been on either side evaporated as quickly as the ink dried on the envelope.

At home, elements of television were becoming a source of intense embarrassment when watched with ones parents. There was a play which focused on the 1956 Hungarian uprising against communist domination by the then Soviet Union. In one scene of what was becoming a fascinating drama, a Russian soldier is interrogating a young female rebel. He puts his revolver between her knees and says,

"Do you want to be deflowered by a bullet?"

"Well, we're not watching this!" says Mum leaping to her

feet to turn the set off and leaving an ominous silence hanging in the lounge while Dad quietly snored.

Then there was the scene in TW3[1] between John Cleese as the Headmaster and, I believe, Ronnie Barker as the parent and Ronnie Corbett as the new prospective pupil.

"Anything more you can tell me about your son?" says Cleese.

"Well, he has just started to masturbate," replies Barker.

"Good." says Cleese "Glad to see he has a hobby."

Cutting short my guffaw, this engendered a similar response, from both Mum and Dad.

In October 1965 *The Magic Roundabout*, a children's puppet programme but with a more mature sense of humour originating in France, became a cult programme to watch, even at sixth form level, followed in June the next year by a sitcom which broke many rules and which would probably not get past the politically-correct police today. *Till Death Do Us Part* had Warren Mitchell as Alf Garnett: a West Ham-supporting, self-opinionated, foul-mouthed, East End racist and mysogynist. He said things that my parents just would not have accepted from my mouth and I found him wonderful! What was not so wonderful was the decision of the BBC not to broadcast a docu-drama it had commissioned from Peter Watkins. *The War Game*, which depicted a nuclear attack on Britain and its aftermath, was deemed too horrific, too graphic – and therefore too politically sensitive – to be shown. Nevertheless it went on to win the Oscar for Best Documentary Feature. I watched it the following year in a screening in the Civic Hall. I have never forgotten it and can still picture its scenes of suffering and devastation in my mind.

One year later, however, it showed a Ken Loach film which,

---

1   *That Was The Week That Was: the late-evening satyrical look at current affairs.*

in its own way, was to have lasting consequences on the socio-political make-up of the UK. *Cathy Come Home*, another docu-drama, was broadcast on BBC1 and viewed by a quarter of the population. It was the story of a British woman who faced a downward social climb thanks to her country's rigid and problem-ridden welfare system in the midst of unemployment and homelessness, and was considered very influential on public attitudes at the time. Indeed, it is still considered to be a break-through moment in social realism on television. The charity *Crisis* was formed the following year as a direct result. It was followed up some fifty years later by the film *I, Daniel Blake*, also by Ken Loach, and also featuring the tragic cruelties of the welfare system.

In America, the escalation (a new use of the word at the time) by the USA of the Vietnam War gave rise to protests and arrests outside the American embassy in Grosvenor Square, London, though I have to say sadly it largely passed me by.

Politically, I was just beginning to hold views which would, nowadays – and I blanche when I remember – put me very much to the right. I recollect thinking the then Home Secretary, Roy Jenkins, overly soft and weak owing to measures such as the abolition of capital punishment, the suspension of birching, the liberalisation of the abortion law, and the decriminalisation of homosexuality. Strictures on divorce – which was still widely considered shameful and an embarrassment – were also relaxed.

The Harold Wilson Labour Government, which had been elected in October 1964 and again, with an increased majority, in March 1966, announced that Britain's pound would, as from 1971, be sub-divided into 100 pence, not 240. The ten-bob note was to go out of circulation in November 1970; half-crowns, florins, bobs, tanners, thrupenny bits – all would disappear, though later I was to begin a collection of the 'old money'. Tourists breathed a great sigh of relief as it was a system totally beyond their experience as all other currencies followed the decimal system of 10s and 100s. My future love of spending more than I possessed began in June 1966 when Barclays Bank introduced the *Barclaycard*, the first British credit card, soon to be followed by Lloyds Bank's 'flexible friend', *Access*. Prior to this, it was seen as only the wealthy who could afford to have the regular credit afforded by American-based cards such as *American Express* and *Diners Club*. Although I was not to lay my hands any card for another four or five years, the seeds of my reckless spending had been well and truly sown!

But in the summer of 1966 and beyond 28 Kingscroft Avenue[1], the country was focused on other names: Alf Ramsey, Bobby Moore, Gordon Banks, and Bobby and Jack Charlton among others. Football's World Cup was taking place for the first time in England. Alf Ramsey's squad overcame all opposition and reached the final at Wembley Stadium on 30th July. An all-time UK record viewing public of 32 million watched England beat West Germany 4-2 after extra time to win the Jules Rimet Trophy (which had earlier been stolen but rediscovered in a hedge by a dog called Pickles) and become football's world champions. And what was I doing that fateful Saturday? I had turned up for my Saturday job at *Elite Decorations* in Albion Street, Dunstable, loyal as ever, and looking forward to my 21/-[2] pay packet: I honestly was not expecting to be able to watch the biggest match of my life so far. Fortunately, my sense of duty was rewarded as Ken Imms, the proprietor, took one look at his shop empty of any customers and sent us all upstairs to watch it on the telly in the lounge above the shop while his manageress, the gently beaming Mrs. Audrey Cole who hated football anyway, kept her eye on things amongst the

---

1   *My second home since 1954. The first was 57 Waterlow Road.*

2   *21/-, or 21 shillings (a "guinea") was worth about £34.00 in today's wages.*

paints and the wallpapers, the timber and the Formica. And I still got paid.

Both my close friend, Graham Lippiatt and I would have something to shout about by the end of the next football season, as well. Taking after his Dad Ted's London affiliation, Graham was an ardent QPR fan. In March 1967 they, a third division team, beat a first division side, West Bromwich Albion, at Wembley 3-2 to win the League Cup, and proved the high point of his supporter's zeal. They were kind enough to take me to some of the matches and to be part of the atmosphere standing near the half-way line, close to the big bass drum that thudded out the chant rhythms while others roared the name of Rodney Marsh, QPR's star player. My own fandom apotheosis was to come the following year but, as a prequel, I was in seventh heaven as Matt Busby's Manchester United won the First Division title – and entry into the European Cup competition – nine years after half the team was killed in the Munich Air Disaster.

The summer and autumn of 1966 saw the country brought down to earth after the celebrations of the World Cup win. On a less serious note, Candlestick Park in San Francisco, California was the scene of the last time the Beatles played a live concert, save for the spontaneous Savile Row roof-top appearance in January 1969. From that moment on, the most famous group in the world became studio recording artists only. I still preferred the lighter side of classical music, including Gilbert and Sullivan. The Beatles were one of only a handful of sixties' groups in which I had something of an interest, though when I look back, I can think of only one other band to which I could be said to have enjoyed listening as they were exceptionally musical: the Moody Blues. Occasionally a song or track might be released by others, which I liked, but on the whole, the pop world could be said to have sailed through my teenage years like a ship in a very foggy night. Not exactly *in with the in-crowd*[1], was I?

Whilst we were all – for the most part – eagerly planning our academic futures, there occurred one disaster which brought home to everyone, in the UK and beyond, the fickleness of fate and the fragility of life. At about 9:15am on Friday, 21st October 1966, a colliery spoil tip, which had been created on a mountain slope near Merthyr Tydfil in South Wales, suddenly collapsed and engulfed the junior school and other buildings in the village of Aberfan. A period of heavy rain had led to the build-up of water within the tip and had caused it suddenly to slide downhill as a slurry, killing 116 children and 28 adults. The tip was the responsibility of the National Coal Board, and the subsequent inquiry placed the blame for the disaster on the organisation and nine named employees.

The New Look (2)

I have said elsewhere that it is difficult not to see Dunstable now as a shadow of its former self. Although I didn't realise it at the time, my home town was about to be relegated to very much an also-ran in Bedfordshire's status ladder. Its arch-rival, Luton, had achieved the status of a County Borough[2] and, although that was to disappear in the Local Government Act of 1972, my town of which I was very proud would, by the same token and in the same year, be reduced to a Town Council – some would say a glorified Parish Council such as is common in villages. How much shopping the new development on the

---

1 *Song by B&G Page, recorded by Dobie Gray in 1964.*
2 *This meant it assumed many of the powers that had been in the County Council's domaine.*

Buckinghamshire/Bedfordshire border took from the town is uncertain, but the New Town of Milton Keynes was formally designated as such by the government on 23rd January 1967. Incorporating nearby towns and villages including Bletchley, Stony Stratford and Newport Pagnell, it was intended to accommodate the overspill population from London some fifty miles away and would become Britain's largest new town, with the area's population multiplying during the seventies and eighties. As I write it stands at a quarter of a million – five times larger than the area was in the early sixties. Many Dunstablians would make the 16-mile pilgrimage to the new shopping centre, though I didn't until the mid-seventies when I had a car. Thirty-four years after it first came into being, I returned to play at its large theatre when on tour with the RSC[1] – though its 1,400-seat capacity was a tad too large for Chekhov's *The Seagull!*

Down and Out (2)

With the cultural and sexual revolution that was the sixties only just beginning to appear over my horizon, my school work limped along in its by now usual, mediocre state. I wasn't learning, I wasn't reading, I wasn't absorbing. Oh, I was pleasant enough in class: I showed interest, gave glimpses or what could be ability, and my French was clearly to benefit from my twinning through the exchange with Brive-la-Gaillarde in France. Brian "Taff" Duncan, my form master and Dunstable Grammar School's epitome of Teddy Roosevelt's[2] dictum of "Speak softly and carry a big stick", did not doubt

---

1   *Royal Shakespeare Company: I was contracted for 6 months, November 1999-May 2000.*
2   *US President 1901-09.*

my ability. But whilst commending in April 1966 the "width of [my] interests" he clearly thought that I was doing too much on stage and far too little in class or at home. Other than the term in which my father became Mayor of Dunstable, this year was to be probably the worst of my school career. One good point was that I had been made a sub-prefect at the beginning of the year – no doubt for my contribution to general school life, i.e. drama, but before the two reports to which I have alluded were issued. Being a sub-prefect involved a few menial duties around the school in the supervising of queues or in dealing with minor problems. Of course, standards of uniform were still adhered to throughout our sixth form existence, the one exception being that we no longer had to wear caps. The badge of office for a sub-prefect was a maroon version of the blue sixth form tie with the school crest dotted on it. A full prefect wore a short gown – shorter, that is, than the graduate gowns worn by the staff, but longer than the very short ones worn by undergraduates at Oxbridge. I never made it up to Prefect. Which was not surprising, given the state of my academic work.

At least, so far as I was concerned, the Lower Sixth meant that PE no longer was on our curriculum and I did not have to try and avoid the Gymnasium, Jack Brennan and rugby balls. Yes, I suppose I missed hockey and cricket to a certain extent, but life was more casual now: names were not checked in on Wednesday's games afternoons and Graham Lippiatt and I regularly skived out of school, walked round to my house (I was one of those who lived closest to the school). Both Dad and Mum were working (Mum had got herself a job at the nearby Courthouse, handling the monies that came in from fines and the like), and we spent the afternoon, drinking tea, eating biscuits, smoking fags, listening to music and chatting – a very innocent way of passing the time compared to what was becoming more and more available. But that was us. And it was me. Another unorthodox use of Wednesday afternoon Games was to go down to Graham's house. He would sit at the piano, vamping away on the keys and singing new words to old tunes, while I tried to accompany him – a chimp could have done better – on his drum set. We even sang in cod French to the tune of the *Marseillaise* about a man on a toilet. It was called "*Où est le papier?*" and ended:

... *Monsieur, Monsieur, / J'ai fait manure. / Où est le papier?*

Despite my various academic inadequacies, I did achieve the publication of two poems in the school magazines for 1966: one a tongue-in-cheek description of the dusty and crumbling, anagrammatic "Eastblund" Grammar School, the other in French entitled *L'Hiver* – Winter. I also took part in the Debating Society, proposing the motion 'This House Believes that the Sentence Imposed on the Train Robbers was too long'. This referred to the perpetrators of the so-called Great Train Robbery in 1963, which I mentioned in another chapter. That the motion was carried by 7 votes to 3 with 2 abstentions gives an indication of how (un)popular the debates were! Unfortunately the 'Parrott' in the teams of the Inter-House Quiz was not me but my father who was representing the fathers of Churchill House boys. Churchill did not win.

That I was then in Churchill House rather than Brown to which I referred in the opening chapters about the School indicates the major change in School life that took place in time for my Lower Sixth. The House names of Brown, Apthorp, Thring and Thompson – all former Headmasters or Deputies – had given way to just three along with a complex point system for all sports and several other activities throughout the school year which would determine the Cock House. Ashton represented the Founder of the School, Bedford was a local name, and Churchill a national one. I am sure the initials A, B and C was also a useful factor!

My first term in the Upper Sixth, my last year at the Grammar School, would grow even more depressing. One of my first tasks was to fill in an UCCA[1] form. It was made abundantly clear to me by supposedly 'helpful' remarks, that certain universities wouldn't even look at me, thanks to my utterly dismal showing in the end-of-year Lower Sixth exams. However, if I was determined to work and make a real effort to get to University to do a B.A. in French, I could put Swansea first and Hull second. I applied to the six we were allowed and had two offers: one from Swansea and one from Oxford Brookes, a small college, totally unallied to Oxford and for which I may not have received a grant[2] anyway. In the end, I gratefully accepted my only real offer: Swansea, who required a B in French and C's in German and English. When compared to the exam results nowadays, it has to be said that, even though grades might appear lower in the sixties compared to the plethora of A's demanded fifty years later, our standards were not a jot lower – indeed, many would claim that they were significantly higher then!

At School, I note with dismay and no little embarrassment from the school magazines for Spring and Autumn 1967 that I supported Keith Sawyer in proposing the motion *This House Supports the Policy of Apartheid.* And it was carried, too, by 11 to 10 with 4 abstentions – I'm not sure whether that says more about the politics of the pupils at DGS or about our prowess in advocating a point of view... Whatever the case, I was to have far less success in a Balloon Debate[3] where Terry Cosgrove's Harold Wilson won with 25 votes, beating Graham Lippiatt

---

1   *Universities' Central Council on Admissions; now UCAS: Universities and Colleges Admissions Service.*

2   *Tertiary education was basically free and grants were freely available to most students to cover costs of living, books etc. Sic transit gloria mundi!*

3   *A debate where only one person can be "saved" from a rapidly descending balloon – the others have to be "thrown out".*

as Mao-Tse-Tung (13 votes), Batman (8), Buddha (4), John Cleese (1). And my contribution? I was General de Gaulle who had just for the second time said *Non!* to Britain's proposed entry into the Common Market. The Balloon Debate echoed that sentiment, as the General and I scored *nul points!*

The Christmas term also saw me join the school choir for the first time. That we were doing a joint concert in the Priory Church with Grace McIntosh's[1] girls' choirs of Queen Eleanor's Grammar School had little to do with it but it was certainly a bonus! Our main work was the *St Nicholas Cantata* by Benjamin Britten and I stood in the basses with Ieuan Adlam-Hill, one of my French masters, who tried to get me to follow him and gave me my first guidance in sight-reading.

I must have seen a showing of Peter Watkins' *The War Game*, the nuclear disaster drama-documentary which the BBC refused to broadcast, during the Easter term of 1967, as the school magazine for Autumn kindly printed, in addition to my report in French about the activities of *Le Cercle Français*, three more poems of mine: *Futilities* and *Watch This Space!*, both anti-nuclear and pessimistic, the second in the shape of a mushroom cloud. The third, *For He is Only Human*, was about a policeman set in a scene of devastation and crying.

Back at the Ranch (2)

Mum and Dad were totally without extremes politically, or, it has to be said, emotionally. On the borough council as an independent, Dad eschewed any links to a political party and

---

1   *I knew Grace already as the Musical Director of the Dunstable Amateur Operatic Society of which Dad was Chairman with Mum i/c the Box Office.*

never discussed council business in my hearing, though he, like his father, was almost certainly a closet Tory of the "one-nation" tendency. My mother, on the other hand, was much more liberal in her views though rarely stated an overtly political opinion on anything. Controversy, it seemed, was banned in our household. Her preference for the Liberal Party, though, was mainly due to her liking of "that nice Mr. Grimond"[1] I never did get to hear what she thought of his successor, Jeremy Thorpe. Later in life, she became more outspoken on issues of importance and displayed a very incisive, a very intelligent outlook on the world. With a fuller education[2] and a greater sense of her own worth, Mum could have had a professional career, in teaching (her preference) or perhaps business or local government.

Home life was consistent: occasionally interesting, occasionally dull, never exciting, never dramatic. They had no extremes with me, whatever I did, good or bad. Both were quiet and undemonstrative in their affections both for me and for each other. I was later to find that such 'coolness' rubbed off on to me in a greater way than I might have wanted and affected my future relationships and my marriage until I was in my forties when I met Amanda and I blossomed – but that's another story! They were concerned, as loving parents, about school work but never exerted any real pressure on me to do well or even to work hard. I was left quite free to choose my own path in life, my own career. Their support was always there, though, but not necessarily apparent; like their emotions, it was largely latent. They seemed invariably to handle me with kid gloves, almost as though I would suddenly explode. We did not have the close relationship that my cousin, Kevin (four

---

1   *Jo Grimond MP, leader of the Liberal Party 1956-67.*

2   *This was denied her by her father in 1936, probably on the grounds that he had not the means to pay for both her and her sister, Eve. – See the earlier section on "Mavis".*

years my junior) for example, had with his mother, Mum's sister Eve, with whom I later heard, he could discuss *anything*, even *sex!* We never talked but superficially – never deeply and certainly not about anything emotional. If Mum were writing this, she would probably insist that she always liked to discuss things but in a non-contentious way – though of that I have little recollection.

I really had had virtually no sex education from my parents. When I was about eleven or twelve, my father once came in while I was having a bath and talked to me about how hair would grow "down there" and how I would find myself "bigger" when I woke up in the morning; and did I know where babies came from? When I assured him that I did, he beat a hasty retreat and left a little paper booklet on my bed. It was dated from the 1920s and doubtless had been given to him when he was a boy. Full of clinical diagrams and drawings and descriptions of biological functions with nothing about feelings, about emotions.

I have had a lifelong embarrassment over body shape and lack of physical ability. I was hopeless at games and in the gym; later my inability to dance and move gracefully would become woefully apparent and I was to bewail the fact that either I was too pale and too skinny, or that I put on too much weight. I'd always had a healthy, some would say large, appetite – Mum and Granny used to say that I had "hollow legs" into which the food would disappear. Those hollow legs seem, in my later twenties and into middle age, to transfer to my midriff. Where they stayed.

Within the wider family I was the first of my generation to drop the 'Aunty' and 'Uncle' titles in favour of plain Christian names. That may not seem a big thing nowadays, but in the mid-sixties it was quite forward. It started not in the family but with Peter and Sylvia Harrison, friends of Mum and Dad's through the Operatic Society. Mum had said that I should call them Aunty Sylvia and Uncle Peter, but they rejected the idea and wanted me to use their Christian names. Eve and Ray also suggested dropping the Aunty and Uncle titles and it spread to Alwyn and Fay, to Ray and Shirley[1] and, much later due to their own preferences, to Keith and Dorothy. It just seemed the thing to do.

Back to the Future (2)

The real, or public, performances – the times I was proud of myself and my costumed and made-up body – came threefold in the Lower Sixth, despite Taff Duncan's reserve about the width of my interests. The first two were in an evening of one-act plays in the first part of the year. Each of the three Houses put on a one-act piece as part of the House competition. I played opposite Terry Doughty and along with Richard Thornton in Sean O'Casey's *The End of the Beginning*. I remember little about it, save for it being my first outing with an Irish accent – or what I thought passed for one. The adjudicator (from another school) commended the acting but in the final analysis placed Churchill second. Perhaps that what spurred me on in my efforts as a director the next year in the Upper Sixth! After the three House plays, I played Prince Hal in a scene from Shakespeare's *Henry IV part 1*, the one in which Falstaff (Mike Bannister) boasts about his exploits but has his bombastic pride punctured by his friend Hal, the future Henry V. This was also the first play in which I was directed by Mr. P.D. 'Pete' Lawman, a member of the English Department, who was later to take me through the speeches for my audition for the RADA[2].

---

1   *Eve (née Estwick, Mum's sister) and Ray Smith; Alwyn, Ray and Keith Parrott – Dad's brothers.*

2   *The Royal Academy of Dramatic Art.*

The highlight of the year for me was undoubtedly the production by Brian 'Chin' Arthur and Alun 'GB'[1] Goodwin of Willis Hall's *The Long and the Short and the Tall* about a platoon of British soldiers who find themselves surrounded by the Japanese in a tin miner's hut in Malaya. The Japanese prisoner was played by Richard Thornton and Mike Bannister was the leader, Sergeant Mitchem. Terry Cosgrove played Lance-Corporal Macleish and added to the occasional humour of the piece when, during a discussion about what to do with the Japanese prisoner, he confused his lines, coming out with *Ye cannae stick a prisoner in an unarmed bayonet*! On another occasion, we were lined up at an angle to the front of the stage to be dressed down by the sergeant, with Terry nearest the edge. When Sgt. Mitchem ordered *Lance-Corporal Macleish, three paces forward! March*!, the third pace took Terry clean off the stage and into the audience. Bruce Royan was Corporal Johnstone, Terry Sycamore the Northerner, Private 'Smudger' Smith, and Michael Griffin the fearful and rather weak-willed radio operator Pte. Whittaker. Verbally sparring much of the time with my Cockney barrack-room lawyer, Pte. Bamforth, was Graham Lippiatt as the full-blooded Welshman, Pte. Evans. We had some good moments on stage, not least singing together as we had been wont to do. But it is not to be forgotten that these were still the years of the 'Blue Pencil' whereby every stage play was censored by the Lord Chamberlain's office and any language or behaviour deemed inappropriate was duly struck in blue pencil from the script. Our song *should* have been:

> *For my little sister Lily*
> *Is an whore down Piccadilly*
> *And me mother is another on the Strand,*

---

1   *GB = Golden Bollocks, due to rather camp mannerisms.*

> *While me father flogs his arse-hole*
> *Round the Elephant and Castle.*
> *We're the finest fucking family in the land.*

but we sang:

> *For my little sister Lily*
> *Takes a stroll down Piccadilly*
> *And me mother has another on the Strand,*
> *While me father flogs his charcoal*
> *Round the Elephant and Castle.*
> *We're the finest flipping family in the land.*

Goodwin and Arthur then exercised even more censorship of the script, often with rather bemusing consequences:

Bamforth and Evans are waking up on the floor of the hut

EVANS: *Had a good kip, then, Bammo?*
BAMFORTH: *What? Kippin' next to you? I'd rather bed down wiv' an eskimo's granny!*

ARTHUR: No, no! Cut, cut!
ME: But Sir, there aren't going to be any eskimo's grannies in the audience, Sir.
ARTHUR: Change it.

EVANS: *Had a good kip, then, Bammo?*
BAMFORTH: *What? Kipping next to you? Not bleedin' likely!*

ARTHUR: Right. Carry on.

And, as if the downgrading of my personal future wasn't enough, I was also told in no uncertain terms by 'Pete' Lawman who, along with Alun 'GB' Goodwin, was to direct the next School play, Molière's *The Would-be Gentleman*, that I, on the instructions of the Head, would only get a small role, thus allowing me "more time to commit to improving [my] schoolwork". I turned out to be a one-scene wonder: the Dancing Master engaged to instruct Monsieur Jourdain, the would-be gentleman, in the art of minuets and other such frivolities. I played my part *as camp as a row of pink tents* as a friend of mine would say, entering with a rosebud clamped between my teeth and imitating Kenneth Williams in his 'Sandy and Jules' sketches in radio's *Round the Horne*. It must have been an appalling performance though 'Maxy' Matthewman described it in the School Magazine as "precious" – probably his euphemism for outrageously camp and way over the top.

It was during this year that Dad, who had just resigned from the Parent-Staff Association in anticipation of my leaving the school, paid the then fee of five guineas for me to have an audition at the RADA. I think, in all honesty, it was done not so much to encourage my desire to be an actor, but rather to get it out of my system – perhaps he and Mum assumed I wouldn't pass anyway! – and it wasn't as though I was intent on doing the rounds of all the drama schools until one relented. Two pieces, one from Shakespeare had to be presented and I chose Beckett's speech from Eliot's *Murder in the Cathedral* ("*Now is my way clear; now is the meaning plain…*") and the (contrasting) speech by Launce, with his dog, from *Two Gentlemen of Verona*. ("*When a man's servant shall play the cur with him…*). 'Pete' Lawman was kind enough to take me through them and give me some advice. I remember waiting in the wings of the RADA theatre until I was summoned to walk out to the front centre of the stage and, to a row of little, tasselled light-shades set about two thirds of the way back in the audience seats, gave my name and what I was going to do. The lights were kind enough to hear both pieces, thanked me and off I went to wait for the letter to arrive at home a couple of weeks later. Of course, I failed: having good parts in school productions isn't the best preparation for training to be a professional actor. I had a decent voice, but very little experience and thought my future career lay elsewhere than on the boards – probably to Mum and Dad's eternal relief as Bedfordshire gave no grants for drama schools in those days.

Nevertheless, my final year was to provide a dramatic high point in the guise of the Inter-House Drama Competition. 1967 was to see the entire production, including direction, done by the boys ourselves. I had volunteered immediately to do Churchill's offering and chose *The Folly of Seithenyn* by Ken Etheridge. This had appeared in *The Best One-Act Plays of 1944-45 selected by JW Marriott* and was what the adjudicator, F.M. 'Tubby' Bancroft, described as a "bold choice" due to its Welshness, and the handling of a submerged village and the drowning of the man responsible, Seithenyn. I had recorded the sound effects – roaring seas and waves – myself, by rolling split peas across a bass drum left over from the days of the school cadet force and I was so screwed up with nerves when it came to the performance that Denis O'Donoghue, who was operating the sound effects, let me operate the tape recorder for him. I also actually smoked a cigarette backstage and 'Pete' Lawman chose quite deliberately to ignore it! Given that the other two plays, Bedford's *The Farce of the Devil's Bridge* by Henri Gheon and Ashton's *The Man in the Bowler Hat* by AA Milne, were both comedies which mine most definitely was not, I was unsure of how much notice Bancroft would take of audience reaction when he marked the plays on his criteria of choice, production and entertainment. However, I was encouraged to hear during his adjudication report that "entertainment is not just making people laugh". With Bancroft being Welsh himself, it was not surprising that he pulled us up on the pronunciation of the name Mair – *my-er*, not *mayor*, but I was praised for an adventurous and imaginative choice and for my handling of a large cast. The final marks out of 80 were Ashton: 61, Bedford: 62, but Churchill – and I remember leaping to my feet and punching the air in a most undignified manner – had won with 71!

Beyond the School (2)

In the aftermath of the Second World War, much thought was given to ways in which the rifts could be healed, not just between the countries of the Allies and the Axis, but throughout Western Europe. One idea that quickly gathered momentum was the twinning of towns to encourage exchanges at municipal council as well as at personal level. From this, it was thought, would stem mutual exchanges of culture, ideas, friendship, tourism, and maybe even business. Through the efforts of Councillor Wilfred T. Lack and for which he was awarded an OBE – you'll have met the name before as my Physics master and Deputy Head of the Grammar School – Dunstable was, in the early days of the scheme, twinned with the French town of Brive-la-Gaillarde in the south-west central *département* of Corrèze. Brive is on the edge of the Dordogne, more recently much beloved region of British retirees, and calls itself *le riant portail du midi* or 'the smiling gateway to the south'. It was then slightly larger than Dunstable with some small industry and, as I was to find out, with its relative proximity to the Central Massif, quite a history of *maquis*[1] activity during the war. To be even-handed, Dunstable was later to be twinned also with Porz-am-Rhein,

---

1   *The name often given to the French Resistance, from the thick, Massif scrubland in which they lived and operated.*

just outside Cologne, North-Rhine-Westphalia, in the then West Germany. But it was to Brive that I asked to go during the Easter of 1966; the only cost to Mum and Dad being the journey, as I would be staying in the home of someone of similar age and interests as me – an ideal opportunity to practise and improve my French with real natives after two terms of sterile, albeit enthusiastic, Whitmarsh[1] orientated 'A' level translations and précis.

The journey was, by today's standards, tortuous: coach to Lympne in Kent, a small twin-prop plane to Beauvais, and a coach into Paris for an overnight stay in the dormitories of a boarding school, the *Lycée Marcelin Berthelot* in Saint-Maur-des-Fossés to the south-east of the city. That gave us our first meeting with some French people when some of us trooped across the road to the *Aux Trotteurs* bar where a kindly lady bought the half-dozen of us all a drink – brightly coloured, non-alcoholic *syrops à l'eau*[2]. The next day the coach took us on a trip round Paris after breakfast before depositing us and our luggage at the *Gare d'Austerlitz* for an six-hour journey down to Brive itself, arriving about 7:00pm.

Having arrived in the gathering gloom outside Brive station, there was a flurry of greetings and handshakes, suitcases being picked up and their owners packed off into cars. I knew I was to be with a Gerard Gourdoux who lived at no.7 Impasse André Chénier and whose parents owned and ran the fruit-and-veg shop in the centre of the town, *Aux Fruits d'Or*. We hadn't exchanged photographs, so maybe it was my shyness, or perhaps it was his as well, but I was the last Brit standing and he was the last Frog, so we must have been destined for each other. Pierre, his father, bundled my case into the back of his

---

1   *A grammar-orientated course for beginners through to 'A' level by W. F. H. Whitmarsh.*

2   *Sweet syrupy fruit juice with iced water*

Peugeot 704 Estate – with three rows of seats, I noticed – and I was twinned.

After a less-than-auspicious beginning, it all turned out to be a great success and I settled down quickly into French family life. Pierre and Ginette, the mother, had vacated their room for me and moved down to the spare room on the ground floor, also occupied by the garage and store, a utility room and a room which Gerard and his brother Jean-Pierre used as their activity space. Next to me on the first floor, the two boys had their bedroom, while the Granny and Grandfather were opposite the rest being occupied by the dining room, kitchen and balcony. Pierre and Ginette left every morning before 5:00am to go to market to stock the shop, leaving Granny to run the house with the pottering assistance of François, as the grandfather insisted on being called. He was a diminutive man with his white hair permanently crowned by a traditional beret and his thick white beard sporting two purplish-brown stripes running down from the corners of his mouth. Our first meal together was to show me their origin: François practised *chabrol*. That is, when he was close to the end of his bowl of soup (which always began both lunch and dinner) he would take the wine, pour a small amount into the remains of his soup, stir it, and then lift the bowl to his mouth and drain it. Some of the wine-and-soup mix invariably trickled down his beard.

Both Pierre and Ginette were very ordinary, hard-working folk without any pretensions. Pierre liked to hint that he'd been in the Resistance, and indeed he may have been – it was just that every Frenchman of a certain age would make similar claims. At table, he always used his pen-knife, peasant-like, to cut his bread, holding it in his hands as he did so and I remember Gerard being very proud when, for his sixteenth birthday, Pierre gave him his own penknife to follow suit. The rule for food was "only take what you can eat." The two boys had had it drummed into them that workers had slaved hard to produce the meal and it was therefore not to be wasted. Me, I wasted nothing, whether it was the oily *salade*, the snails, the shredded leeks in vinaigrette, the rabbit, the cheeses, the *babas au rhum*, or the wine. Particularly the wine. And the *Marie Brisard* aniseed *digestif*.

The visit of Dunstable's youth group was also fêted with yet more wine at the *Mairie* by two *Maires-adjoints*[1], *messieurs* Dignac and Amon. We were also taken out on day trips to places of interest in the area such as the Chastaing Dam, the underground lakes of the Gouffre de Padirac, and the cliff-top-and-side town of Rocamadour. Whilst we had been well-behaved on the train, the coach carrying both English and French groups would echo to the sound of raucous singing – pop numbers, folk and patriotic songs, old pub and musical hall ditties, and the occasional rugby vulgarity – as our groups gelled almost immediately, meeting almost daily at the central *Café du Théâtre*: my school mates Graham Lippiatt and Steve Matthews, aka "Tank" for his size and prowess in rugby, plus Murray Pakes, Tony Parsons, Sally Smith, Anne Wibberley, and Lindsay Tawell amongst a group of about twenty. Whilst not conscious of it at the time, it was undoubtedly the singing that brought us all together. How different from nowadays when everyone would have their earpieces in and their eyes glued to their smart phones!

On the rare occasion I found myself alone at home with *Mamie*[2], she and I played draughts or, on one occasion, I helped her 'kill' a rabbit with karate chops to the back of its neck – I think it was already dead! One weekend, after a massive Easter Sunday lunch of many successive courses, not to mention copious amounts of alcohol, we drove up into the Central Massif to an Uncle's place where, before sitting down to yet

---

1   *Deputies or assistants.*

2   *Granny.*

another meal, we took inebriated pot-shots at wine bottles on a wall with a rifle he said he had used *pour tuer les Boches*[1]. After that and some camomile tea I gently dozed off until the evening meal was served on his long dining table. This was no ordinary piece but had ten places carved out of the thick, solid oak, so that soup, food etc. could be placed in the hollows thus avoiding the need for plates.

In our time together – that is, when we weren't going out with the rest of the group, Gerard and I would do what came naturally to two teenage boys of different languages and cultures: we exchanged all the rude words we could think of for their counterpart in the other's language. Slang is frequently limited in time. Suggest to a French girl that the two of you 'go to the strawberries'[2] now would mean little more than an invitation to Pick Your Own at a local farm. In 1966, according to Gerard, you'd probably get your face slapped. Some crude Anglo-Saxon did not translate with quite the same vigour of expression, though some French phrases were quite picturesque: who would have thought that 'to sharpen one's pipe'[3] would then mean to get oral sex? Gerard was, if anything, more advanced in some things than was I – as I found out when I heard about him and one of our English girls: more strawberries than Wimbledon.

Back in England later that summer, language caused some confusion at least with my mother when we entertained Graham Lippiatt and his French correspondent Joël. Over the evening meal, an animated conversation in French took place between Gerard and Joël in which could be heard many repetitions of the same word – well, it sounded, much to my mother's concern and the worried looks she was giving my

---

1   *to kill the Krauts (Germans).*

2   *aller aux fraises.*

3   *se faire tailler la pipe.*

father, very much like 'bollocks'. Noting their anxiety, Graham and I grinned at each until, in the end, I was able to explain to Mum and Dad that Joël and Gerard were talking about the television programme *The Magic Roundabout*[1] in which the character Dougal the dog was called *Pollux*.

My link with Gérard and his family was to last longer, in that during the Upper Sixth Easter holidays – a good escape from the rigours of revision – I went back to Brive by myself, learning to stomach the cross-channel ferries in the days when modern stabilisers hadn't been invented. I soon found that two or three large duty-free brandies in the bar were the best stabilisers I could find. Dad had booked all the tickets at the local branch of Thomas Cook's, but it still left me the task of getting on the right transport at the right time. Being the first time I had travelled independently – and abroad, too – this was a considerable step forward for me and probably also for Mum who was normally the world's greatest worrier. Yes, I rang home as soon as I arrived at the Gourdoux's, but that was after travelling to London and to Dover by train, by ferry to Calais and then by train again to Paris. There, I had to cross from the Gare du Nord to the Gare d'Austerlitz by the *Metro* and find my way through a large mainline station to my reservation in the train for Brive. And cases did not have wheels then. Heaven knows what torments Mum endured while I was travelling, while I was in France and while I was coming back, but let me go she did. I didn't think much of it at the time: it was just something that seemed quite natural and well within my abilities both as a traveler and as a speaker of some French. And, of course, these were the days before mobile phones, and before the internet: any contact with home was either through a postcard which would invariably arrive in Dunstable a week after I had returned, or by an expensive telephone call just to let them know I had arrived safely.

---

1   *Le Manège Enchanté*

This stay was notable in particular for one name: Oradour-sur-Glane. Gérard drove me to this village north of Limoges in the heart of the *Haute-Vienne* countryside which, on 10th June 1944, had been surrounded by a Waffen-SS company in reprisal for the abduction by the Resistance of a German officer. All bar a handful of the residents were murdered – some 642 civilians – and the village burned. Gerard and I walked round the remains of the village in silence. It had been left exactly as it had been on that day, save for the cemetery – the stone houses roofless, a car slowly rusting away in a garage, likewise a sewing machine on a table and a bicycle hanging on a wall. Later, in the early nineties, I was to take my parents there. The bike had fallen from the wall and the car's suspension had collapsed completely. The silence, again, was absolute.

"You know, Rog.," said my father after a while, "I can't hear a single bird."

At the end of my eleven days there, I came back with Gèrard who was to stay with me in Dunstable for a similar time. Apart from lasting improvements in my oral French, the one thing I acquired from Gérard was a love of the French *caporal* tobacco as in *Gauloise*, *Gitane*, or *Disque Bleu* cigarettes. Their smell was pungent and instantly recognisable, their taste unlike any other. Trendy they were not, at least not in France except to the older age bracket, but to me they encapsulated the authenticity of everything that was French, and which I wanted to imbibe to its maximum. Apart from occasional dalliances with a pipe, this was an association I was to maintain until my mid-fifties when I finally gave up smoking in January 2004.

Three years later in 1970 I was to visit the family again, though only for a weekend as it was during my three-month stay in Paris whilst training to be a teacher. I had done a little teaching of English to gather together sufficient funds to buy a return ticket to Brive, but neither Gérard nor Jean-Pierre was there. François, the grandfather with the wine-stained beard, had died, but Granny entertained me, along with Ginette and Pierre so I felt my visit had not been in vain.

Thereafter I was to lose touch with the family completely. When, some forty-five years later, Veronica and I travelled to the Dordogne for a wedding, we spent part of one day in Brive during which I returned to the *Hôtel le Quercy, the Café du Théâtre,* and to the *Impasse André Chénier* and the last house on the left, number seven. Still recognisable, I was astonished to find *M. et Mme. Gourdoux* on the letter box attached to the front gate. I was too shy to call on the off-chance to see perhaps if Gérard now lived there, or Jean-Pierre. Later, I wrote to the occupants saying who I was and telling of my connection to the Gourdoux. But it was in vain as I did not receive a response. Neither did the other searches I made bear any fruit and have now assumed that the Gourdoux name on the letterbox was an oversight by the new residents.

Now in the Upper Sixth, I must have felt that I was growing up and becoming more my own person as I suddenly decided that I should have a party! When I found that Mum and Dad were going out to some big evening do, all black-tie and long-dresses, the scene could be set for 28 Kingscroft Avenue to become the party centre of the universe with me, who had been to others' parties but never thought sufficiently 'in' to host one, opening my door to those with whom I wished to be considered friends.

The best one can say is that the house, fortunately, was not trashed. Bottles of *Strongbow* and large cans of *Watney's Party 7* and *Party 4*[1] were in ample evidence with the addition of a few packets of crisps. My music system was, by now, a second-

---

1   *Large cans of beer containing 7 pints (the "normal" party offering) and 4 pints the "mean" party offering) respectively. They had to be opened with a pointed cutter which pierced triangular holes in the top of the can to enable the beer to be poured into glasses.*

hand radiogram – and mono, not even stereo! Since the classical highlights of Alan Keith's *Your Hundred Best Tunes* wouldn't exactly cut it, I had to invite others to bring records to play. I remember sitting there on the sofa with Graham Lippiatt at about 7:30, wondering if we were going to be the only ones there and consuming the larger part of a bottle of *Strongbow*, but little of the actual evening itself remains in my mind, save for, at one point – probably about ten-ish – stumbling upstairs locked in an embrace with E., a girl from Queen Eleanor's Grammar School (the girls' equivalent to DGS). She was not pretty, but attractive – and probably made all the more so by the *Strongbow*. She had short cut hair which curved round her jaw in the points popular at the time, a large mouth and a figure which was more East Anglia than the Pennines, but I was drunk and eager to try out the little packet which I'd bought at the barbers' and kept in my wallet. The next I knew was Mum kneeling by the bed, propping me up and trying to pour black coffee down my throat. She and Dad had probably come home a tad earlier than expected and, after their initial shock, cleared the house, tidied up, bless them, and were busy, if not with me, then with containing their evident disapproval. Our next-door neighbour, Roy Walker, was later to tell Dad that he had thought to intervene but was "worried about flick-knives!" Fortunately, E. had disappeared. And I still had all my clothes on. Nothing came of that evening either from my parents or from my friends – who might have been expected to make fun of my parents arriving home and being horrified. There again, perhaps they had had the same experience themselves on different occasions.

Equally embarrassing were my efforts in the 'A' level exams that summer. My lack of work, commitment and revision had certainly come home to roost with a vengeance when I earned only a C in French, an E in English and an 'O' level pass in German. *The Forester's Arms* – about which, more another time – consoled me briefly, while Swansea University understandably chose to do without me. In the meantime, I occupied myself, albeit for very modest pay, by joining the land staff at Whipsnade Zoo during the summer holidays. In the mornings, we were sent out round the various areas of the zoo litter-picking, sack in one hand and a stick with a sharp metal nail stuck into the end for skewering the papers left all over the pathways and the lawns in the other. The afternoons were usually more interesting in that we had to help with the various facilities, such as the rides (elephants and camels) or the Children's Zoo. I was never allocated the former, but the latter, I quickly learned was where one could, if so inclined, make the odd half-crown[1] extra by re-selling tickets that people had thrown away…

A Gap Year 1967-68

Having won the House Drama Competition for Churchill House during my final year at the Grammar School and having leapt up on to the stage to be congratulated by Bancroft, it had been obvious to me that there had been no trophy to grasp and lift triumphantly. All the other aspects of inter-House competition had an array of silverware in all shapes and sizes, but not Drama. So, as an end to my drama career at the School, I got together with Graham Lippiatt and Michael Griffin and we bought and presented the school with a gilt column, topped with the two masks of drama and on a plinth with a small plaque advertising its purpose and the names of the three of us who donated it. I don't think Philip Banfield, the Headmaster, really liked the style as it was somewhat brash and different from the staid silver cups awarded for everything else, but he did appreciate the thought. Thinking back, it was

---

1   2/6 – *two shillings and sixpence or about £4.00 in today's wages.*

probably one of those acts designed to leave ones mark behind one in some way: some had done it with their outstanding academic achievements, but my legacy in that domaine had, of course, been mediocre in the extreme.

I knew I wanted to do something that could use languages. I don't know where the suggestion of a career in the Civil Service came from. Possibly Mum and Dad. Dad had also previously arranged for an interview with someone in Barclays Bank in London on the supposed strength of my languages rather than any enthusiasm on my part to be involved in balance sheets and the like, but that did not appeal so I filled in the necessary forms for the Executive (post-A level) grade[1] of the Diplomatic Corps and sent them to the Civil Service Commission then in Savile Row. Meanwhile, I went back to school to see if Banfield had any pearls of wisdom to cast before the academic swine which stood before him.

"I thought you were at one stage interested in teaching?"

"I had thought about it, Sir."

"Well then, Roger, [a sign of being an 18-year old leaver was the use of one's Christian name rather than the traditional surname] why don't you give it a try? You could contact the county education offices to see if there's any possibility of doing a spot of teaching, unqualified of course, to see if you like it".

"Yes, I will. Thank you, Sir." And I did. And he gave me an open testimonial to the effect that I bore an "unimpeachable personal reputation". Whilst taking a year out after A levels is now common place and known as a Gap Year, the concept was not as commonly accepted in 1967 as it is now, the only opportunities then being in working overseas in third-world countries, known as VSO or Voluntary Service Overseas. Started in 1958, a sign

---

1   *Clerical Grade was post-O level, while the highest grade, the Administrative, was postgraduate and predominantly Oxbridge. And ne'er did the three mix!*

of the times was that this was initially only for male volunteers before starting university. Volunteers offered unskilled help in return for basic accommodation and pocket money. But five years before my own gap year, the practice changed to using university graduate volunteers who would have greater maturity and a more defined skill-set to offer.

In the meantime, however, I was invited up to Savile Row for an interview. Suit on, shoes polished, bus to Luton, train to Kings Cross-St.Pancras, tube to Piccadilly and then walk. When I was invited into the interview room, it was to sit on a lonely chair in front of a long table around which five city-types, all black jackets and stripy trousers, old-school, club and regimental ties impeccably knotted, and greying hair slicked back, displayed the regulation half-inch of white shirt cuff beyond the jacket sleeves. Before going and never having been interviewed in my life before, Dad had given me a little advice on the interview, much of which was concerned with speaking up for myself appropriately and politely, but also on how to deal with a question to which I did not know the answer, the main thrust of which was not to pretend to know, but to be honest.

After explaining to me the outlines of the Corps and the fact that I could be posted to any far-flung outpost of British influence and expected to learn one of the lesser foreign languages of the world (Dzongkha? Uzbek? Igbo?), the questions were, to my memory fifty-odd years later, heavily political. What did I think of the Iron Curtain? – At least I could talk about having been into East Berlin through Checkpoint Charlie – nods of interest and approbation. Which newspaper did I read? – My parents took the Telegraph – more positive nods of approval. Did I read the Peterborough column? – I'm afraid not, Sir – never mind. What did I think of the Common Market[1]? Ah. Problem.

---

1   *The European Economic Community, now (enlarged) the European Union.*

"I'm afraid I know very little about the Common Market, Sir, but I would be very willing to read up about it and talk to you another day." A couple of raised eyebrows and a slight, inclined nod to each other. Thanks Dad. What did I think of General de Gaulle? A topical question in that the French president had already vetoed Britain's application to join the Common Market in 1963 and, two months later, in November 1967, was to do so again. When I said that I thought he was "an old man trading on his wartime reputation", the whole table resembled a troop of nodding *Churchill Insurance* bulldogs.

But before I could hear from the Civil Service, I journeyed to Bedford for another interview, this time at the offices of the education department of the County Council and about the possibility of an unqualified teaching position. There I was immediately successful, being offered the chance to help with French either in a secondary school in Stewartby some 20 miles from Dunstable and with no direct bus (I was still unable to drive), or in Downside Primary School, Dunstable. I chose the latter at a salary of £490.00[1] per year. No sooner had I reconciled myself to teaching than the Civil Service wrote to me to say that I had been selected for the Home Civil Service but that I was still being considered for the Diplomatic Corps, although there were only twelve entrants per year. So, not fancying the Home Civil Service as I thought being abroad a great deal more exciting, I went ahead with my appointment to Downside County Primary School where my cousin, Diana[2], was in the top class. Downside lay at the southern end of Dunstable and at the foot of Blows Downs and was reachable by pushbike. Under the charming and gentle, francophile Head Teacher, Ron Fowler, I was to use the

---

1   *About £12-15,000 in today's wages.*

2   *Diana Duncan, née Parrott, elder daughter of Alwyn, the youngest of my father's brothers, and Fay.*

Nuffield En Avant teaching packs – lots of pictures and display cards – all listening and speaking – and I was to support the class teachers in doing a little French almost every day with every class – except for with my cousin Diana, as Mrs. Nellie Bullock, the Deputy Head and French speaker, taught the 10-11 year olds. The children all took on French names, some the equivalent to their own, others something totally different, and threw themselves into all the activities with gusto. Yes, and they learned as well.

This job at Downside CP School also meant that, for the first time in my life, I was the proud possessor of a Lloyds Bank current account and cheque book, along with a plastic card which guaranteed my cheques up to £30.00. I could not apply for the new Access credit card as my then salary did not qualify me for it.

I had just got settled in and was really enjoying myself when another letter came from the Diplomatic Corps section of the Civil Service Commission congratulating me on being one of the twelve entrants for that year… I weighed up the pros and cons, talked to Mum and Dad who said they would support me in whatever decision I made, and turned the men in suits down: teaching had started to appeal to me. Mum and Dad never gave any indication as to which they would have preferred for me, save for my mother making it clear that she had always wanted to be a teacher herself. Uncle Stan[1], my godfather, was later to express his disappointment in no uncertain terms, telling me that, as a teacher, "You'll be a pauper all your life". There are times, even over fifty years later, when I still wonder where and what I might be now had I taken the road *less traveled by*[2] of the Diplomatic Corps. No regrets – just a fascination that can stir my imagination occasionally.

---

1   *Stanley Bearton, brother to Ronald and Sarah Parrott, my granny.*
2   *Robert Frost "The Road Not Taken".*

I was to have a great year at Downside. My monthly pay cheque amounted to barely £40.00 of which I was to give Mum £30 for my keep – I later found that she'd put it all to one side to help support me later at Uni., bless her, thereby leaving myself £10.00[1]. I applied to Coventry College, the School of Education of the University of Warwick, to do a B.Ed (Hons.) four-year course to become a secondary teacher of French and Drama. Back at Downside I taught French, helped with boys' games, and went out for a few months with another teacher, Gill Luff, who had the bonus attribute of a smart, dark blue, soft-top Austin-Healey sports car. Anxious to get behind her wheel, so to speak, I learned to drive with Terry Mead, the son-in-law of the Tom Cowper from whom Mum got her weekly grocery delivery. My lessons through the year went from 24 to 25 to 26/-[2] an hour during which Terry one day turned up in a brand new white Ford Cortina Mark 2 which I almost refused to drive for fear I'd damage it. But Terry was a superb teacher in whom I had total confidence. I'm proud to say that, with neither Mum nor Dad driving and consequently no car to practise in (though I once drove Grace McKintosh's[3] new Vauxhall Viva with her and Mum and Dad inside and we all wondered why I wasn't driving very smoothly: I'd left the hand-brake on) I passed my test first time after only sixteen lessons… but I never got to drive Gill Luff's Austin-Healey.

I also joined a local drama group, the Priory Players, who performed in the Parish Hall, connected to the Priory Church. They had Robin Hadcroft, Stan Knowles, whose son Graham was at DGS[4], Denise Barber who taught at Downside, and Lois Counter, and I was to do three productions with them:

---

1   *Approximately £1300; £900 and £300 – which seems an awful lot now.*

2   *25 shillings would be about £40.00 in today's wages.*

3   *Head of Music at Queen Eleanor's GS, Musical Director of the Dunstable Amateur Operatic Society and family friend.*

4   *Dunstable Grammar School.*

Robert Bolt's *Flowering Cherry*, Alec Coppel's *The Gazebo*, and a scene from Noel Coward's *Present Laughter* which was entered into a local drama festival in the Queensway Hall. I played a student, Roland Maude, and was devastated when the adjudicator tore me to shreds before a large audience, saying that my performance was grossly exaggerated and my mannerisms way over the top. Afterwards, I asked the director why she hadn't pulled me up, why she'd let me be like that. All she could say was,

"You were so keen and I didn't want to discourage you." I suppose she had a point, though it wasn't the most helpful direction I'd ever had! Perhaps, however, given the dire problems I faced when I finally went to drama school, I should have paid more attention to the criticism...

Early in 1968 I was invited by the Dunstable Town Twinning Association to take charge of the annual exchange visit to Brive at Easter. Why, I don't know: I can only assume that they could think of no one else. At this time there were no 'risk-assessments', no DBS[1] screening. In our health-and-safety consciousness of today, a callow nearly 19-year old youth would never be allowed to be responsible for a group of some twenty teenagers up to the age of 16 or 17, even though it were in company with an even younger – at 18 – good friend, Steve Matthews. I had experience of going to Brive, yes, and post-A level spoke decent enough French, but really had little idea of what it meant to take care of and lead such a group. I even remember at a meeting for those going on the exchange and their parents that, when asked about standards of behaviour, one of the naïvely embarrassing comments I made was that I hoped we didn't bring back any "budding *Pierres*"!

Steve and I were put up in the *Hotel le Quercy* in the centre

---

1   *Disclosure and Barring Service: screening to protect children and vulnerable adults, formerly CRB (Criminal Records Bureau check).*

of the town, and catered for at its restaurant across the car park – though after a couple of days of excellent food, one of the *Maire-Adjoints* had to remind us that we were expected not to choose the *à la carte* menu, but the (cheaper) set-price one! I feel sorry, now, that I did not stay again with my family, the Gourdoux. Still, it went with the role and status, I suppose, and Steve and I kept each other company. A hotel room also had its uses in that at a disco one evening I'd 'got off with', so to speak, one Marie-Christine. We met up the next day – though I have to say I didn't recognise her at first as she'd been wearing a wig at the disco for stylistic purposes – and went back to the hotel. Thus, I finally got to break into the little packet that had, figuratively speaking, been burning a hole in my wallet for too long. To my shame, and for the rest of our stay there, I did my utmost to avoid any contact with her and pushed that all too quickly-accomplished milestone of my life equally quickly to the back of my mind.

The exchange, on the whole, went well: I only lost one student! Experience soon makes you actively count heads and tick off names every time before setting off in your chosen transport. On one trip to Rocamadour, a picturesque town both perched on the top, and set in the side of a cliff, we boarded the coach that would take us back to Brive, and I merely asked "Is everyone here?" to which, of course, came the cries of "Yes!" And off we went and no one missed John.

John was a pleasant lad of about 13 or 14, probably not the brightest button in the bag and with floppy conventional hair and big, strong lenses in his black-framed glasses on a rosy-cheeked, moon face. It was the same glasses that had misted up one evening in a bar in Royan. The whole exchange group had gone for a weekend to the Atlantic seaside town of Royan, heavily bombarded during the war but now a very modern reincarnated resort. A few of us had, quite innocently, chosen a bar in which to have a drink one evening when suddenly the lighting changed and a young lady with short blond hair and a six-foot python appeared and proceeded to take her clothes off, more or less in time to the lurid music and the writhings of the snake. That, unsurprisingly, was my main memory; the secondary one was of John trying his hardest to peer through his steamed-up spectacles.

Back in Brive and Monsieur Amon, I think it was, one of the *Maire-Adjoints*, was waiting for me outside the *Hôtel de Ville*.[1] John had started to walk the 39 miles back to Brive, but then had had the good sense to telephone his correspondent's family, who had driven out to pick him up.

"*Vous êtes le **re-spon-sable** anglais!*"[2] Monsieur Amon stormed into my face in front of all the parents and students. So I was; but at that moment, I didn't feel it.

I have said before that I was never one of the 'in-crowd' and always found myself very much on the fringes – except, perhaps in two areas: drama and the exchanges with Brive-la-Gaillarde in France. Speech Day at School never had a prize for Drama. Throughout my seven years there, I only ever won one prize, a rather nondescript one, along with several others, for 'Contribution to School Life' – well, drama, I suppose – an AC-Delco sponsored award. I chose François Mauriac's biography of de Gaulle – more for the status of it, I think, than for its potential use since I never ever read it.

Yes, I tended to be a 'leader of the pack' when it came to the French exchanges, a leading voice in deciding what we should do, where we should go and in the singing of raucous songs on the coaches. Certainly travelling by myself as I had done in the Upper Sixth year gave me a sense of achievement, of independence which compensated, at least in part, for the fact

---

1   *The Town Hall.*

2   *You're the person responsible for the English!*

that I always wanted to be best in something, but never got there. It takes the wisdom of years to realise that there will always be someone better – and someone worse – than you, in whatever you do.

Perhaps the highlight of my year, was nothing to do with Brive, with Downside School, with teaching, with acting or with Gill Luff, but came as a result of a telephone call one lunchtime. It was Wednesday, 29th May 1968. I was out on the playing field at Downside School doing cricket with some boys (a male game only in those days) when one of the teachers ran out to say that my father had been on the phone and would I ring him back? Strange: Dad hated personal calls at Kent's[1], believing that work time was precisely that and domestic affairs had their place but not during the working day. Anyway, I phoned him and found that Ray, his brother, had offered him a spare ticket for that evening's European Cup Final match at Wembley but he, Dad, would pass it on to me. Was I was interested? Was I? Matt Busby's Manchester United versus Benfica of Portugal! You bet I was! United had taken the First Division championship the previous year and had won their way through all the rounds – it was all knock-out, no Champions' League, in those days – beating Real Madrid on aggregate in the semi-final. Denis Law, one of United's star players was out with an injury, but with George Best, Brian Kidd and John Aston up front, Paddy Crerand, Bobby Charlton and Nobby Stiles in midfield, Shay Brennan, Bill Foulkes, David Sadler and Tony Dunne in defence and Alex Stepney in goal, United were almost at full-strength, with everyone an international. Moreover, Charlton and Foulkes, along with the manager, Matt Busby, had survived the Munich Air Disaster ten years previously in 1958 and stood now on the threshold of Busby's lifelong ambition.

---

1   *George Kent Ltd, Luton.*

The first half passed without incident, but eight minutes into the second half, Charlton opened the scoring for Manchester United with a rare, headed goal. However, the lead only lasted for 22 minutes before Graça scored for Benfica. Benfica had a chance to win the match near the end of normal time, but Stepney made a crucial point-blank save from Benfica's international, Eusebio who, a sportsman to the end, congratulated Stepney. In extra time, Best put United in the lead again after just three minutes. Picking up the ball 25 yards from goal, he dribbled round the Benfica defence and their keeper and rolled the ball into an empty net. Kidd, who was celebrating his 19th birthday, headed United's third a minute later, before Charlton hit the fourth, hard from just within the penalty box. And we were sat on a level with the goal where United had put three away. It would be 31 years before Alex Ferguson led United to victory in the European Champions League. Thirty-one long, long years.

My future years were, meanwhile, becoming clearer as I had been offered a place at Coventry College, part off the diversity of Warwick, after attending an interview – during which I had to write an essay on why I wanted to become a teacher. Rumour had it that a girl, who had written about how much she liked children, was later told by an unsympathetic interviewing lecturer to go away and have some.

During the summer holidays and to earn some money for my transition to tertiary education, I worked under my Uncle Alwyn[1], up at Hawthorn Baker, a manufacturer of printing machine parts, the highlight of my day being when I got to take the parcels from his despatch department over to Luton station, taking the country route through the village of Caddington and thrashing the firm's little, grey Mini-van for all it was worth.

---

1   *Alwyn Parrott, my father's youngest brother.*

The one space where I would always feel quite at home without being at home – or, indeed, at anyone's home – was in the back lounge of the Forester's Arms up Chapel Walk behind the Methodist Church on The Square. In 1973 the pub's passing was mourned by many as it made way for a car park. The Forester's Arms was run by Conrad and Sylvia Eccleston and served mainly Whitbread Tankard ('best') and Trophy draught beers. My memory is of paying about half a crown for a pint of Tankard and two shillings[1] for a pint of Trophy. Your age was less important to Conrad than good behaviour and sensible drinking. By 18 I had my own tankard hanging up on a hook over the bar, waiting for Conrad to fill it. Occasionally, a little old man with bad teeth, called Harry, would sit at the piano in the lounge and we'd all have a sing-song: old music hall songs such as *Down at the Old Bull & Bush, Any Old Iron, Nellie Dean, Underneath the Arches, I'm Henery the Eighth I am, Maybe it's Because I'm a Londoner…* and so on. The non-teetotal Methodist Youth Club would meet there, including my cousin, Cheryl. No bigger than a standard lounge in a small terraced house, it had brown, padded bench seats which ran round the small room, a few round tables with ashtrays piled high, and some padded stools. Dim beiges, ochre yellows and dark browns from the open fire and copious cigarette smoke, mixed with the wafting odours of the Jeyes fluid from the tin-roofed gent's urinal outside and colluded to make the air a warm and gentle fug.

The best evenings were Christmas Eve. These were the years of strict pub hours, but on special occasions, the bar stayed open half-an-hour longer until 11:00pm (that made drinking-up time 11:30). We'd drink and sing and drink until about 11:20 and then dash down Chapel Walk, over High

---

1   *Half a crown, 2/6, is worth about £4 in today's wages, with 2/- about £3.20.*

Street South, through Priory Gardens and into the packed Priory Church for the 11:30 start to the Midnight Service. If you had kept an eye on the back seats, you would have noticed a constant procession of bodies nipping out of the church during the service to relieve themselves of an excess of Conrad's *Tankard* behind the gravestones.

Every year has its highlights and its depths, but this particular period of 12 months from leaving the Grammar School and going to University appears, on reflection, to have been notably significant. I've already spoken of France, females and football, and of Downside, drama and driving. In addition, on 30th September 1967 I unwittingly became a listener of the new Radio 2 and Radio 4 as the BBC had christened the Light Programme and the Home Service. The Third programme had, of course become Radio 3, whilst Radio 1 was the BBC's answer to the pirate pop stations which had sprung up in the sixties, several of which, like Radio Caroline, had been broadcast from ships in the North Sea, thereby avoiding the UK's broadcasting regulations. Although I listened regularly to *Round the Horne* and loved the *Julian and Sandy* sketches from Kenneth Williams and Hugh Paddick, the real world of the homosexual community – the word 'gay' was still some years from being used, and 'LGBT'[1] some 25 years away – was brought home to me for the first time by press coverage of the murder of the playwright Joe Orton by his lover Kenneth Halliwell, who had battered him with a hammer before killing himself with sleeping pills. Private homosexual acts between men over the age of 21 had been decriminalised on 27th July 1967. Prior to these two events, homosexuality had been a subject of fun and of mockery at school. Yes, there were boys who had been clearly interested in other boys, leading to casual

---

1   *Lesbian, Gay, Bisexual, and Transgender.*

groping 'behind the bike sheds' so to speak, but it had generally been viewed as a transient phase in their lives. If a boy showed any degree of 'camp' behaviour or interest, he would probably have been mocked, such as the one nicknamed "Bumbly" and who had to endure (unjustified) chanted cries of "Bumbly is a homo!" The murder of Joe Orton and the surrounding story seemed almost at once, and very properly too, to take away from me that joking, that jeering.

One television series, first aired in July 1968, is still being shown in repeats: *Dad's Army*; whilst I now live not far from the Colet Court Preparatory School where, in March of the same year, Andrew Lloyd-Webber and Tim Rice's first musical collaboration, *Joseph and the Amazing Technicolour Dreamcoat* was first performed. I was later, in my sixth year as a teacher, to direct the show at Haybridge High School in Worcestershire.

November 1967 was a bleak month for the economic well-being of the UK. Within ten days we had the outbreak of foot-and-mouth disease in the farming community, the 14% devaluation of the pound by Harold Wilson's government, and de Gaulle saying *Non* for the second time to the UK's entry into the EEC[1]. The UK's relationship with France did rally, however, with the unveiling of *Concorde*, the supersonic passenger aircraft which would, after several years of testing, grace the skies for 27 years[2]. Now, as I write, I have been on board Concorde – sadly, only as a museum piece at Bristol – and our break away from the EU is causing economic mayhem at all levels: industry, commerce and agriculture, all over again.

Violent demonstrations, especially outside their embassy in Grosvenor Square London, against the involvement of the United States in the war in Vietnam continued, with cries

---

1   *The European Economic Community or Common Market, now the European Union.*

2   *From 1976 to 2003, when Michael Bannister of my year at DGS and fellow-actor, flew Concorde's final flight as its Chief Pilot.*

of "Hey, hey L.B.J.[1] How many kids have you killed today?" Johnson was then followed by Richard Nixon who later resigned before he could be impeached over the Watergate affair. But it was a speech, widely viewed as racist, in April 1968 by the then Conservative Shadow Secretary of State for Defence under Edward Heath, Enoch Powell, which ignited a fierce debate about immigration and led to his sacking. It became known as the *Rivers of Blood* speech, a popular mis-quotation from the words Powell, a formidable classical scholar, took from the Roman poet Virgil when, talking about the apprehension he felt over the levels of immigration:

"As I look ahead, I am filled with foreboding. Like the Roman, I seem to see the River Tiber foaming with much blood."

That I became more interested in politics and moved to the Left – though my later student activity was, the more I regard it with hindsight, a need to 'belong', to feel a part of a larger organisation, rather than a deeply rooted belief – was largely down to that speech and to the furious reaction afterwards, both for and against Powell. Powell was no Hitler; that he was on the right of the Tory party was beyond question. It was not only his views on immigration along with his radical free-market economic policies which marked him out as a bogey figure: it was also the simplistic analyses offered by the national press where things were either black or white, good or bad – all very similar to the media reaction to Brexit and the question of immigration which was to loom large in 2016's referendum.

One good thing about 1968 was that the Kray brothers, London's most notorious gangsters, had been arrested on charges of murder, fraud and blackmail in May. Then, the criminals seemed largely home-grown, whereas the modern-day serious crimes of drug and people-trafficking, terrorism and knife-crime all have a considerable international element.

---

1   *Lyndon Baines Johnson, 35th President of the USA 1963-1969.*

Nowadays, transplant surgery is, if not common-place, then fairly routine, the main problem being getting enough organs to satisfy the demand. One of the great advances in medical history took place – on the 3rd May 1968. This was notable not for my nineteenth birthday but for when the first heart-transplant in the UK took place. The recipient, one Fred West, only survived for 45 days and it was not to be until 1979 when a really successful transplant took place.

And, as if to balance lives and deaths, only a week earlier, the 1967 Abortion Act had come into force, something which I remember feeling quite opposed to. Even to this day, it still creates both doubt and revulsion in my mind. In the case of abortion, I cannot accept the premise that we are the sole owners of our bodies and thereby able to do as we like with them. And yet. I cannot help but feel that if it were my daughter who had been raped and left pregnant, I might feel differently. By the same token, I am instinctively against assisted suicide, but would be the first to admit that I may have a completely different view when faced with the fatal, undignified and agonised future either of a loved one or of myself.

STUDENT YEARS 1968-1973

Coventry College of Education

Sunday 22nd September 1968 saw four of us in a grey Morris Oxford saloon, the same in which I had travelled on several occasions to Loftus Road, home of Queens Park Rangers. In the front were two of the club's foremost supporters: Ted Lippiatt, driving, and my close friend Graham, his son; with me on the back seat was Dad. In Ted's copious boot was a brand new green trunk with glinting brassy corners, edges, and a hasp and staple locked together by a dull steel padlock. It contained the beginnings of a new life for me: my clothes and toiletries, a small weekend bag (Mum had hopes that I would want to come home occasionally – oh dear!), a few books, some pens and paper, a French/English dictionary, and some ring-binders – we had been sent instructions as to what to bring. Up the A5 and then across on the M45 to the southern side of Coventry and to the suburb of Canley, mainly a working-class housing estate, where, on its edge and also on that of the Warwickshire countryside, lay the 1,400-strong Coventry College of Education, soon to be the School of Education of the University of Warwick. The Uni. itself was only just across the fields a few miles away and it was their Bachelor of Education (with Honours) degree course that I was to be following.

I remember feeling quite confident in myself. After all, I had just completed a whole year's teaching – quite successfully from what I had been told – and was about to further my prowess in my two best areas: French (main subject) and Drama (subsidiary). The college boasted a social hall for discos and general socialising, with a fully-stocked bar which would no doubt stand in well for Conrad Ecclestone[1]'s *Foresters Arms;* there was a large hall with a decent size stage, and a purpose-built drama centre, a good-sized library (this was long, long before computers and the internet), and a CCTV[2] suite, while the Modern Languages suite had a language laboratory, something which I was eager to try for the first time. It had its own stationery- and book-shop, as well as a small 'tuck' shop which sold cigarettes – Jim Cobbett, the student manager, was to make sure he had some *Disque Bleu* for me – toiletries, biscuits and other snacks. But then there was the 'personal', for want of a better word, side: there were three on-site halls of residence for males[3], but eight, yes eight! for females[4]. After the homogenous gender of Dunstable Grammar School, life was about to look up!

The City of Coventry Training College for Women had opened on the site in 1948, replacing the Men's Emergency College and had been set up in a former wartime workers' hostel to address a shortage of teachers. When I joined, the principal was still Miss J.D.Browne (1912-2009) who had been Principal of Coventry Teacher Training College (later called Coventry College of Education) from its inception in 1948. Joan Browne was a rather forbidding lady in the latter part of her career, with white-grey hair and glasses and a tongue which could lash and drip acid. She was held in great respect by all, not least for her

---

1   *See a previous chapter.*
2   *Closed Circuit Television suite of rooms in which students could be filmed and recorded teaching a class of imported children.*
3   *Gosford, Hampton and Knightcote.*
4   *Arden, Bericote, Compton, Dunsmere, Emscote, Felden, Loxley, and off-site: Maxwell.*

alleged reputation as an ambulance driver for the Republican side during the Spanish Civil War (1936-7), and also for her pioneering work in "showing what women could achieve, long before it was fashionable to do so[1]".

Her right-hand man or Vice-Principal was Gordon Lawrence, an astute, humane and kindly educator. Beyond the academic life of the College, the day-to-day well-being of the institution was in the hands of the college Bursar who was in turn in charge of the College Porters, led by the militaristically redoubtable Bill Street. Sir Francis Bacon once maintained that *Knowledge is Power*; for Bill, keys were power, as they were the agents whereby he could help your life, or make it a misery. Yes, Bill could be officious but he could also be kind – if you were on the right side of him. His job, and that of his colleagues, was difficult and made worse by demanding staff and thoughtless students.

Neither was Joan Browne always easy to deal with and did not suffer fools gladly – as I found to my cost when President of the Students' Union some three years later and ill-prepared for a meeting of the Academic Board. JD, as she was known, did occasionally find herself well out-of-step with modern trends, as in a dispute in my third year over, shall we say, students staying a long time – and occasionally overnight – in halls which were not for their gender. Whilst she did not wish to deter guests staying occasionally for the weekend – each hall had a 'guest room' which could be rented, she was keen to distinguish between proper guests and – in her view – illicit, nay immoral, stop-overs. She then issued a statement, part of which defined guests and visitors as follows: "A guest is one who stays the night; a visitor is one who comes and then goes".

---

1   *Estelle Morris, MP for Birmingham Yardley 1992-2005; Secretary of State for Education under Tony Blair, now Baroness Morris of Yardley. Coventry College 1970-74.*

That this statement was humorously misinterpreted goes without saying.

The issue was resolved shortly after one of the men's halls, Hampton, 'declared UDI[1]' i.e. defied any attempts to regulate the timing and the gender of those visiting. In the end, as was only practical and reasonable – it was impossible to regulate – students were allowed to come and go as they pleased.

I had been placed in K.53, sharing a double room on the third floor of Knightcote Hall with one Peter Parker, a generally genial, slightly rough and hefty rugby player from Manchester – and a City supporter too! Still, it was our given role to get on together for a couple of terms or so and get on we did, more or less. The allocation of rooms to new students, or 'Freshers', had probably been on an alphabetical basis, given that one Bob Prince – who was to become my closest friend there – was two doors down the corridor. Every student's room had its own wash basin and wardrobe and cupboard area which, in my case, separated my sleeping area from Peter Parker's. And we each had our own desk and chair, easy chair and bookshelf. There was a large cupboard or Trunk Room for suitcases and trunks in the middle of the corridor, opposite the kitchen area.

In those days – unlike today's spiralling of student debt – most students enjoyed totally free tertiary education. My room and all meals had been paid for and, even though I came from a comfortably-off family, I also had a grant of £90[2] per year from Bedfordshire County Council, ostensibly for books and other necessary educational expenditure – ha! Kitchen facilities existed for the interminable cups of coffee offered as everyone sought desperately to get to know everyone else, and particularly

---

1   *Unilateral Declaration of Independence – term used by the white minority government of Ian Smith in Southern Rhodesia, the future Zimbabwe, when it defied and split from the UK and the Commonwealth.*

2   *Roughly £2,600pa or £850 per term.*

those of the opposite sex, and for those who would delight in filling the upper floors with aromas of turmeric, coriander and chilli as the more established curry devotees showed off their burgeoning skills at the weekend. Showers and baths were in a separate area on each floor, along with a clothes-drying and ironing space. There again, it was not unknown in those days for a pair of jeans – close-fitting round the hips and thighs then flaring widely from the knee downwards (*Loons* were the trendy make) – to be washed while on their owner in the bath and then to dry whilst still remaining on that owner in order that, since jeans invariably shrank, the close fit could be made even tighter or more body-shape displaying. Every student's room had its own wash basin and wardrobe and cupboard area which, in my case, separated my sleeping area from Peter Parker's. And we each had our own desk and chair, easy chair and bookshelf.

Coming from a boys' grammar school and fairly sheltered home life, the freedom offered by this tertiary education came as a welcome release, a great sense of freedom and a feeling that a new life had just begun. I felt at home in Coventry College of Education. I could put posters on the walls (my half of the room, anyway) and, within the structures of our learning, were free to come and go more or less as we pleased. Throughout the rest of my life, I've never had any problem changing from one house to another and have been able to feel at home more or less wherever I have happened to be. Oh, we were bound by a timetable which, when compared to my university counterparts, resembled more a straitjacket than a freedom pass. In fact, it was not too dissimilar from a sixth-form timetable of today with precious few free periods – sorry, private study sessions. Timetables were even heavier for PE Wing students – those (girls only) who had chosen to specialise in Physical Education and for which the college was known for having a specialist course. We also did compulsory PE – only really to give us the wherewithal to do a spot of fill-in PE in a junior school, should we as future class-room teachers, ever be asked. Not only that, but it was at nine o'clock on a Monday morning, too!

Our studies in Education practice and theory with Miss Beryl Jones tended to be generalised in the first year, diverting to its four main areas, Philosophy, Psychology, History and Sociology later on. Then there was teaching practice in various schools throughout the Coventry area. I think I remember about a couple of weeks in the First Year rising to a full term in the Third. Of course I finally got to experience the rigours and delights of the Language Laboratory in the French department led by Brian Rigden, Bernard Kavanagh and an apt tutor for a student called Parrott: a certain Tom *Swallow*. The department had developed its own programme of work they called *Approfondissements*[1] in which a paragraph or two from French Literature was voiced and recorded on to reel-to-reel tapes – no CDs or even cassettes in those days! – and we each sat in our own little booth with our headphones on listening to the recording and then repeating it back in short phrases building into sentences. The tutor in charge would listen in to each of us at the click of a switch and correct our pronunciation. Thereafter, there would be exercises on chosen points of grammar and translation exercises, ending with a *rédaction imitative* whereby we would endeavour to write an essay in a style similar to the main text.

It was in these *approfondissements* that occurred my first disagreement with the French department. Fair enough, it was their job to ensure that the French we would subsequently teach should be standard in grammar, syntax and lexis, and pronunciation. It was in the latter that a problem arose. Most of my spoken French, most of the colloquial French, most of the most recent French I had learned had been in Brive-la-

---

1   *"extensions" or "deepenings".*

Gaillarde, a town which,, was also the place where a typical southern accent seemed to begin. Take, for example, this opening sentence from George Sand[1] which, because of the accent-argument, I still remember:

Et d'abord salut à votre septantaine, qui me paraît plus robuste que la vingtaine de bien d'autres![2] which then, in 1968, emerged from my lips roughly like this:

Et d'aborrr salut à votrrre septanntaineu, qui me parrraît plus rrrobusteu que la vengtaineu de bieng d'ôtrrreu!

Now I cannot claim that my accent and my transliteration are perfect, but it may give some idea. And yes, I did – eventually – bend to their wishes!

Day-time free-time tended to be spent, if not in one's room or in the Library – yes, books: no internet and Wikipedia for forty years or so – then in the Junior Common Room (JCR). Coffee and tea were, mid-morning and mid-afternoon, provided free of charge, served by kitchen ladies for whom a lovely and sometimes wicked sense of humour appeared to be a necessary job qualification. Morning newspapers were provided free by the Students' Union, which had its office there as well as its Social events' office and print room which, in those days, produced multi-copies from Gestetner stencils, cut on typewriters where the ribbon had been dispensed with. It also invested in a proper cutter whereby any document, e.g. a picture, could be fed into it, a stencil cut, and then copies printed on the Gestetner ink-drum-printer. And we could get coloured inks! Totally primitive compared to today's computer print-outs but a certain student I knew, cut a stencil of a £1.00[3] note and mixed a shade of green ink…

---

1   *The pen-name of the 19th century female writer Amantine Dupin.*

2   *And firstly, greetings on reaching the age of 70, at which you seem stronger than do many others at 20!*

3   *Worth about £20 in today's wages.*

The JCR also had a free-play juke-box on which the track that seemed to be playing for ever was the Beatles' *Hey Jude*. By the time of Third Year term-long teaching practice, that seemed to have changed to *My Song* by Elton John. It was also in the JCR that, for the first and only time in my life, I reached the quarter finals in a competitive sports event – and damaged my self-winding watch at the same time with my wrist action – the College Table-Football Knockout Competition.

Outside the JCR, in the main concourse of the central block were the Hall, the two shops, the Porters' Lodge, and the Dining Hall with long refectory tables where, when chicken was being served, one always waited for one of the serving ladies to ask you:

"Do you want stuffing, love?" The answers ranged from the jocularly humorous to the downright rude.

I must put in a word for Frank Shaw. In these impersonal days of account managers and customer service, of everything-must-be-done-online and press-one-for-this, press two-for-that, Frank Shaw was like the advert on television whereby an avuncularly friendly bank manager would step out of the wardrobe, give you good advice and hopefully solve your financial problems. Frank Shaw didn't live in my bedroom but in a branch of Lloyds Bank in Earlsdon, an area of Coventry between Canley and the city centre. Once a week, on a Wednesday, he also inhabited, along with an assistant, a Portakabin-type hut on the college site, the better to deal with our finances. Of course, these were the days long before computers and online banking and ATM's had yet to be invented. The main way of paying and of getting cash was by cheque. You had a cheque guarantee card – up to £30 – for purchases in shops, or you presented a 'Pay Cash' cheque in a bank – and a bank where there were usually five or six people waiting to serve you! Customer service was not always brilliant, but at least it was there, unlike today. The advent of plastic, or credit, cards was in 1966 with the arrival in the UK of Barclaycard, followed in 1972 by Access. As a student, I qualified for neither as credit was infinitely more difficult to get in those days than ever it is now. The one thing I learned in my first term was the error of my ways in asking my parents to open any of my post that came home to Dunstable. I had my father on the phone:

"I've just opened your statement from Lloyds [*oh shit!*] and found that you're ten pounds[1] overdrawn. Your mother and I have never been in debt in our lives – save for our mortgage – and we expect you to be equally careful with your money. I've paid off the £10 and put another £5 in as well – and that's got to last you!"

All mail was, in future, directed to my college address!

The Easter holidays of April 1969 were memorable for one family event: Granny and Grandad's Golden Wedding. The whole Parrott family was able to gather together first at a hotel in Woburn for lunch and later at Ray's house in First Avenue, Dunstable. Not for the first time was Ray able to come out with a few appropriate words when the family was watching Granny and Grandad moving slowly down the garden path towards Ray's front door and he remarked.

"I bet Dad moved Mum a bit quicker than this fifty years ago!"

"Life…"

I have remarked before on the new found freedoms that college life afforded. Perhaps the one word I have not yet used is the word opportunity. In my case, a certain level of opportunity tended to be rather abused, especially in my first year while I

---

1   *Worth about £300 in today's wages.*

savoured the novelty fruits of student life. Rather than form bonds of friendship with various groups through shared activities and interests, drinking in the bar or doing politics or dope, my drug of choice was females and I tended to move from one to another in a manner which, I think, gave me a poor reputation at the time and on which I now look back with no little embarrassment and shame. As the first year passed, so my weekends eventually became rather dull, lonely times as I played no sport, did not possess a strong work ethic and had no constant companions, save for Bob Prince when he wasn't being sporty or with Chris, his girlfriend (and future wife).

Yes, there was the college bar and disco hall with its dart-boards, its ever-changing brightly coloured oil shapes projected on to the ceiling and the small group of Geordies always at the same table, always getting pissed on Newcastle Brown. Saturday evenings in the Social Hall would inevitably be divided between those who insisted on playing darts, those who just sat with the intention of drinking the whole evening, and those who preferred to demonstrate how 'cool'; they were by their moving and dancing to the latest music. The real intentions of probably 95% of those there – mainly males, but also some females – would emerge at about 11:30pm when the lights were at their lowest and the disc jockey would put on an appropriate "smoochie" such as the Moody Blues' *Nights in White Satin* whereupon most of the afore-mentioned would take to the floor in a sweaty mêlée of lips and hands with the one they thought they could most likely entice back to their room.

The television room was always packed on a Thursday evening for *Monty Python's Flying Circus*, the now legendary cult comedy series. I'm not sure whether I actually enjoyed it and laughed out loud or whether I just went along with it all because everyone else did. Back in my room, it was the Beatles' double *White Album* that I played constantly on my reel-to-reel tape recorder. Others had stacks of vinyl LPs, stereo decks with massive speakers and kept showing off about tweeters and woofers. But for a freer and more anonymous atmosphere of red-and-green psychedelic swirls and the background music of Fleetwood Mac or Lindisfarne, I preferred to go to the Airport Lounge at Warwick Uni. The journey there and back, however, was not terribly easy and it usually had to wait until later in my fourth year of five when I had my first car.

Mind you, I still felt like a fish out of water in so far as my appearance was concerned. Whilst I did possess tops and bottoms which didn't look too much out of place in the general student *mêlée* and my hair was getting longer day by day (it eventually reached my shoulders), trendy I was not and still did not possess a pair of jeans, (preferably Levi's, the mark for those not willing to go as far as Loons with the very wide-flared bottoms). There again, a teacher-training college or School of Education was always likely to be more conservative in its appearance than a university campus.

Beyond the college itself, the Dolphin pub on the Canley Estate occasionally proved a welcome alternative – a working-men's pub where, on a Saturday evening, the ladies would all be in their best frocks and coats and handbags, while the gents swanned around in three-piece suits and watch chains, marred only by cigarette ash or a beer-stained tie. Occasionally the college itself would host a decent live band instead of a disco and I remember listening to jazz with George Melly and John Chilton's Feetwarmers, or getting lightly stoned just on the heavy atmosphere of Osibisa (*criss-cross rhythms dat explode wid 'appiness*), such was the quantity of cannabis being smoked that evening. My weekends might also get disrupted by the shouts that there was a phone call for me. In those pre-mobile days, we relied on the pay phone situated in the entrance of each Hall of Residence and, if it were answered – which was not always the case – then shouts for the person requested would echo up and down the stairs, or a message would be taken and stuck on the noticeboard or, more kindly still, slipped under your door. My parents had the number, though their first comment was always to ask why they hadn't heard from me.

I did manage to involve myself to some extent in the drama in the college – and beyond what I did as my subsidiary subject under Larry Surridge, Walter (?), and Rita Human. In my first year, I auditioned for *A Man For All Seasons* and was offered the part of Richard Rich, the upstart who, having been nurtured by Thomas More, turns against him and, at Thomas Cromwell's behest and bribery, perjures himself over Henry VIII's divorce with Katharine of Aragon, causing the inevitable guilty verdict and More's subsequent execution. John Hurt had played the role in the film with Paul Schofield as More, and has always been, since then, my favourite screen actor. Later, I was to musically direct *A Funny Thing Happened on the Way to the Forum*, and play the baddie, Sir Despard Murgatroyd, in Gilbert and Sullivan's *Ruddigore*, but it was in the first term of my second year that I spent far too much time away from my academic work when I directed what had been the first play I had been in at the Grammar School – and one I still love greatly: TS Eliot's *Murder in the Cathedral*. Jeffrey Kissoon, today a professional actor of some note, played Thomas Beckett as we performed both in college and in the still new Coventry Cathedral, murdering Thomas at the High Altar in front of the backdrop of Graham Sutherland's tapestry of *Christ in Glory*. Although directing, I was also to play the 3rd Tempter and 3rd Knight as the student due to play those roles had not, with a fortnight to go, learned his lines and I sacked him. The performance in the Cathedral led the Coventry Evening Telegraph's reviewer to comment that I might be using the Trinidadian Kissoon to exemplify the "modern upstart Beckett". No: he was just the best actor in the college at that time. The one thing we all had to learn – Jeff, my Chorus of Women of Canterbury, the Priests and we Tempters and Knights – was how to cope with an acoustic whereby everything you said was subject to a three-second echo. In the end, we either ignored it or, if possible, chose a point on the floor down the centre aisle and towards the back where we literally aimed our voices. I also put the four Tempters in white and black, full-face masks denoting their character and their temptation and removing them from the reality of the rest of the cast. As I was to be away in Paris during the following term, the Drama Department of the College kindly allowed me to write up my production plans and analysis as one project of some 20,000 words, as I was to miss their in-house assessment in the coming term.

I also had the opportunity of singing Britten's *St Nicholas* cantata again, this time with the college choir and boosted my singing abilities with the freely-given help of Janet, the wife of minor English composer Graham Whettam. But it was the end of year 'Going-Down Ball' that was the highlight of my years at Canley. With black-tie and long dresses we were transported in coaches to the Solihull Civic Centre which we took over for the evening, and with tickets costing less for a pair than for singles, great fun was had in pairing up for the evening as it frequently led to even greater 'fun' back at college afterwards. We, along with the staff, gathered in all our fineries in two halls and three bars to the music of discos, minor bands and headline groups for the late-sixties/early-seventies such as Fleetwood Mac, the Moody Blues, Fame and Price, and the Kinks.

Life at Coventry College and at the University of Warwick was, for me, as close as I ever got to the 'permissive sixties' denied to me in Dunstable and at the Grammar School. I didn't really work much harder than I had done at school, doing little more than the bare necessity to get by safely and provide myself with a means to an end – the qualification to enter my chosen profession – but it did prove something of an awakening in me of things social, political and sexual. As I have already said, there was no internet and, of course, no social media. Whilst the internet might well have helped in my essay-writing, I cannot for the life of me imagine how social media would have improved the social life I had at the time – unless that betrays my present attitude to such as Twitter and FaceBook!

La Vie Parisienne

Having been immersed in Eliot for the first term of my second year, the second term, January to March 1970, was to be equally, if not more, absorbing. Those of us doing French as our main subject were sent to the *Institut Britannique* in the heart of the *Quartier Latin* and near the *Sorbonne* to follow a course in *Langue et Civilisation Française*. We stayed in rooms in the *Collège Franco-Britannique* in the residential student area towards the south of Paris known as the *Cité Universitaire*[1]. Reached by the then *Ligne de Sceau* of the Metro and on the *Boulevard Jourdan* in the 14th *arrondissement*[2], this wonderful site housed thousands of students in blocks each for both French students and for those of a particular nationality. Most of the blocks also had a facility open to students from all over the *Cité*. We had a bar which sold bottles of *Kronenbourg* and *Tuborg*, along with hotdogs, made by thrusting a piece of *baguette* over a spike to warm it, then dipping a large rubbery frankfurter in mustard and inserting it into and through the bread until it protruded from the other end. I need not add the number of comments which would be made as to its somewhat phallic appearance. I should add that

---

1   *British Institute; Latin (University) Quarter; French Language and Civilisation; Franco-British College; University Village.*

2   *An administrative district of Paris.*

it was after an evening indulging in these hotdogs and beers (well, I was serving behind the bar...) that I found out how to tell the cleaning lady that my basin was blocked. She took care of it, bless her: probably wasn't the first or the last time a student had thrown up in his own basin. For a spicy omelette one could go to the *Maison de l'Inde*, whilst we usually took breakfast in *Mexique*[1] where fried eggs – *oeufs sur le plat* – seemed to be the norm. There was also a massive student canteen in a purpose-built block in which, should one enter committing the heinous crime of wearing a hat, the tradition was that the perpetrator be bombarded with shouts of *"Chapeau! Chapeau!"* and by pieces of *baguette* until the offending hat was removed.

In the *Quartier Latin* itself, my standard lunchtime fare was a North African sandwich roll or *Pan Bagnat* with salad, tuna, egg and olives, or perhaps the stereotypical toasted cheese and ham *Croque Monsieur*. There was much still to be learned though, as I found out when sampling the delights of a new self-service restaurant on the Boulevard Haussmann. My starter of what I thought to be a *chou-fleur au gratin* or cauliflower cheese turned out to be a rather unedifying dish of sheep's brains in a white sauce!

In the March of that year, 1970, Mum and Dad had said that it would be a nice surprise for Granny if I could ring her from Paris while they were down with her and Grandad on the Saturday evening of her birthday. This I did, and Granny, bless her, could really not get over the fact that I was in a foreign country and speaking to her.

"In Paris? It sounds just like he's in the next-door room." That same month, Mum made her very first visit abroad when she and Dad came to Paris by train for the weekend. Over three days, the three of us covered all the main sites, walking – and much to Mum's credit, given her arthritis – for miles!

---

1   *India and Mexico.*

During that term, I binged on Paris, getting to know it better than any place other than Dunstable and which, after London of course, remains my favourite city. From the *Cité Universitaire* in the south, to the *Marché aux Puces*[1] up at the *Porte de Clignancourt* in the north, via *Montmartre*, and *Pigalle*, and from the *Bois de Boulogne* – well before the modernist structures of *La Défence* – in the west to the *Bois de Vincennes* in the east, I must have walked in all twenty of its *arrondissements*, spiralling outwards from the 1st near the *Louvre*, round the *Marais* to the 4th (*Île de la Cité*), the 5th (*Quartier Latin*), 6th (*St Germain*), 7th (*Tour Eiffel*), 9th (*Opéra*) and all the way round to the posh 16th (*Place de l'Étoile*, now the *Place Charles de Gaulle*, and the *Arc de Triomphe*) the 18th (*Montmartre* and the *Puces*) to the 20th (*Vincennes*) in the east. Paris, of course, was still reeling somewhat from the anti-government, anti-de Gaulle student demonstrations and riots of *les èvènements de mai '68*[2] and it was clear in the *Quartier Latin* from where the cobblestones ended and where the tarmac began just where the barricades across the roads had been and where the *pavés* had been sourced to hurl at the CRS[3]. I still remember an advertisement for Kleenex tissues in the Metro which said

"*Zut! un rhume. Chic! un Kleenex*" and which had been altered to read

"*Zut! un CRS. Chic! un Pavé*"[4]

Whilst my spoken French was steadily improving, I did learn one lesson from a monsieur Chevalier (not Maurice!) who taught *Phonétique et Diction Française*[5] at the *institut* and who, one Saturday morning when we both found ourselves down in the bar of the *Institut* chatting, invited me back to meet

1   *Flea Market.*
2   The *"Events" of May 1968.*
3   *Compagnie Républicaine de Sécurité, or riot squad.*
4   "*Damn! a cold. Great! a Kleenex.*" "*Damn! a copper. Great! a cobblestone.*"
5   *French Diction and Phonetics.*

his wife and have lunch (sautéed kidneys). I readily accepted the invitation and was sitting in his car going out east towards *Vincennes*, he rabbiting away in his excellent English, when a lady driver cut him up.

"Bloddy seely cow!" he exclaimed. Suddenly, he ceased to be almost English and reverted in my mind to the Frenchman he always was. I've always remembered that when tempted to swear in French – even if I now think my French accent better than his English one was!

My sojourn in Paris, albeit for barely three months, gave me a deep, visceral, love for the place. In my mind, Paris will always remain as it was at the beginning of the seventies – without *La Défense*, or the *Boulevard Périphérique*[1], without the arterial roads running alongside the Seine or the miasmic tunnels of the *Réseau Express Régional* which used to be just a suburban network rather than cutting its way through the city (however helpful to Parisian commuters that may be!). Paris had suffered little structural damage in the war, compared to London which had endured and survived the Blitz, though on the Metro one was still expected to give up ones seat to a *mutilé de guerre*[2] and one didn't have to walk far before coming across a neatly attractive wall placard commemorating some *résistants* who had been *fusillés par la SS*[3]. Although the Paris of the post-war era and the fifties was changing slowly, there was much that was still the same. Mine was a slightly old-fashioned view of the French capital, seeing it not so much through the eyes of Johnny Halliday, Sylvie Vartan, Françoise Hardy or Antoine[4], but more through those of one who, for me, is the ultimate

---

1   *Ring Road.*

2   *War-wounded.*

3   *Members of the resistance... shot by the SS [World War II German elite corps].*

4   *Rock, pop and folk singers.*

Marianne[1] or symbol of France: Edith Piaf. It was her songs I hummed, walking through the fleshpots of Pigalle and climbing the hill to the *Sacré Coeur*. I hummed her in *Gibert Jeune*, the second-hand book sellers on the Boul'Mich (Boulevard Saint-Michel) where I bought my copy of *Grévisse*, the bible of French grammar, along with dozens of French *Livres de Poche*[2] thinking they might come in useful one day. I hummed her in the cafés over *un verre de rouge* and *un sandwich à jambon* or *un pan bagnat*[3], and the inevitable *Gauloise* or *Gitane*. I hummed her all the way round the *Puces* as I hunted for bargains in the flea market and particularly amongst the then-trendy – and smelly – embroidered Afghan fur coats; and I hummed her in the Metro carriage first thing in the morning as the aroma of *Bien-être* mixed with *Gauloises* and *eau de javel*[4] wafted over me. Those three months rated as probably the best of my young life. I had sufficient funds to enjoy myself, was foot-loose and fancy-free, and not really looking forward to the academic grind at college along with the inevitable teaching practice.

Back in Coventry, I completed my year as an RAL – Resident Approved Lodgings. After spending my first two terms resident on site in Knightcote Hall, I along with the rest of my year, had been turfed out into digs with landladies throughout the Coventry area. I had found myself – alone, this time, not sharing – with a sweet old dear in Green Lane some 2½ miles from the college. This was in Stivichall to the south of the city but near the bus route which I joined at the Burnt Post Pub on Charter Avenue to the College at Kirby Corner Road. Bob

---

1   *The female symbol of France, modelled on Brigitte Bardot.*
2   *Paperbacks.*
3   *A glass of red, a ham sandwich and a round bap filled with salad, olives, boiled egg and tuna, a speciality of the Nice area.*
4   *A cheap cologne, cigarettes with 'caporal' tobacco, and a common cleaning disinfectant.*

Prince and Dave Parker were a few doors up the same road. Thanks to Paris, though, I only spent two terms in Green Lane.

May 1970 saw my twenty-first birthday celebrated, thanks to Mum and Dad, in the former coaching inn that was the Saracen's Head in High Street South, Dunstable. All the family were invited, along with friends from the Forester's Arms and a few friends more of Mum and Dad's than mine such as Grace McKintosh. It was quite a staid, conventional evening with a buffet and drinks and was the last family get-together to have both Granny and Grandad, as well as Aunty[1], all there. I remember being particularly pleased with three presents I received: a Simon and Garfunkel album from Fay and Alwyn, a set of sherry glasses – I still have one! – from the Rev. Vernon North and his wife, Beryl, and a typewriter from Mum and Dad. This was a good twenty five years before computers and laptops were commonplace and they had sought out, with the help of Arthur Buck, the local Scout Commissioner and director of a typewriter firm, a good quality *Imperial*. It had a metal body and zip carrier-case, and 'dead keys' for French accents whereby on, for instance, hitting the '^' dead key, the carriage would not advance, allowing me to then immediately type an 'a' thereby getting an 'â' and advancing the carriage. I loved it and used it for years. My handwriting, poor since my primary years, never recovered, and was never to improve. Now I do all of my writing on a keyboard and perhaps writing by hand is, for the vast majority of people, a rapidly fading art. Albeit via keyboards, I did write a series of four hundred and sixty-four letters, some two million words about anything and everything in our lives, to my friend Rosemary Askew over twenty years – and that is, today, quite exceptional by any standard. I still keep them all, both on the computer and, along

---

1   *Sarah and Harold Parrott, and Doris Child.*

with hers, in hard copy. I wonder if, in 50 years' time, whether anyone reading this will have kept all the emails they had ever sent?

Being twenty-one also meant that I qualified for the odd part-time job, one of which was with Hertz, the car-hire company. It seemed then easier for hire cars to be left wherever the hirer wanted, rather than returned to the central office, and I became part of a team which would be picked up in a mini-bus and dropped off at various outlying points and told to return the car at that point to Hertz in Coventry. The pay was derisory, but it meant that I could at least practise my driving. Fortunately, I didn't let Hertz or myself down in any way.

Getting Plastered

But, before I could use my new typewriter to complete my basic teaching qualification, I was to find myself in hospital looking like an Egyptian mummy. By the seventies there was still only one curry house in Dunstable, and when we met up, home from University or wherever during the summer holidays, Terry Cosgrove, Graham Lippiatt, others and I would go out for a few beers, then get a take-away curry from the *Gulistan*, our first Indian restaurant which stood between the Nags Head and where the old Town Hall had been until 1966. Prior to the arrival of the *Gulistan*, post-pub food had usually been limited to 'fish and sixpennorth'o'chips', but this was the beginning of the Indian take-away curry or Chinese era. My house being central to Dunstable, I'd ring Mum and Dad to put the plates in the oven to warm, and we'd take it all back to Kingscroft Avenue as Mum and Dad loved to see everyone. One memorable occasion involved us ordering Vindaloo curries and Terry asking for them to be "Extra hot, please." To which the very young, small, Indian waiter replied "Would you like it to kill you?" "Yes!!!" said Terry. It almost did.

It was on one such evening in the summer of 1970 and while I was spending a few weeks in gainful employment in the comptometer[1] office at George Kent Ltd., thanks to Dad, that I was coming home from one such summer holiday drink out in Redbourn. Michael Griffin was in Terry's Luton-bound car and I was in Stuart Fraser's along with Graham Lippiatt and his girlfriend Sally heading back to Dunstable. When we left the pub we were under the impression for some reason that Terry's car had set off first so we were encouraging Stuart to put his foot down to try and catch up. Of course we never did catch a glimpse of the phantom we were chasing and, because we going too fast in a futile pursuit, that's when the accident took place. The irony is that we found out later that Terry's car was actually behind us and that they must have passed the scene of the accident without realising we were off the road.

Stuart's grey Triumph Herald, a car not renowned for its reliability or for its ability to hold the road, left the A5 on a bend south of Markyate. Basically, we were all very lucky. The row of telegraph poles on the A5 were on the side of the road that we went over. A few feet either way and the car would have hit one, with much more serious consequences. We were also fortunate that as we slewed across the A5 out of control, nothing was coming the other way. I remember seeing a hedge rushing towards us and then nothing until I came to, sitting on the damp ground on the opposite side of the car from which I'd been sitting – seat-belts were not compulsory in those days . The car had gone through the hedge and down, some four or five feet into a field, rolling over sideways completely. Sally had some cuts and bruises and had been thrown out of the

---

1   *A large mechanical counting and printing device for maintaining accounts with suppliers and clients.*

car; Graham had cuts to his legs and a broken collar bone, and remained in the car all the while with the radio playing. Stuart was found propped up against the front passenger door, a cracked bone in his back. My head had been cut and my neck hurt. A lot. I made it up the bank to try and attract some attention – this was some twenty-five years before mobiles became common-place. Eventually someone called the ambulance service and we were taken to St Albans Hospital. There, despite complaining about my neck, they didn't check it at all, only dealing with the cut on my head of which my significant memory was it being stitched up and the stitches being pressed flat against my skull with a pad. That hurt. The next day, my Uncle Alwyn[1] brought Mum and Dad to collect me and take me home. My neck was growing more and more painful, though, and over the next week I found it more and more difficult to sleep at night or to sit in a chair without loads of cushions to support it. What was more worrisome was that over that week, my head gradually tilted to one side.

The GP who took the stitches out of my head sent me straight down to the Luton and Dunstable Hospital where I was admitted after x-rays on my neck showed that cervical vertebræ 3 and 4 had been dislocated. Very fortunately, neither had touched the spinal cord. In the orthopædic Ward 1, a harness was fitted round my jaw and hooked behind my head onto the back of the bed, which in turn was upended, allowing my body's weight to pull down from my neck thus allowing room for the said vertebræ to slip back into position. The intense pain of this was eased by drugs which, according to my parents, made me less than welcoming to the friends and family who came to see me. Granny, however, was not allowed to come as it was felt that, not being over-steady on her legs, she might reach out suddenly, grab something to

---

1   *Dad's youngest brother – Mum and Dad never drove, never owned a car.*

support herself and there were so many pulleys and cables on almost every bed stretching broken leg bones back into place. Fortunately, my harness worked as the alternative would have been drilling holes in my skull to allow the fixing of a frame which would have done the same job only another way: by connecting weights on to a cable over a pulley and over the back of the bed.

After five days, the bones were declared restored in situ and I was sent home with a surgical collar and instructions about how to stand, sit and lie. A week later I was back in the orthopaedic ward to be plastered round my head, neck and upper body with only the crown of my head, my face, my arms and my abdomen free. I was told it was called a Minerva Jacket, though nowadays, I think it would probably be all plastic and chrome-steel struts and strapped round with velcro. A square opening was cut in the back of the neck to allow the ensuing operation to take place. Bone was taken from my right hip and grafted between the two offending vertebræ which were then bound with silver wire which remains in place to this day.

Mum and Dad were understandably appalled to see, when they came in later that day, this white effigy sitting up in bed amidst drips while at my side lay a massive pair of sharp what looked like wire-cutters: the explanation being that they were there in case they needed to cut the plaster open quickly in order to resuscitate. Great. However, I was up the next day, carrying my drip and drain to the loo as I hated using a bedpan. After five days – and sooner than the hospital expected (they had originally estimated up to a fortnight) – I was sent home with a three months-in-plaster sentence.

That summer was warm and they had lined the plaster with a sort of thick woollen vest which, combined with my trickling sweat, set up an irritation which only Mum's knitting needles, strategically inserted and agitated, could solve. I could not wash, nor cut my hair, nor shave. Nonetheless, I did chance my arm and took out to dinner at The Sugar Loaf one of the nurses who had attended me in the orthopaedic ward. Fortunately, after 4 weeks, and before I went back to College, they offered to change the cast for me – and I could wash and shave! I was resident in Knightcote Hall again at the time and had to sleep sitting upright. I think it safe to say that no-one had ever seen or experienced this Minerva Jacket at the college and I proved something of a curiosity. I wore the new one until the end of November and then a plastic collar for a while. I had asked the plaster technician if I could keep the first, blood-stained (from the operation) plaster and took it back to college where, appropriately lined with silver foil and with a light-bulb inside, it was to adorn my window sill and look out over the College grounds. If that were not ghostly enough, the sight of me in October walking slowly into the Methodist Church on The Square in Dunstable with my parents, Grandad, Aunts and Uncles behind my Granny's coffin and garbed from head to waist in white plaster, caused a few hearts to miss a beat, or so I was told.

At the time of the car accident I, in common with quite a few lads of my age, carried a condom around in my wallet – another example of how I followed the Boy Scout motto of *Be Prepared*. Needless to say, this condom had been in my wallet for some considerable time and had rubbed clear its unmistakeable outline in the leather. After all the business at St. Albans hospital when, as was normal, my personal effects were gathered together and handed to whomever came to collect me, I noticed when I got home, that the said condom was missing. The hospital would not have removed it, so that left only one other possibility – the person who collected my effects: Dad. Nothing was ever said, no comments were ever made, but I never got my condom back! Perhaps he had been taken short, so to speak, himself? Had I ever tackled him about it, he would no doubt have voiced his disapproval and said that he hadn't wanted Mum to see it.

And so I passed into our final year at the end of which we would be qualified teachers, though I and others would be staying on for one more year for the B.Ed (Hons.) degree. I seem to remember not doing terribly well in my Easter term-long teaching practice. Not that I couldn't hold a class' interest and attention, or communicate or even actually *teach* them something. It was that I didn't do it the *way* they wanted it done and the manner in which they deemed *appropriate*. Oh, I passed it all right – a B grade, I think.

While all that was going on, Dad had, quite sensibly, put the matter of the accident in the hands of his solicitors, Gutteridge & Co, who occupied the oldest premises in Dunstable save for the Priory Church, next to the Anchor Gateway. Stuart Fraser had admitted that he had taken the bend too fast – 'driving without due care and attention' they called it in those days – but I had to wait and have my neck and other parts tested after about a year to see how, if at all, my movements were restricted and to make as assessment as to future deterioration etc. for "quantum" to be assessed by a barrister. For the time being, and sensing my new-found freedom, I announced that I had obtained a holiday job working for Coventry Parks Department for a few weeks during the summer holidays, thus severely limiting the time I could spend home in Dunstable. This lack of time at home was to go down like a lead balloon at 28 Kingscroft Avenue. Not only that but, unbeknownst to them – such was my arm's-length relationship with my parents that I hadn't even consulted them, i.e. sought permission from my 'bankers' – I had also committed myself to taking a year off before completing the final year of my B.Ed (Hons) course…

President

I don't know how the idea came to me. I think it was just one of those things that I fancied doing and, once the idea had taken hold and I had decided how interesting, how much 'fun' it might be, and probably that it would give me some sort of status, a purpose and a belonging (which, looking back, I must have craved), I decided to go ahead with it, regardless of the fact that it would mean another year at Coventry College, another year for Mum and Dad to put up with me and, moreover, a year away from what I was beginning to find exceptionally boring: my courses in Education and French. I talked to the existing incumbent whom I knew tolerably well: Ian Tunnicliffe, and went to a few meetings. I had little fear of standing in front of meetings, large or small or of public speaking – which I already thought I did fairly well (he boasted!) thanks to the acting. The only other person after the same thing as me was one Roland Baker. Whilst I had hair down to my shoulders, invariably sported a roll-neck jumper and cord jeans, Roland was very different both from me and from your average student in that he invariably wore a tie, a sports jacket, and grey flannels, had short hair combed and parted neatly, was a member of the right-wing Monday Club and consequently espoused views which were poles apart from the left-of-centre norm frequently found in a teacher-training establishment. I canvassed round all the Halls of Residence, something not normally undertaken, spoke at the one hustings organised and, although I forget the ultimate margin, was in the end elected the next President of the Students' Union, 1971-1972.

This was a sabbatical post in that I was given a year off my studies and a full grant – about £120.00[1] for the year –

---

1   *About £2,500 in today's wages.*

plus expenses for going to NUS[1] conferences etc. In the other posts available, Cynthia became Union Secretary and Ken, the Treasurer. Angie Donnelly was in charge of Internal Affairs and Gordon Young, someone with whom I did not get on at all, looked after External Affairs. Gordon was later to resent my incursions into national student politics and tried to get me removed, even to holding a vote of no confidence – which, I am pleased to say, I won, though I'm not sure that I deserved to. Stevie Deverill was our Social Secretary and, as such, responsible for booking all the entertainments throughout the year: discos, live bands and the end-of-year 'Going-Down Ball'.

That I could chair the regular meetings of Hall reps was beyond doubt, but my commitment to the nitty gritty of daily life – like making sure the newspapers were in the JCR[2] – eluded me as I became more and more interested in the wider student movement. My first NUS conference had featured a young Labourite, Jack Straw[3], in the chair as national president, soon to be followed by one Digby Jacks, a ginger haired and massive-bearded member of the Communist Party of Great Britain (CPGB). Whether it was he who was instrumental or a couple of friends I made who were at Warwick Uni., but I soon joined the Communist Party and went along to my first meeting on the Canley Estate, keen to be seen as a supporter of the working class of Britain but soon doubtful about my commitment as it was made clear to me that I would be expected to take on some organisational role in the Party as that was the 'best way' to learn about the Party, its work and its history. Whilst I managed to dodge that commitment – I didn't attend any more meetings – I took great satisfaction in *belonging* to something which, when others knew of it, made

1 *National Union of Students.*
2 *Junior Common Room.*
3 *A Labour Party Home Secretary and later Foreign Secretary in Tony Blair's Government.*

them look twice at me – though, with hindsight, probably more out of derision that admiration. And it is, perhaps, wanting to be seen as a *part* of something that harks back to my secondary years when I wasn't, save for the odd play, part of *anything*.

Possibly the best NUS conference I attended was a 'Presidents' Informal' in Edinburgh to which I drove via Manchester University, meeting DGS friend Terry Cosgrove there for lunch on the way. The discussions in Edinburgh I forget; the sampling of malt whiskies at half-a-crown[1] each I do not. But whilst I enjoyed the camaraderie, the carousing and the endless jawing of NUS conferences, they were, if anything, an eye-opener and a total farce: a make-believe world of student power, whatever that might be, which tried to align a load of largely privileged, middle-class students, with the 'downtrodden' working classes. For the life of me, I just could not accept that those who ground out their lives in factories and pits could ever take seriously the fortunate few who could while their time and their grants away in student bars pretending to be 'leftier than thou' – and I was one of them. Conferences were battles, not so much against the intransigence of Heath's Tory government and his Education Minister, Maggie-Thatcher-Milk-Snatcher[2], but internal fighting for supremacy between students in the Socialist Labour League, in the International Marxist Group, in the International Socialists, in the CPGB and so on. Labour Party members were outside all that and considered hopeless, revisionist capitalists. The Federation of Conservative Students was ignored completely and treated as though it didn't exist. The real enemy was the one closest to you, who failed to follow exactly the same working class, far-left socialist, revolutionary ideology and dogma as you

---

1   *2/6 (12½p) or £2.50 in today's wages.*

2   *Margaret Thatcher, later Prime Minister, had done away with school milk for primary-aged children.*

did. There was no real discussion, just interminable, formulaic speeches. I joined the occasional march such as the one through the centre of Birmingham where we seemed to be shunted through interminable concrete underpasses where the more fundamentalist brethren delighted in pointing out what they assumed to be, and may well have been, MI5 long-lens merchants on the rooftops. That particular march was anti-Thatcher, aimed at the education policies of Heath's Government and started at Aston University to the refrain of the Strawbs' *Part of the Union*. No-one seemed to appreciate that the song was meant to be satyrical! The march was accompanied by a parody of Rod Stewart's song *Maggie May*:

"Wake up, Maggie, I think I got something to say to you: Fuck off!"

Such was the depth of serious political analysis by the student movement.

I was also selected to speak at one NUS conference about the James Committee Report on the future of teacher training and felt my status enhanced when a reporter from the communist daily, the *Morning Star*, approached me afterwards and wanted some details, saying that I would have front page coverage the next day. I failed. Not because what I had said wasn't the party's view or because I hadn't spoken well. No. It was because I, unlike another 'comrade', hadn't mentioned 'the working class'. I had not learned that speeches on behalf of The Party were deemed to be successful only if formulaïc and stuck to an agreed vocabulary and content. I think it was then I finally decided not to continue my subs to the CPGB.

Just as I felt totally disillusioned by my experiences of far-left student politics, so I do not have a very roseate view of my year as President. My focus was not, as it should have been, the well-being of my fellow students, but more my own adventure into the new world of student politics. Neither was I well prepared for some of the other duties I had, such as my membership of the College's Academic Board, remembering full well the moment that the Principal, the doughty Joan Browne, condescendingly requested – perhaps due to my hitherto lack of contribution – the 'student view' on a topic and turned to me – and I had nothing of any consequence to say.

If I had begun my year determined to throw myself full-heartedly into the left-wing maelstrom that was student politics, I ended it in ultra-conventional fashion: a wine and cheese evening to which, in addition to my closest colleagues in the Union, I invited a selection of the lecturing staff, including Joan Browne the principal, and my parents who seemed even more delighted than they had been during Dad's mayoralty to get an invite to a Royal Garden Party.

Did this sabbatical year, this presidency, do me any good? Yes, in that it took me into a world of which I had no previous knowledge and which, with all its rules and standing orders, its cultures and compromises, and the amoebic nature of its principles, gave me a good grounding in some form of political life, but one into which I was never to enter during my working life. Yet there was to be an occasion, nearly fifty years later when, as Chairman of the Board of Directors of the (Harrod's) Village Estate Management Company Ltd. where we live in Barnes, I thought back frequently to the lessons I had learned as a student president. Many bore absolutely no relevance whatsoever of course, but having had to deal with one or two students whose aim was not the good of the union but their own sense of status and importance, not to mention using or ignoring the rules for their own ends, it may have been some help in dealing with one, a Russian, whose end was only his family's economic well-being in the maximising of their rental profits of their several properties. *Justitia omnibus fiet*[1] as the Dunstable motto proudly has it. And yes, that is what I tried to

---

1   *Let Justice be done to All.*

do whilst keeping everyone together as I hate division. It was also the nearest I was ever likely to get, then in my late 60's, to my Grandfather's and Father's work on the borough council.

Escort-ing Helen

There was, however, one other aspect of which I have not yet spoken, and that was my burgeoning love-life. After my ill-spent first year and my forays into drama and France, it took until my presidential year for things to turn around. And turn around they did, namely in the shapely form of Helen Sinnett. Helen lived in Felden Hall and was one of her Hall's reps on the student council whose meetings I chaired. Helen's home was in Torquay where her father was Head of English at a secondary school. Up until that year, our paths had never crossed and when they did so I was to find that she was already engaged to one Alistair, a bachelor fortunately not of our Parish and with whom she met up but once a month at the most. Bright eyes, a winning smile, long brown hair (a deal longer than mine though that was down to my shoulders) a cashmere top, a mid-calf length suede skirt and deep-red suede boots – those are my visual memories of the Helen I knew and wooed like mad that year. Not that I had to make that great an effort as I believe her faith in the existing engagement was already becoming stale and was, with a few hiccups, about to die. She soon became a regular visitor to K.53, my large room in Knightcote and the one I had originally started off in, sharing with Peter Parker, but of which I now, as President, had exclusive use. I think I planned my every move, not necessarily well in advance, but remember assessing words and deeds for their likely maximum effect, being close and loving one moment or pulling back and seeming to give up or to play 'hard to get' the next. Looking back at this stage, I sometimes wonder whether it was all just an adventure, a game I needed to win; whether I was more interested in chasing the quarry than in catching the prize, but I think that would, in all reality, be unjust and too harsh a judgment. Hindsight can be a cruel weapon in that our memory is not always accurate or complete and can block whatever suits our current psyche.

By Easter, life had moved on apace. My settlement from Stuart Fraser's insurance company following the accident had come through via our solicitor and I had been awarded £1,200.00 – about £25,000 today – in compensation for 'pain and suffering'. I had been through various independent assessments and had, of course, been making ample use of the fact that my neck might not tilt sufficiently to enable me to play my 'belovèd' violin again (or, in reality, for the first time in about six years!). Still, that wasn't a bad amount and I went straight out and bought myself a pale blue Ford Escort 1300 – RNX 589F: don't you always remember the registration of your first car? – for just under half that amount, and then spent another £40[1] on a rather nice reddish-brown leather blazer: something I had always wanted. These were the days before I had any sort of plastic and, having found this jacket, the shop wouldn't accept a cheque so I had to bus back to College, and get Ken the Union Treasurer to cash a cheque so that I could complete the purchase.

But I could also be downright stupid in spending this new-found fortune. On some strange whim I thought it would be rather good to possess the ultimate symbol of my surname: a real, live parrot. Thus, from a pet shop in Coventry, I came back to college with a large cage containing Percy, an African grey parrott which boasts a bright red tail. Eventually, and at least three years later (and after he had bitten my father) I passed him on to someone I knew through Droitwich High School,

---

1   *Over £800 in today's wages.*

my first teaching post, and who was moving down to a small-holding in Cornwall.

Having a car parked outside Knightcote was a considerable status symbol and had tremendous practical value. Of course, it was easier to pop down to Dunstable for the day, perhaps a Sunday, have a good lunch, get given some petrol money, and then drive back again. Or for more nefarious purposes such as driving K – an amiable sort who regularly won the college table football competitions and who was a bookie's runner in his off-moments – up to his supplier in one of the halls on the main Warwick University site. There I watched as the supplier carefully weighed down to the last gram various types of hash and grass and then ferried him back again to Knightcote, gratefully accepting a spliff as my reward.

Status symbols can come back to bite you, though, as on the day when, finding myself blocked in, I decided to drive down on to the grass bank in front of the hall in order to escape via the end of the lawn. Unfortunately, the weight of the car combined with the slippery grass meant I slid down and ended up broadside-on to the wall of the hall, much to the merriment of several onlookers and had to get myself removed and repaired as a result.

On the brighter side, Helen's engagement was behind us and we were 'an item' with me being invited down to Torquay at Easter to meet her parents, Ron and Mary, and her two younger brothers, Roger and Richard. On the chosen day during the holidays that I was to go down to Torquay to meet Helen's parents, I gave my Dad a lift to his work in Luton before heading for Devon. Mum and Dad were still to meet Helen and Dad was talking to me – quizzing me – about her in the car.

"You seem to be quite keen on her, then?" Heaven forfend that he should use the word 'love'!

"Yes, I am." The answer would have been the same, anyway.

"Well... Don't do anything to... to... *rush* matters." Which was his way, probably, of saying "Don't get her pregnant." I didn't. Get her pregnant, that is. Not for another seven years.

The end of my presidential year also coincided with the end of Helen's training and her qualification as a teacher and she quickly found her first job in a village primary school just outside Coventry. We also decided that I should live out of college and, with Helen, rented a two-up-two-down in Harnall Lane East, just round the corner from where Coventry City's football ground was until 2005. I remember our budget then was £7.00 a week for the rent, and £5.00 for food and other expenses.[1] This arrangement was kept, quite deliberately from both sets of parents who believed – for their own sakes, we thought, given that they were all very traditionally conservative when it came to sex and living together – that we were sharing a house with two other girls. I had my own room, Helen shared with another girl who was also a teacher, and the fourth had the front room downstairs.

"That's lovely, dears! Why don't we come up and visit you one Sunday?" Mary, Helen's mother, beamed. Ah. Problem. The solution was to kill two birds with one stone and invite my parents on the same day. The two sets of parents could meet each other and Helen and I would beg and borrow to make the house look as though four people were living there. Books, photographs, ornaments, cases, trunks, chairs and tables were borrowed and arranged. The appointed day came and went. All seemed a tad bemused that four people could exist in such a small space, but appeared to accept what we presented to them. What they thought in the depths of their hearts was left – at least to us – unsaid. In a strange sort of way, they were probably grateful that we apparently cared for their

---

1   *£140 and £100.00 in today's wages.*

sensitivities, that we didn't thrust it in their faces or flaunt it.

Later, I was to take her home to Dunstable for the weekend. No one talked of the sleeping arrangements but I knew my parents only too well and didn't dream of discussing it with them: Helen was to sleep, alone, in the third bedroom. On the Saturday evening, she and I had been out for a drink up the Forester's. By the time we got home, Mum and Dad were already in bed; I was a tad peckish and so quickly made and toasted a cheese sandwich. Helen and I sat and chatted while I ate and then went up to our respective rooms. Just before I got into bed, I popped into Helen's room – quite innocently, I should add – to say goodnight. Immediately, I heard my father's meaningfully pointed voice:

"Roger, have you turned the grill off?"

"Yes." I called back and continued talking to Helen. A couple of minutes later:

"Roger, are you sure you turned the grill off?"

"Yes, I did!." More talking until:

"Roger, I think I can smell something burning…"

Mum was clearly unhappy and had kept nudging Dad to persuade me to leave Helen's room. I did, and went downstairs to check. All was fine, of course. I returned to my own room and my parents slept contented that 28 Kingscroft Avenue's reputation had not been sullied.

My final year at Coventry College concentrated solely on Education – and, of the four main areas[1], I had chosen the Sociology of Education – and French. Unfortunately, the French department had been the exemplar object of a fairly vitriolic article on grading and assessment I had published in the Student Union journal, *Boeufmerde*[2]. I had little enthusiasm

---

1   *History, Psychology, Philosophy and Sociology.*

2   *Made-up French for 'bullshit'.*

for returning to their tender mercies and requested of the authorities a change to Drama as my main subject. This was denied and so it was back to the *Approfondissements* about which I have already spoken, and the works of Baudelaire, Mauriac, Camus, Balzac and co. Returning to academic work after a year of swanning around in union politics was not easy and I struggled with work deadlines, and with preparation for classes, staying up all night on more than one occasion to get an essay done, cutting up all my hand-written notes and sellotaping them in order and then thrashing away on my birthday typewriter throughout the night, gulping coffee and getting through numerous *Disque Bleus*. I did not do well: my marks were low; I claimed I'd 'lost' my Sociology of Education special study because I had not left myself anywhere near enough time to complete the reading, research and writing, and it was only thanks to the kindly tolerant lecturer, Les Bell, that I struggled through to a Third Class Honours while the French Department hadn't wanted any more than a 'Pass' for me – and they had their doubts about that!

As much as I loved my Ford Escort and as much as it was proving a boon in so many ways – though I had pranged it again, broad side-on (again!) against a stone bridge on one frosty morning while taking Helen to school – and although it was prone to the gear lever coming out in my hand in the busiest parts of Coventry, I nevertheless needed some more cash so sold it. I first laid hands on an old and very rusty, tatty Ford Anglia with holes in the floor and a bolt I fitted myself to keep the driver's door closed. A policeman eventually told me to get it off the road and so from a small garage and petrol station I knew in Earlsdon, I bought a little, red, second-hand Mini with an impressive-looking dashboard – though the rest of the car wasn't up to much.

Helen and I were married in the June of 1973 in Cockington, the pretty tourist village just outside Torquay and treated ourselves to a one-night stay at the Waldorf Hotel in London before Helen had to go back to her school on the Monday.

My degree ceremony was held in Coventry Cathedral where three years earlier we had performed Eliot's *Murder in the Cathedral*. I don't think Mum and Dad cared a fig about the 3rd class honours: they were just glad that I'd got a degree, a means of getting a job for life with prospects and with a pension, such were Dad's criteria and he'd wrapped himself in that thick layer of cotton wool ever since he'd come out of the RAF in 1946. Only once to my knowledge had he toyed with the idea of moving and that was when he saw the job advertised of bursar to a major Symphony Orchestra. He couldn't bring himself to risk the possibility – inevitability – of George Kent Ltd. finding out that he was looking elsewhere when some people were being made redundant there. He also seemed to prefer the older, paternalistic, patriarchal system of management that was still current at Kent's.

I, meanwhile, was about to start my professional career as a teacher of French, Scale 1, at Droitwich High School in Worcestershire.

Epilogue

Over twenty years after starting my teaching career and after that day in Cockington, I was sat one Sunday in my flat near the River Severn in Worcester with Mum, Dad and Eve[1]. They'd come to join me and Sarah and Heather, my daughters, for the day. I was 44, divorced, living on my own, and a very disillusioned senior member of staff at Pershore High School who was spending his every spare moment with the Worcester Swan Theatre, the Worcester Operatic and Dramatic Society, the Malvern Festival Theatre, with a group that performed murder mystery events in restaurants and hotels and with another group providing regency banquet entertainments. For some time I had been giving thought – not without encouragement from those who knew me best – to a change in my career, in my life. Nearing seven o'clock, Eve, who was driving, said.

"Well, I think we ought to get our coats on, now."

"Just a moment," I said, "there's something I need to tell you." There must have been something in the tone of my voice as my father's face was a picture, expecting bad news. Was I about to emigrate? Had I found another wife and hadn't told them? Was I seriously ill? Had I realised that I was gay? No, I announced that I was giving up teaching to widen and deepen my life-long interest and go to drama school to become an actor. All those criteria of steady job with a pension, a house and no

1   *Mum's sister, Evelyn Smith, née Estwick.*

debts save for the mortgage he had nurtured since leaving the RAF were suddenly shattered in his son. Mum just sat, fearful of the worst, but with a rather strange look on her face.

"Why?" was my father's only, furrowed forehead-shaking response.

"Because I don't want to get to 60 and look back and think 'If only…'" was my reply to that perplexed and worried man.

And Mum, who always regretted never having had a career of her own, said,

"Oh, I know exactly what you mean!", bless her.

Appendices

PLAITING

Until her final days when she bemoaned her fate in losing my Dad, Mum was always one to count her blessings and the benefits of being in a democratic country with a good health system, and of the great advantages of going to school and having an education At one stage, later on in her life, she wrote down this little piece which, she said, her Granny[1] had learned at school in about 1870 and had subsequently taught her. Luton and Dunstable were centres of the straw-hat industry (hence Luton Town FC being known as The Hatters) and my Grandad's company, Parrott & Jackson, began life making cardboard boxes for the hat industry.

In the poem, Dunstable is where straw is plaited (a plait used 7 strands of straw) and Luton is the centre of the hat making industry, i.e. where the plaits are sewn together into hats. It is set in the first part of the 19th century:

Beside a country cottage gate and sitting in the sun,
I saw a girl of eight years old, and a tiny little one.
Each left arm held a loop of plait, fast growing by a score,
And quickly moved their fingers small as I drew near the door.
"Well done, my little maid," I said unto the elder one.
"Is that your little sister there, so busy at her score?"

---

1   *Ellen Alice Child, 1863-1956 – "Mummisgranny"*

"Yes, sir," she said, as from her mouth another straw she took,
"And that's my brother Billy there, a-playing by the brook."
"Do children plait so young?" said I, "Yes, sir, in course they do.
There's Billy, he are less than she and Billy, he plaits too.
When Father had the fever sir, we little money got
Till a kind lady buyed all our plait and then we got a lot.

But mother splits the straws for me, and she does more 'n that,
She clips the ends, and mills it too, afore she sells the plait.
Then Mother takes all that we made, whether it shines or snows,
To sell it all on market days. To Dunstable she goes.
And Mother says if I makes haste and grows,
That I may go to Luton, sir, where everybody sews."

"Can you read this little book which in my hand I hold?"
"No, sir," she says, "but I means to try, that is when I are old."
"What! don't you go to school ?" said I. The child hung down
    her head;
"Oh ! Please sir, we don't go to school, we has to earn our bread."
I sadly turned away and, musing o'er the chat ,
I sighed that children are not taught to read because they have
    to plait.

CHRISTMAS GAMES

I'll Sell My Bat and I'll Sell My Ball

A ring is formed with one in the middle who is the "drummer".
Everyone sings:

I'll sell my bat and I'll sell my ball,
I'll sell my spinning wheel and all;
And I'll do all that ever I can
To follow the drummer wherever I can.

Then the drummer adds: "*I can play the [instrument]*"
Anyone who does not immediately imitate the action –
or know what instrument it is – of the "drummer" must pay a
forfeit/is out/takes the place of the drummer.

Fish, Fruit and Flower

A list is produced of the above plus countries, rivers, towns,
cakes, puddings, sweets, birds animals etc. etc. A letter is
chosen and you have to name each item on the list beginning
with that letter. Points for each one and especially for unique
ones (i.e. one which no-one else has got) may be awarded…

Consequences

Everyone has a piece of paper and a pencil and begins by writing a Man's Name, folding it over so it cannot be seen and passing it to the person on the left who then adds "… met [woman's name]". The process continues with the place they met, what he said to her, she said to him, he gave to her, she gave to him, The Consequence Was, and The World Thought, before they are all folded up completely, tossed in a pile and everyone draws one out and proceeds to read the often nonsensical, occasionally rude, "story".

Last Will and Testament

A similar procedure to *Consequences*, except that the categories are who died, when, where, what of, what they left (several items), and to whom they left them, and any further comments… Expressions of disgust usually arise when the "Wills" are read out.

Adverts

Adverts are cut out of magazines and newspapers beforehand and the name of the product either cut out or obliterated and the names have to be guessed.

Adverbs

One person leaves the room and the rest choose an adverb (e.g. slowly, happily etc.). That person comes back and asks each of the rest int turn to perform a simple action. From the way they do it, the person who has come back has to guess the chosen adverb.

Faces

Faces from newspapers, the Radio Times and magazines are cut out, pasted on sheets of paper, numbered and everyone has a pencil and paper and writes down who they think it is.

Charades

One person (or a small team) choose a word, a book, play, song or film title, give the number of syllables (words) or words (title) and then act out those words or syllables for the other people or team to guess.

Come and Sit in My Chair

Half the people leave the room. Those remaining stand behind chairs conveniently placed, armed with a rolled-up newspaper and each chooses the person who should sit in their chair. One by one, those outside are invited in and everyone invites them to sit in their chair. If the person chooses the wrong chair he or she is thwacked with the newspaper.

1950's TV

Adventure

The Adventures of Robin Hood
Lassie
The Adventures of William Tell
Ivanhoe

Children's

Andy Pandy
Blue Peter
Muffin the Mule
Playbox
Crackerjack
Popeye the Sailor Man
Bill and Ben the Flower Pot Men
Watch with Mother
Mr Pastry
Pinky & Perky
Zoo Time
Billy Bunter

Crime

Dixon of Dock Green
No Hiding Place

Perry Mason
Highway Patrol
Boyd Q.C.

Western

Wells Fargo
The Lone Ranger
Gunsmoke
Wagon Train
Bonanza
Rawhide
The Cisco Kid
Champion the Wonder Horse

Drama

Emergency Ward 10
Classic serials – various, e.g. *Oliver Twist*

General Entertainment

Double Your Money
What's My Line?
Sunday Night at the London Palladium
Six-Five Special
Take Your Pick
This Is Your Life
The Black and White Minstrel Show
Candid Camera
The Good Old Days

CHILDREN'S FAVOURITES

with Uncle Mac (Derek McCulloch) Record request programme, BBC Radio Light programme, Saturday mornings:

The Banana Boat Song / Day-O	Harry Belafonte
You're a Pink Toothbrush	Max Bygraves
When you Come to the End of a Lollipop	Max Bygraves
You Need Hands	Max Bygraves
Tulips From Amsterdam	Max Bygraves
A Mouse lived in a Windmill	Max Bygraves
Rudolf the Red-nosed Reindeer	Max Bygraves
Don't Jump off the Roof, Dad	Tommy Cooper
Mad Dogs and Englishmen	Noel Coward
Hole in the Ground	Bernard Cribbins
Right said Fred	Bernard Cribbins
The Runaway Train	Vernon Dalhart
Does Your Chewing Gum Lose its Flavour	Lonnie Donegan
My Old Man's a Dustman	Lonnie Donegan
My Boomerang Won't Come Back	Charlie Drake
Mr Custer	Charlie Drake
The Auctioneer	Leroy van Dyke
The Gnu Song	Flanders & Swann
Hippopotamus Song	Flanders & Swann
Transport of Delight	Flanders & Swann
When I'm Cleaning Windows	George Formby
St George & the Dragonet	Stan Freberg

Ying Tong Song	The Goons
George, Don't Do That	Joyce Grenfell
The Teddy Bears' Picnic	Henry Hall
The Blood Donor	Tony Hancock
The Lion and Albert	Stanley Holloway
Three Little Fishes	Frankie Howerd
The Ugly Bug Ball	Burl Ives
The Owl and the Pussy Cat	Burl Ives
I Know an Old Lady	Burl Ives
Big Rock Candy Mountain	Burl Ives
Robin Hood	Dick James
Ugly Duckling	Danny Kaye
Tubby the Tuba	Danny Kaye
Sparky's Magic Piano	Lee LeDoux
Nellie The Elephant	Mandy Miller
Ballad of Davy Crockett	Fess Parker
How Much is that Doggy in the Window	Patti Page
The Laughing Policeman	Charle Penrose
Puff the Magic Dragon	Peter, Paul & Mary
My Brother	Terry Scott
Goodness Gracious Me	Peter Sellers, SophiaLoren
Hello Muddah, Hello Faddah	Alan Sherman
Mole in the Hole	The Southlanders
Twenty Tiny Fingers	The Stargazers
Little White Bull	Tommy Steele
Christopher Robin at Buckingham Palace	Ann Stephens
Donald, Where's Your Trousers	Andy Stewart
Hand up your Sticks	Kenneth Williams

PRIMARY YEARS' BOOKS

Peter Pan	JM Barrie
Rupert Annuals	Alfred Bestall et al.
Jennings & Derbyshire (various)	Anthony Buckeridge
Alice's Adventures in Wonderland	Lewis Carroll
Detective fiction – various	Agatha Christie
Just William (various)	Richmal Crompton,
The Adventures of Robinson Crusoe	Daniel Defoe
Oliver Twist	Charles Dickens
Christmas Carol	Charles Dickens
The Black Tulip	Alexandre Dumas
The Wind in the Willows	Kenneth Graham
The Adventures of Robin Hood	Roger Lancelyn Green
King Arthur	Roger Lancelyn Green
The Biggles Adventures – (various)	Capt. WE Johns
Just So Stories,	Rudyard Kipling
The Jungle Book	Rudyard Kipling
The Call of the Wild	Jack London
London	Arthur Mee
Winnie the Pooh	AA Milne
The Scarlet Pimpernel	Baroness Orczy
The Fifth Form at St Dominics	Talbot Baines Reed
Black Beauty	Anna Sewell
Treasure Island	Robert Louis Stevenson
Kidnapped	Robert Louis Stevenson
Tom Sawyer	Mark Twain
The Adventures of Huckleberry Finn	Mark Twain

Looking at History	RJ Unstead
Around the World in 80 Days	Jules Verne
20,000 Leagues under the Sea	Jules Verne
Ben Hur	Lew Wallace
Swiss Family Robinson	Johann Wyss
The Sea Wolf	?
No Famous Five or Secret Seven (Enid Blyton)!	

ASHTON VOLUNTARY PRIMARY SCHOOL

A Brief History

The building of 'The Ashton Elementary Schools' as they were then called had begun in 1861 and they were opened just over three years later. There were two schools, one for boys and one for girls, in the same building. There were about 90 children in each department. Mr. Frederick Hatt was Headmaster of the Boys' School and had two pupil teachers. It consisted of one large schoolroom, 103ft by 20ft, and one smaller classroom, 14ft by 20ft. Miss Page was in charge of the Girls' School with the help of three pupil teachers. They had three classrooms, one 51ft by 20 ft and two 14ft by 20ft. One of these latter was used as the Managers' meeting room when needed. Both schools employed a few Monitors at a time, at 1 shilling per week. Pupil teachers worked under the direction of the Head teachers. They had to teach in the style of their Head and keep control without shouting at or striking the children.

In 1870 a survey of existing Elementary education provision showed that the Ashton schools were by then catering for 301 boys and 159 girls. Funding appeared to be dictated by the results of the previous year's examination which had a constricting effect on the curriculum. The children were examined annually on basic skills and the Inspector's report commented on the running and discipline of the school.

Teachers were therefore under considerable pressure to ensure that their children met required standards in reading writing and arithmetic. The one headmaster who failed to secure the full grant for the school was a Mr. Alfred Wire who became Headmaster of the Boys' School in 1873. He subsequently resigned and the Managers made no immediate moves to replace him, leaving the Headmistress of the Girls' School in sole command of both boys and girls. She found that the boys were "behaving so fearfully bad that not knowing what to do" she "dismissed them till next morning while awaiting further instructions". A temporary Headmaster had to be found quickly! To be fair, Mr. Wire was something of a pioneer in education, trying to widen the curriculum to give the boys science lessons. In doing so, the standard of the all-important basic skills had diminished, but in time such progressive ideas became more widely accepted and children were given a more liberal education.

The diocesan Inspector examined the children in knowledge of the Bible and the Catechism. The Rector of Dunstable taught the boys Scripture. Boys and girls were taught songs, which they performed when visitors came to their schools. Children were also taught geography and the girls spent much time learning to sew. Physical education was led by an army drill instructor, one Sergeant Field. A future head, Mr. Knight, also introduced agricultural studies which must have been helpful to many of the boys who lived on farms and were expected to help with the work on them as the Bedfordshire economy then was largely rural.

By 1894, boys were studying history and having to learn poems for repetition, such as *The Homes of England* by Felicia Hemans. or Sir Francis Hastings Doyle's *The Loss of the Birkenhead*.

One of the greatest problems all schools faced at this time was that of attendance. In 1871 the Inspector's report noted that the Headmistress of the Girls' School was doing excellent work but such efforts were hampered by the fact that children attended school; for barely half the week! Outings organised by churches in the summer month, attractions such as the Statute ('Statty') fair or a travelling menagerie which visited the town would see many stay away from school. The prevailing agricultural economy would also see large numbers of children required to stay at home to work in the fields in addition to the official harvest holidays. Heavy rain would deter the many without weather-proof clothing; weather would also affect those who had no shoes. Parents also had to pay a nominal sum sum for each child to attend school and many then stayed at home in times of hardship such as the recession in the straw-plaiting trade which affected many people in the Dunstable area.

The curriculum gradually widened and by the 20th century, drawing had been introduced, the girls went to cookery classes at the local Cookery Centre, and shortly afterwards, the boys went to woodwork. Miss Wilkes, the Headmistress of the Girls' School was keen that girls should be given some instruction in the management of a home and family. On one occasion, a Health Visitor was invited to the School and she "gave a lesson to the elder girls on How to Undress, Wash and Dress a Baby" – in this case a real, one-month-old baby was brought along to the "intense interest" of the girls. During this time, most of the teaching was done by unqualified pupil teachers who would be trained by the Head and also given further education in a variety of subjects for at least five hours a week by him or her, usually early in the morning before school began. Heads would also give demonstration lessons which were then expected to be copied by the pupil teachers who were reprimanded if found to be 'loud speaking' since it was important for them to talk quietly when more than one class was being taught in the same room! Over the turn of the century, the pupil teachers (unqualified) were gradually replaced by qualified Assistant Mistresses and Assistant Masters. Mr. Knight, mentioned above, who was Headmaster of the Boys' School for 37 years, was particularly commended by the Inspectors for the careful instruction he gave his pupil teachers.

In the first decade of the 20th century, both schools had risen to three Assistant Masters or Mistresses along with a pupil teacher and one monitor. Miss Wilkes had organised the Girls' School into four classes, each having between 28 and 38 girls. The two lowest classes were taught together in the large schoolroom which, although more crowded than the other rooms was at least warmer in winter when, yes, even the ink in the ink-wells froze! During the First World War, the Boys' School lost two Assistant Masters to the forces and the school was under-staffed throughout this period.

A picture of the school in the immediate post-World War I era was given by Vera Day in a 1974 copy of the *Bedfordshire Magazine*. Her father, Frank Sharman, was headmaster and she could peer through the "church" windows of the school to see the boys running to arrive before the bell stopped ringing from its steeple. A few of them , she noted, had iron hoops which she coveted as she only had a wooden one. Swopping cigarette cards was a popular activity and she needed the number 19, the 'Common Mallow', to complete her set of country plants called *Struggle for Existence*. She even tried to get a Mr Smith, a tobacconist, to peek inside a 6d packet of ten Players, just in case! She and the other girls would wear white, starched pinafores and were taught by a Maud Wilkes, her sister Emily and others. When school had finished for the day, Vera would play among the empty desks which to her smelt of inkwells and chalk and read adventure story books by GA Henty and RM Ballantyne from the school library. Above the fireplace were carved deep into the stone the warning words, appropriate to a Church of England-aided School: "The fear of the Lord is the beginning of wisdom" and she would stand on the Headmaster's platform and imitate her father saying "Grace!" and imagine dozens of pairs of boots clattering to attention, their voices intoning "Be present at our table, Lord" before marching out to the strains of *The Minstrel Boy*.

On 31st December 1935, after 71 years as an elementary school, the two schools were combined, and some alterations were made to the building so that The Ashton Church of England Junior Mixed School could open on 6th January 1936. The initial roll was 329 children and Miss J.M. Mapley was the Headmistress. The rest of the staff consisted of three Certificated and five un-certificated teachers. The first week was occupied in establishing the routines of the new school and Miss Mapley described the rain during this time as "incessant"

At eleven years of age the children transferred to one of the local senior schools.

During World War II, education was much interrupted by air raid warnings – Dunstable was never bombed, however – and by the advent of evacuees from London as in some instances, timetables were halved in quantity the better to accommodate the new influx). Children were initially sent home when the sirens went, presumably to avoid a mass catastrophe! Later, corridors were strengthened to act as shelters. The passing of the 1944 Education Act resulted in the school becoming a Voluntary Aided (VA) Primary School, taking children from the age of five to eleven. By the end of the 20th century the building had become unfit for purpose.

At the end of the Summer term 2006 the school moved to new buildings on part of Ashton Middle School's (and the former Grammar School's) playing field, a move made possible only by allowing – of all things! – an Aldi store to be built on the Church Street site of this lovely school.

ARITHMETIC

1. Add:

£.	s.	d.
9	13	7½
+4	18	11

2. Subtract:

£.	s.	d.
7	6	3
-1	15	6¼

3. Multiply

£.	s.	d.
5	9	2½
	x	8

4. Divide

7) £18 1   4½

5.   In my pocket I have eight coins: half a crown, a two-bob bit, a shilling, 6d, 3d, a penny, a ha'penny and a farthing.
How much have I all together?

6.   The coal man delivers 4 sacks of coal, each weighing 56lbs. Coal is priced at 15/8 per hundredweight.
What is the total cost of the coal he has delivered?

7.   I have 2lb 12oz of potatoes, a pound and a half of

apples, one and a quarter pounds of sausages and a small cabbage which weighs 13oz.
What is the total weight of my shopping?

8.   I go to a timber yard and buy four odd lengths of wood. Two lengths each measure three foot six inches, one is 4 ft 8 in., and the fourth is 5 ft 9 in.
What is my total length of wood?

9.   I divide seven yards of material into four equal curtains.
What is the length of each curtain?
(Give your answer in yards, feet and inches)

10.   Three boys measure their heights: Jack is 4 ft 11 in. Sam is 3 inches taller than Jack, but Leo is 8 inches shorter than Sam.
How tall is a) Sam; and b) Leo?

"L" STREAM DGS 1961

Michael Abbot
Steven Barker
Alan Beat
David Bray
Robin Burgess
Michael Cheshire
Peter Chiodini
Keith Clements
Terry Cosgrove
Stuart Fraser
Michael Griffin
Michael Hepworth
John Howard
Graham Hadfield
Graham Lippiatt

Roy Lipscomb
John Mawson
Neil Parr
Roger Parrott
David Pateman
?? Paye
Keith Sawyer
Malcolm Skipper
Graham Smith
John Smith
Richard Spring
David Tearle
MalcolmTupper
Roy Wilcox
?? Wright

ARITHMETIC ANSWERS

1. £14. 12. 6½

2. £ 5. 10. 8¾

3. £43. 13. 8

4. £ 2. 11. 7½

5. 6/4¾

6. £1. 11. 4

7. 6 lb 5 oz.

8. 17 ft 5 in.

9. 1 yd. 2 ft 3 in.

10. a) Sam is 5 ft 2 in
    b) Leo is 4 ft 6 in.

BIBLIOGRAPHY

Austerity Britain 1945-1951, David Kynaston, Bloomsbury 2007

Bourne and Bred, Colin Bourne, Book Castle, 1990

Days from a Different World, John Simpson, Pan 2006

Family Britain 1951-1957, David Kynaston, Bloomsbury 2009

Fry Chronicles, The Stephen Fry, Penguin 2010

History of Modern Britain, Andrew Marr, Pan 2008

Keeping On Keeping On, Alan Bennett, Faber & Faber 2016

Making of Modern Britain, The Andrew Marr, MacMillan 2009

Modernity Britain 1957-1962, David Kynaston, Bloomsbury 2014

Our Times, A. N. Wilson, Arrow 2009

Proud Heritage, Vivienne Evans, The Book Castle 1999

Utterly Exasperated History of Modern Britain, An John O'Farrell, Black
    Swan 2010

Short History of Dunstable School 1888-1963, A F.M.Bancroft, Dunstable
    Grammar School

Stop the Clocks, Joan Bakewell, Virago 2016

This Boy, Alan Johnson, Corgi 2014

1940's Childhood, James Marsh, History Press 2014

1950's Childhood, Paul Feeney, History Press 2009

1950's Childhood, Derek Tait, Amberley 2013

1960's Childhood, Paul Feeney, History Press 2010

Report by HM Inspectors, Min. of Educ., HMSO 04/53

Bedfordshire Magazine 1974, Vera Day, Bedfordshire Magazine 1973

Back in Time For Dinner, BBC2, 2015

1966 Dunstable film, East Anglia Film Archive

WEBSITES

Looking at everyday things in the past

http://www.whirligig-tv.co.uk
https://www.retrowow.co.uk
https://images.google.com
https://www.downthelane.net
https://www.facebook.com/groups/152614321467277/
[Dunstable Way Back in the Day]

Historical research

https://www.ancestry.co.uk *[census record, births, marriages &
deaths]*
https://www.nationalarchives.gov.uk
https://ondemand.bl.uk/onDemand/ *[British Library]*
https://www.ons.gov.uk*[Office of National Statistics]*
https://forebears.io/surnames/
https://www.dunstablehistory.co.uk/timeline.htm – Rita Swift
https://www.associationofdunstablecharities.co.uk/history –
H.Garrod
http://forebears.co.uk/surnames/
http://vk.ovg.ox.ac.uk/polio

Entertainment in the past

https://www.bbc.co.uk/archive/
https://genome.ch.bbc.co.uk

Topic-based research

http://www.massobs.org.uk
https://en.wikipedia.org/wiki/Rationing_in_the_United_
    Kingdom
https://www.historic-uk.com/CultureUK/

Calculating money

http://inflation.iamkate.com
https://www.measuringworth.com/calculators/ukcompare/

ACKNOWLEDGEMENTS

The birth of my grandson Sam Golledge motivated me to start this book, but I needed the spur and encouragement of working with the lovely u3a Belsize Park *Writing Your Life Story* and *Writers' Workshop* groups to make my copious notes into connected text.

My thanks to Bedfordshire County Archives, to the Dunstable Gazette, the Town Clerk's Office and to the Library for their willing help and question-answering, and to BBC Three Counties Radio for allowing me on air to beg for information about Ashton VP School. I am also indebted to two noble local institutions, the Dunstable School Old Boys Association and in particular to Den O'Donoghue for all his help and advice and equally to the Dunstable and District Local History Association in the person of John Buckledee.

It was not easy to find personal recollections about Ashton School but I am very grateful to Anona Browne (ne Maskell), Edwina Byass (né Smith) and Doreen Cove for their help and comments.

I am fortunate still to have friends who were at the Grammar School with me and in particular Prof. Terry Cosgrove and Graham Lippiatt who both advised, commented and helped enormously, aided by their wives Maggie and Sally respectively, along with Mike Abbott, Mike Bannister, Chris Harding and Steve Matthews. I especially thank Fr. Keith Sawyer for his encyclopaedic memory of DGS times past.

Thanks are also due to my friends Rachel Bull and David and Jo Bridgwater for reading, enduring and commenting on various sections, and to Alison Fleming for her professional eye, expertise and critique.

The family mentioned in this book are largely departed this existence, but I am grateful to my cousin Cheryl Dear (née Parrott) for her memories, to my daughters Sarah Stephens-Lewis and Heather Nightingale for their interest, and to Jenny Thompson (née Bearton) for her contributions to our family history, as I am to my wife, Veronica, for her willing and very able trawling of the internet, her steadfast encouragement, and her patience as I shut myself away to write.

RP, March 2023.

All photographs are from a personal collection except where courtesy of Dunstable Gazette. Front cover photograph courtesy of the Dunstable and District Local History Society.